New Romantics Who Never Were
THE UNTOLD STORY
OF SPANDAU BALLET

New Romantics Who Never Were
THE UNTOLD STORY
OF SPANDAU BALLET

DAVID BARRAT

New Romantics Who Never Were:
The Untold Story of Spandau Ballet

Orsam Books
www.orsam.co.uk

First edition published 2018

Copyright © David Barrat 2018

David Barrat asserts his moral rights to be identified as the author of this work.

All rights reserved. No significant part of this publication may be reproduced in any form without the prior permission of the publisher (the author).

Book design by Maureen Cutajar
www.gopublished.com

ISBN: 978-0-9570917-2-6

FOREWORD

DOES THE WORLD NEED A book about Spandau Ballet?

Well, obviously, I thought so, and, as you are reading this, maybe you thought so too.

You will note that I did not ask if the world needs *another book* about Spandau Ballet. That would have been silly. In 1984, as you may know, an official biography by Robert Elms and David Johnson was promised, said to be called 'Angel Boys,' but that never materialized. There were, it is true, a couple of what appear to have been officially sanctioned and uncritical glossy books published during the Eighties, with lots of photographs accompanied by the most basic text, but they contained little in the way of real information and one of them, *Spandau Ballet: The Authorised Story* by John Travis, was described by *Smash Hits* as 'a load of rubbish', and, 'one of the most swizzly pop books ever "written".'

During this twenty-first century, we have had books by three of the band members which have certainly added a lot of detail but, being each written from a personal perspective, are somewhat partial in their accounts, as one would expect. A couple of years before the announcement of a reunion, news emerged that a new official biography of the band by Paul Simper was going to be published but, when Gary Kemp completed his autobiography, which covered much of the same ground, this project was put on hold, where it remains. In 2014, a documentary film, *Soul Boys of the Western World*, was released into cinemas and on DVD but, inevitably for a visual approach, it featured a rather superficial treatment of the band's history.

Most of the articles about Spandau Ballet published in the music press during the 1980s, from which fans obtained their information about the band, were written by a small group of insiders who all knew each other from the early days. None was likely to include anything that would upset Steve Dagger, a manager who was brilliant at controlling the band's image and portrayal of its history. Perhaps the one independent viewpoint which exists can be found in Tony Hadley's *To Cut A Long Story Short* – independent in the sense that it was wholly outside of the control or influence of Steve Dagger. Tony did reveal some new information about the band but his book was inaccurate in a number of respects and naturally only represented Tony's, somewhat disgruntled, viewpoint. So, to the extent that anyone is interested in the story of Spandau Ballet, I do feel that a completely independent look from the outside has long been required by someone who is not influenced by a desire to please (or displease) the band and who does not have an agenda of his own to pursue.

What you are reading now is a wholly unofficial, unauthorized and unapproved book about Spandau Ballet and the key point I want to make here is that I have not spoken, for the purposes of this book, to any of the following six individuals:

> Gary Kemp
> Tony Hadley
> Martin Kemp
> Steve Norman
> John Keeble
> Steve Dagger

When I started to give consideration to writing this book, which was more than ten years ago, my intention was for it to be created like a work of academic history, taken purely from written or recorded sources which I would assess and analyze to piece together the true story of the band. I didn't want to trouble anyone or take up anyone's time simply to satisfy my desire to write a little book about Spandau

Ballet. In the event, and fortunately, I did contact a small number of people connected with the story who were enormously helpful and who gave up their time willingly to help me. To those people I am eternally grateful – this book simply would not have been possible without them – and I acknowledge their assistance individually in the Acknowledgments section at the end.

Of course, when I told people I was writing this book, the first question they would always ask me was: Have you spoken to Gary Kemp, Tony Hadley, etc.? As you already know, but it's worth repeating, I did not speak to any of them. In the first place, I doubt they would have had time in their busy schedules to speak to me, even if they had wanted to, which I don't imagine they would have done. For any interviews with the band members to have been useful, I would almost certainly have needed to spend a number of days with each of them to cover the story properly and would probably have gone over ground which they have covered many times in interviews in the past. Secondly, they have almost all had their say in their own books and it's unlikely that they even remember much more of any importance. Martin was first out of the blocks in this respect, followed by Tony (who wrote his book in collaboration, of a sort, with John) and then Gary, who would no doubt have had the assistance of Steve Dagger. Other than Steve Norman, therefore, they have pretty much all published their collective memories of events. What more could they have realistically told me?

While, in their books, they have all added to our knowledge of Spandau Ballet, they nevertheless all make elementary factual mistakes about the band. Martin thought his brother had written 'over one hundred hit songs', Tony thought Spandau performed five songs on stage at Live Aid in 1985 while Gary said that the famous 'debut' performance at Halligan's recording studio was in October 1979 (the correct facts, incidentally, which will already be known to all dedicated fans, are to be found in this book). It's a curious fact that sometimes fans actually know more about a band than the band members themselves!

Thirdly, while I would have absolutely loved to have chatted to them all about the band's history and heard all the inside stories, I have always nevertheless thought it best to remain totally detached from the band members to retain my independence of mind and thought.

In the book, you will see that I have illustrated certain points with quotes from some of the aforementioned five band members (plus manager) and I want to stress that these quotes have invariably come from television or radio interviews transcribed by me or, alternatively, from published articles and interviews in the music or national press. I have tried to include only rare and unusual quotes which have not featured in other accounts of the band. But none of those quotes were said to me personally and I certainly don't want to give that impression. Where it is of any importance, and does not disrupt the flow of the story, I have provided the source of any quotes in the text. To the extent it will be of any interest, a pretty full biography is included at the end of the book listing all the main sources referred to by me during my research. At certain parts of the book, where the precise chronology of events is important, I have included the publication dates of all relevant magazines and newspapers, something which I hope is not too tiresome for you, the reader.

Accuracy, like truth, is needless to say, very important to me and I have made every possible attempt to ensure total accuracy of everything that you will read in this book. Nevertheless, as I did not witness the events described, my information necessarily comes from contemporary documentation and published sources uncovered during many years of research or from what I have been told by those I have interviewed. I have tried very hard to tell the story of the band, and the period in which the band existed, as it unfolded and as it was viewed at the time without the luxurious benefit of hindsight. One of the problems of relying on memory is that memories can easily be coloured by subsequent events whereas documents, even if they may not always reveal the full story, don't (usually) lie.

I should state, however, that this book is not an actual biography of Spandau Ballet, although it contains some biographical information. Nor is it a book containing glossy photographs of New Romantics dancing or posing at nightclubs. If you are looking for those in this book you will be disappointed. It is a book about a number of aspects concerning the band which interest me and which have not been included in a publication before. It does tell a story but it is by no means the whole story and I am sure there is much that is not known by me. No doubt the story could be told in other ways but this is how I wanted to tell it.

Although this book is naturally written from my own perspective, it is not written from a personal perspective in the sense that it is not concerned with my own feelings about the band. I have tried to keep myself out of the story as much as possible but, on occasion, I have had to include, to a limited extent, my own subjective judgments about the value of the band's songs, otherwise every song is as good as another and no song is better or worse than any other. Even here, however, I have tried to remain as objective as possible and to remember that everyone has different views about which are the best and worst of Spandau Ballet's songs. Some, of course, would say that they are all bad. If you are one of them, perhaps this book is not for you.

Who am I to write a book about Spandau Ballet? Well I'm really just an ordinary fan of the band. I became one at the age of sixteen after hearing and seeing a live version of 'Gold' broadcast on television in the spring 1983 – which I thought then was the best song I'd ever heard – although I had already liked and purchased the seven-inch version of 'Lifeline' in the previous year. Over the next six years I purchased all of the band's albums and singles (in twelve-inch format) and attempted to read everything I could in the music magazines about Spandau Ballet, not so much about the band members – I was usually trying to find out information about the songs and, most importantly, when the next album would be released – but I was generally interested in anything to do with them. I remained loyal – even when I was at university, during which time the *Through the Barricades* album was released – until the band's final album in 1989, which I purchased, then forgot about them for the next ten years. The internet rekindled my interest, as it did for many others. In 2004 I created a cult Spandau Ballet related website, or rather an MSN group, called Deformation. Although this was essentially a light-hearted site devoted to identifying Spandau Ballet related mistakes (mainly those made by journalists) aimed at a small number of fans, containing various in-jokes, it also contained some serious articles which I had spent time researching in the British Library and British Newspaper Library (then housed in separate buildings) relating to two particular subjects which I found interesting.

The first of these was the origins of the band's unusual name. I had noticed some contradictory statements had been made about this and I wanted to get to the bottom of it. The trail I followed led me to an unexpected and quite surprising conclusion which forms a central part of this book. The second topic had arisen as a result of a question asked by an online friend who had been told by her mother that Spandau Ballet joined the New Romantic movement very late and were not real New Romantics. My online friend asked me if this was true. I had no idea. It started to make me wonder when the term 'New Romantic' was first used and by whom. The internet contained a whole mass of inaccurate and conflicting information, including an online article which stated that 'THE NEW ROMANTICS ARE HERE' was 'the most frequently used heading in most English papers in 1979'. I was to discover that the exact opposite was true; it was a heading that was used in precisely no English (or other) papers in 1979 and this spurred me on to attempt to get to the bottom of the issue.

Another issue that interests me is the legal battle that tore the band apart during the late 1990s and which was, in part, resurrected in 2001. Having missed the main court battle, I actually attended the extremely short hearing at the High Court before Mr Justice Jacob in January 2002, which ended for me in some confusion, but I was able to piece the story together and was, in fact, the first to reveal online a number of important facts about this legal action. Until that time I had barely posted on the internet but, suddenly and unexpectedly, I was embroiled in a variety of online disputes.

Whether these topics are of interest to you, the reader, remains to be seen. I hope you find them interesting. What this book certainly is not about is the personal lives of the band members or about any type of scandal, personal or otherwise. If you are looking for that type of thing here then, just like those wanting glossy photographs, you will inevitably be disappointed. It really is a straightforward history of a group of men who have brought musical pleasure to many people, myself included, and who are of interest to me for that very reason.

In many respects, I seem to have been fated to have written this book and I rather think I am the only person who could have done it, but, when the idea of such a book came to me, I had never written one before. Would I even be able to get it published? In order to ensure that this would see the light of day, and to avoid having to submit to agents and publishers, I decided that self-publishing was the way forward and thought it would be a good idea to self-publish a book on another topic, by way of a test, to see how easy or difficult that would be. While researching the history of Rotherfield Street, the street in which Gary and Martin Kemp lived and grew up as children, I found the story of a fascinating unsolved murder committed during the First World War at number 114 Rotherfield Street (the Kemps later lived a short distance away at number 138) and, with an existing interest in True Crime, decided it would be perfect for my first book, which became *The Islington Murder Mystery*, published under my own imprint of Orsam Books. While researching that topic I stumbled across a rather more famous murder from 1907 in Camden Town and self-published my second book about it: *The Camden Town Murder Mystery*.

There are, I'm pleased to say, no murders involved in this book, not even murders of music, thank you.

On a grammatical note, I would like to mention that it's not entirely clear if a band such as Spandau Ballet should be referred to in the singular, being one group, or, being comprised of five individuals, in the plural. When the band played a gig did 'they' play the gig or did 'it' do so? I don't think there is a hard and fast rule so I have used whatever feels appropriate in any particular context. Don't let it bother you too much.

One other thing. In this book, I have tried to avoid making sweeping statements or spouting grand socio-political opinions about the role of Spandau Ballet and the New Romantics. Did Britain suddenly transform from black and white into colour when the New Romantics appeared on the scene in the late seventies as some people would have us believe? I don't really think so – the exact same thing has been said about Britain in the sixties – but it's a compelling image. In truth, at the time, certainly at the start, very few people were even aware of the small numbers of oddly dressed people dancing in little known clubs. One can draw all kinds of parallels with the election of the Thatcher government in May 1979 and the influence of socio-economic factors on youth culture and the influence of youth culture on society and the relationship between music and politics; I'm sure there are some valid points to be made but I personally find this kind of thing rather dull and, in any case, everything that can be said about these types of connections has already been said in a variety of different ways in other publications. I'm more interested in the unadorned facts and the interesting story those facts reveal, so let's get cracking with the story.

CONTENTS

―◀O▶―

FOREWORD	....	v
CHAPTER ONE	A Star Is Born	1
CHAPTER TWO	The First Spandau Ballet	29
CHAPTER THREE	From Gilly's to Billy's	55
CHAPTER FOUR	From Holborn to Halligan's	75
CHAPTER FIVE	The Second Spandau Ballet	99
CHAPTER SIX	What's In A Name?	123
CHAPTER SEVEN	Hopeless Romantics	145
CHAPTER EIGHT	The New Romantics Who Never Were	161
CHAPTER NINE	Golden Years	199
CHAPTER TEN	When the Monolith Cracks	221
EPILOGUE	And Then There Were Four	249
AFTERWORD	The Two Spandau Ballets and the Three Bass Guitarists	253
APPENDIX 1	The Boy and the Bishop	259
APPENDIX 2	Rocking at the Roxy	271
APPENDIX 3	Spandau and the Music Press	283
APPENDIX 4	Spandau Ballet v.1 Images	289
APPENDIX 5	Spandau Ballet v.2 Images	295
ACKNOWLEDGEMENTS	....	299
BIBLIOGRAPHY	....	301

CHAPTER ONE

A Star Is Born

'I was a wide-eyed boy of twelve and looking out from my TV screen was a space aged messenger giving voice to my burgeoning sexuality. Pointing a painted figure he spoke to me. I'd been chosen.'
—Gary Kemp, speaking of seeing David Bowie on *Top of the Pops* in *Passions: Mick Ronson*, Sky Arts documentary, first broadcast on 6 April 2017

A BISHOP FROM THE EAST appears unannounced outside a modest north London dwelling in the year one thousand, nine hundred and seventy one. According to the gospel interpretation of this account, it is a cool Thursday evening in October. Heretically speaking, however, it is probably on a warm Thursday evening in August when the Bishop makes his extraordinary and unheralded appearance. Rather like the three wise men arriving in Bethlehem with gifts for the baby Jesus, this particular wise man carries a precious gift of his own; not gold, frankincense or myrrh – although Gold will one day emerge as a result – but a brand new cassette tape recorder, acquired specially for the Chosen One. The gift is presented and accepted. The Chosen One's mother is delighted, albeit astonished and not a little flustered at the surprise visitation to her humble abode from such an important personage. The Chosen One is unaware of the unique symbolism of the visitation but he knows instinctively, as does the perceptive

Bishop, that he is destined for greatness. He does not, however, think of himself as having been 'chosen' until the following summer when David Bowie seems to point his finger directly at him while performing 'Starman' on *Top of the Pops* on 6 July 1972.

The years that follow will involve the Chosen One helping to give life, in a manner some will describe as an 'immaculate conception', to a band of loyal associates who will assist him in fronting a new 'cult' whose influence will permeate many aspects of society and generate a group of devoted followers. The Chosen One's words and passions, as delivered and interpreted by his associates, will be heard, admired and even revered by thousands if not millions of people around the world. There will be 'sermons' delivered to the masses and, at times, on his personal journey to glory, it might even appear that the Chosen One can walk on water. But there will be difficult times ahead too: a challenge to his supremacy, betrayal by his closest associates and even an attempt to crucify him in the High Court near the Temple. In due course, this will be followed by the astonishing conversion of his sworn enemy on the road to Damascus, otherwise known as the road to Docklands, and, of course, the story will end, almost unbelievably, in glorious rebirth and resurrection.

But that is all in the future. Now, in September 1971, shortly after the most likely date of the unexpected arrival of the Bishop, the Chosen One – eleven-year-old Gary James Kemp – is a new starter in Mr Thompson's class 1CT at Dame Alice Owen's Boys' School in Owen Street, Islington, along with another new pupil named Steven Anthony Norman. Although the two boys have not previously known each other, and support rival local football teams, they will one day, in a few years' time, become great friends through a mutual love of music.

Starting at Owen's on the same day, but in another class, is a tall and rather gangly Anthony Patrick Hadley who has only just recovered from the effects of a serious bone marrow infection he suffered the previous year. Like Gary, he is also given a cassette recorder (by his parents) and takes to recording himself singing along with records obtained from his uncle's record shop. Already at the school, now starting his second year, is a beefy John Leslie Keeble, while a much older boy, Stephen Charles Dagger, the son of a trade union official, is about to begin his fourth year but, as yet, has nothing to do with anyone in Gary, Steve and Tony's year, or John's for that matter.

All these boys have a bright future ahead of them but the school itself is doomed. Having been built as a charitable gesture for the education of boys from the Parish of Islington and Clerkenwell at the start of the seventeenth century by Alice Wilkes (who had married Judge Thomas Owen to become Dame Alice Owen), its time is almost up after nearly four hundred years. The school's name will survive but it is controversially moving out to Potters Bar in Hertfordshire: the result, according to the school governors and the Inner London Education Authority, of a rapid decline in Islington's population, leading to a reduction in the need for school places. It is also necessary because of planned road improvements at the Angel intersection, including a large roundabout due to be built outside the school, which is not only likely to make it extremely noisy but also difficult for children to cross the road in the heavy traffic. These are the official reasons at least but there is a suspicion in some quarters that the governors simply want to move to a brand new building in a nicer area with government funding.

Parents of children at the school had written a formal letter of protest to the Department of Education against the move in the summer of 1971 – with the most vocal, Mrs Nina Dowson, commenting to the local press, 'I think it is dreadful that a small school like this should leave Islington' – but to no avail. The 1971 intake will be the last at Islington, which is why Gary's younger brother, Martin, is later forced to separate from his sibling and commence his secondary education at the Central Foundation Boys' School off Old Street. The plan at Owen's is to allow the 1970 and 1971 intakes to stay at the Islington school until they reach the sixth form in 1976 when they will have the choice of transferring *en masse* to the new building – which is to take on new pupils starting in the first year from 1973 – or moving to a different school in Islington. Those who started at the school before 1970, such as Steve Dagger, will not be affected but a number of the teachers know they will not be moving to Potters Bar and become demoralized, so the standard of teaching slips somewhat.

Although they are all together in the same building in September 1971, it is not until October 1976 that Kemp senior, Norman, Keeble and Hadley come together to form a band. The story told by Gary is that, during the school summer holidays, at the age of sixteen, he went with his brother Martin, Steve Norman and the nineteen-year-old Dagger to see the Sex Pistols play an exciting late night/early morning gig at Islington's Screen on the Green on Sunday, 29 August 1976, with no less than Buzzcocks and The Clash in support.

If the Bishop can be said to have played a role analogous to the three wise men in Gary Kemp's life then his John the Baptist figure, if not David Bowie, must be John the Rotten, otherwise known as Lydon. He certainly appears to have captivated the young Gary, not least by managing to knock out his front teeth with his microphone while on stage. But more than this: watching ordinary young working class men singing and playing their musical instruments with apparent limited technical ability but vast amounts of creative energy, it seems to have dawned on Gary, in a moment of epiphany, that there was absolutely no reason why he too could not form a teenage band of his own. Until this time, as he told music journalist Paul Simper in 1983, he believed that to be in a band you had to have 'so much backing of money and unbelievable musicianship' but the success of punk showed him that this was not the case.

Gary was, in fact, already proficient as a musician. He had been playing music in earnest for nearly six years, since Christmas Day 1970 in fact, when his father had bought him an acoustic guitar after he had shown interest of a sort in his cousin's toy guitar. He soon started writing songs and even recording them (in a little kiosk at Waterloo station) and ended up playing a couple of his own compositions at a prize-giving event at Rotherfield Junior School on Thursday, 8 July 1971. His talent was recognized by the watching Ernest Urban Trevor Huddleston, Bishop of Stepney, there to present the prizes, hence the arrival, probably a month or so later*, of the Bishop at the Kemp family home, armed with a cassette recorder, allowing young Gary to record his future songs. Gary's development as a musician was such that, during the summer of 1975, he was performing on a Thames TV tea-time children's programme, *You Must be Joking*, along with the band Flintlock.

By 1976, Gary was playing in a jazz-funk band called The Same Band which included amongst its members a teenage Ian 'Jess' Bailey, who had been in the same year at Owen's as Steve Dagger. It also included one of Gary's school classmates on drums, Chris Ostrowski, and an older man of about thirty, Ian Fox, which is no doubt why Gary now recalls it as 'a band with guys in their 30s', although in reality its members were of a mixed age range. According to Gary, they used to play Average White Band style music and Eagles covers, although they did play some of his original songs too. Gary himself was a precocious teenager who, having attended the Anna Scher School of Drama at an early age, had already starred in a Children's Foundation feature film, *Hide & Seek*, which had premiered in Leicester Square in 1972. He had his priorities straight though. With the money earned from the film, he bought himself a new electric guitar.

Some, like music journalist Dave Rimmer, have doubted that Gary was present in the crowd at the Screen on the Green in August 1976, not least because it was an exclusive audience comprised almost entirely of art students, music journalists and industry insiders, but there are compelling reasons to believe he was there. The assistant manager of the Screen on the Green was another ex-Owen's pupil, Stephen Woolley, who was a friend of Steve Dagger, having been in the same year as him at school.

---

* See Appendix 1.

Dagger had a longstanding dream of managing a band and had been hanging round The Same Band, which he was connected with through knowing Jess Bailey, offering to do various tasks for them. He must have been impressed by the talented sixteen-year-old guitarist who wrote his own songs and, assuming, as is likely, that he used his connections with Woolley to wangle himself into the Sex Pistols gig, it would only have been natural for him to invite Gary along too, despite the three year age difference between them.

Thus enthused – 'It gave me goose bumps', he said in a 2001 Radio 2 interview, 'I knew I wanted to form a band and was inspired by the energy that was going on with punk' – when Gary returned to school at the end of the summer holidays to commence sixth form he appears to have had some kind of desire to do something new musically. Jess Bailey was on his way to university and Chris Ostrowski left Owen's at the end of the fifth form to get a job in the summer of 1976 so The Same Band could not continue; in any event, Gary was no longer interested in the type of music they played. At the same time, while he might have had a 'eureka' moment during the Sex Pistols concert, the formation of Gary's next band came about not as a result of anything *he* did but rather as a result of the curiosity of another Owen's boy.

MICHAEL HENDERSON ELLISON WAS BORN in Sunderland in January 1959 and, at the age of two, developed measles which left him with some minor permanent hearing damage and difficulty in picking up certain frequencies. However, he was by no means deaf, being able to follow conversations perfectly well, and he never had any form of speech problem as Gary Kemp mysteriously suggests in his autobiography. When he was ten years old, Ellison's family moved down from the north-east of England to Hornsey Rise in London; his coal mining father had decided that the mining industry was in decline and that he should seek new employment in the south, taking a job as a warehouse manager for a carpet company in Islington.

After six months at Ashmount primary school in Crouch Hill, Michael, who had been educated at a good Catholic primary school in Sunderland, was one of the select few from Ashmount to be accepted by Owen's in 1970, having passed an examination and impressed in an interview with the headmaster. Not that the eleven-year-old Ellison was particularly pleased. He had never heard of Owen's before and was dismayed to learn that it was miles away from his home which would necessitate taking a bus to Archway and then the tube to the Angel, a journey of about half an hour compared with the five minutes or so it took him to walk to Ashmount. Moreover, the school day began at 8:50am (finishing at 3:40pm) which was earlier than he was used to. However, his mother was happy and proudly told her friends that her son had 'got into Lady Owen's'.

The young Mike Ellison had become interested in music at Ashmount, where vinyl records were played at lunchtime, and both his parents were musicians – his father having played in brass bands, his mother being a pianist – but his own moment of musical epiphany came in his first year at Owen's when he heard the sound of electric guitars coming from the art room. Drawn towards the noise, he discovered some sixth formers playing Black Sabbath's 'Paranoid' and thought, 'Wow! This is really powerful stuff.' Discovering that the music teacher at Owen's had arranged with a local music shop for pupils at the school to be able to buy acoustic guitars for a special discount price of eight pounds, Mike took advantage of the deal but was disappointed by the fact that the music teacher would only teach classical music, whereas he just wanted to play the Sabbath.

To make matters worse, as Mike recalls, in the mid-1970s the Inner London Education Authority introduced a ban on electric instruments in schools within its jurisdiction. This was in response to incidents of professional musicians being electrocuted on stage through poorly earthed instruments. Les Harvey of Stone the Crows, for example, died at the Swansea Top Rank on 3 May 1972 when his wet hands touched a poorly grounded microphone.

Consequently, Mike could not even go and play loud guitar in the art room like the sixth formers he had seen and admired. However, Mike had a friend, Clifford Manley, who lived near him in Hornsey Rise and was also learning the guitar. The two boys used to jam together and swap musical ideas outside of school. Eventually they wrote to the local council to ask if there was anywhere they could play and were rewarded for their precociousness by a booking at a council hall for an old people's dinner where they nervously performed two or three cover songs, although, appropriately, it was more like the Osmonds than Black Sabbath they played on that occasion.

Mike also learned to play the drums when his uncle, a drummer in a band called Five Links, showed him how to hold the sticks and find his way around a drum kit. He would practise by putting on headphones and playing along with songs on the radio, to the undoubted annoyance of anyone in the close vicinity. His drumming ability was the reason he was asked to play the drums in a school production of the Sandy Wilson musical, *The Boy Friend*, featuring a fourteen-year-old, singing and dancing, Gary Kemp. By this time, things had improved in the music department at Owen's following the hiring of a new music teacher called Denny Wright, a professional jazz and skiffle recording artist, who had performed with Lonnie Donegan, amongst others. He was a fantastic guitar player who was happy to teach modern music to the boys, including both Mike Ellison and Gary Kemp, who attended his classes. Frustratingly, though, due to the continuing ban on electric instruments, the boys were only allowed to play acoustic guitars when they really wanted to play loud rock music.

Outside of school it was a different matter and, upon learning that a friend's band needed a bass player, Mike bought himself a Columbus Fender jazz bass copy guitar for about a hundred pounds after having received a small inheritance from his late grandmother. He started playing in his friend's band at a local church and was spotted there by members of an Irish folk band who were short of a bass player and who invited him to join them every Friday evening after school, as well as on Saturday and Sunday evenings, when they played at local dance halls. This resulted in a willing Ellison being paid sixty pounds a week for his contribution. During the long hot summer of 1976, after having completed his 'O' Levels, Mike also earned himself an additional sixty-five pounds per week working for a building firm and was thus able to afford not only driving lessons but an impressive new Carlsbro PA speaker system: an essential but expensive (at around £300) requirement for any self-respecting band.

In about October 1976, shortly after starting in the sixth form at Owen's, which had now relocated to Potters Bar, converted from a voluntary aided grammar school to a comprehensive and merged with Dame Alice Owen's Girls' School, Mike was idly rooting around in a cupboard in the music room where he was surprised to find an old drum kit and an amp. Surely amps were prohibited in school, he thought. He asked the music teacher and was both amazed and delighted to be told that pupils were, in fact, allowed to play electric guitars within the school building. Being out in Potters Bar, the school had escaped from the authoritarian jurisdiction of the Inner London Education Authority and the ban on electric guitars no longer applied. It was a major discovery and an important turning point.

Mike, who used to drive to school in his father's Rover 3, brought in his bass and amp in the car the very next day and started playing in the music room, which immediately interested the watching Gary Kemp and his now best friend, Steve Norman, who was both a drummer and guitarist. However, it was John Keeble who took over the drum kit that Mike had found in the cupboard. He quickly demonstrated superior drumming skills which he had learnt since the day his parents had bought him a toy drum kit but which he had kept secret from just about everyone. Mike had sat next to him for two years in maths class but John had never dropped the slightest hint that he could play the drums. With two lead guitarists in Gary and Steve, a bass guitarist in Mike and a drummer in John, it suddenly looked possible to form a school band, or at least to commence playing songs together.

No doubt Gary and Steve were eager to start a band but it was the forward thinking Mike who organized matters to get it off the ground. He arranged for a friend who owned a Land Rover to collect Gary's and Steve's guitars and amps from their homes in Islington and transport them to Potters Bar.

Their instruments now at hand, the four sixth formers started playing together and found they had an instant musical chemistry with everyone making their own individual contribution to the overall sound. The first song they played together was the Rolling Stones' 'Silver Train'. Gary knew the riff to it and taught the others. They all added their own interpretation to the song and started to learn other covers such as 'Sandman', 'We've Gotta Get Out Of This Place', 'Oh Carol', 'I Saw Her Standing There' and 'Midnight Hour', all played very energetically. The sound of music attracted other pupils, as well as some teachers, to the music room, just as Ellison had been attracted to the art room by the refrain of 'Paranoid' some five or six years earlier. One of those drawn in, and obviously liking what he was hearing, was Tony Hadley.

Steve, Mike and Gary had been sharing vocal responsibilities, with some girls from the fourth form joining in as backing singers, but it wasn't working and the band clearly needed a dedicated lead singer. A hopeful Tony informed Steve that he could sing and was consequently brought into the elite group by Gary and Steve (who jointly made the important band decisions at the time). Gary has explained that, 'we needed a singer and I thought, you know, this big tall kid, Tony Hadley, he's got a leather jacket, you know, maybe we should ask him – and everyone in the year above hated him so that seemed like good credentials to be in a band' but, as Tony had a fine strong voice, honed through years of participation in holiday camp talent competitions, as well as experimentation on his tape recorder, it seems more likely that it was his vocal skills that secured his entry into the band rather than his leather jacket or his unpopularity with the upper sixth.

Mike Ellison was certainly impressed with Tony's voice in those early days. 'Boy could he hold a note,' he says, 'when he held it, it just went on forever. It didn't waver. It was really good.' In his laid back manner, Mike might have given the impression that he didn't care one way or the other as to whether Tony joined the band but, he says today, 'just because I didn't jump around and scream doesn't mean I didn't care.' Tony also looked good, not only because of his leather jacket but also because he wore fashionable cowboy boots which drew attention to him and attracted some hostility at the same time because they made a loud noise as he walked along the school corridor.

Perhaps the most interesting point to emerge from the story of the band's formation is that the members of the band, despite being at the same school since 1971, barely knew each other before they started together in the sixth form at Potters Bar in 1976, and were certainly not all friends while the school was based in Islington. Although Gary and Steve had been close pals for some years, Tony was practically unknown to them and Gary admits in his autobiography that he had never even spoken to him during the first five years at school. In a 1984 interview, John Keeble admitted that, until his final year at school, 'I never really knew Steve, Gary and Tony' and it seems he had positively disliked Tony from what he did know of him and his cowboy boots. Indeed, when the idea of Tony joining the band was first mooted, Mike remembers John saying, 'If he's singing, I'm leaving', a stinging remark also recalled by Gary in his autobiography.

Although the band mainly played cover songs, they also rehearsed an original Gary Kemp composition called either 'I've Got Roots' or just 'Roots'. It was as a result of this song title that they named themselves, simply, Roots. All their songs were played very loud and at a furious speed in a sort of punk or new wave style. They were proud of playing 'I Wanna Be Your Man' by the Beatles from start to finish in less than a minute. At one point, as if to confirm their punk roots, they rehearsed 'Anarchy in the UK' together. Gary brought in one or two more of his own songs in embryonic form which Steve and Mike would develop musically, with Tony suggesting amended lyrics. Their first gig was in December 1976, for the fourth form Christmas party, in the school dining room, at the request of one of their fans from the music room and it went down a storm, particularly with the girls in the audience. It was soon followed by their first gig outside of school: a charity concert on behalf of the Hornsey Centre for Handicapped Children at the Queen's Head public house in Green Lanes, Haringey, a few days after Christmas 1976. This came about through Mike Ellison, who was already due to perform at the concert with the Christian/folk band he played in, performing songs like 'Jesus Christ Superstar', although he was not a devoted Christian as some imagined.

The evening did not go well for Roots and sowed the seeds of the band's eventual demise. The guitar that Steve had been playing until this point wasn't very powerful and he had been finding it difficult to extract volume from his amp, meaning that he was being drowned out within the very loud band. Consequently, that evening, he borrowed an expensive Les Paul copy from a friend of Mike's called Marco who was a member of Mike's other band that had already finished its own set. This guitar somehow got broken – either Steve accidentally dropped it or Gary knocked it over – which was rather embarrassing for Mike who had to apologize profusely to the distraught Marco.

Gary was also having terrible trouble with his own guitar. In his autobiography, he says he thinks he was slightly drunk and, as a result, could not manage to get it in tune but Mike thinks that he had just put on new strings, which were stretching, and that was what was causing the problem. Either way, Gary took ages to tune the guitar while sitting at the front of the stage which caused bored audience members to wonder what was going on. The delay annoyed Mike Ellison's father, a strict perfectionist of the old school, who believed that a musician should have tuned his instrument in advance of a performance. He was also eager to see his son perform and approached Gary to instruct him to get a move on, thus irritating the proud young guitarist who did not like to be told what to do. Tony appears to recall a loud stand-up row between the two although Mike, who was on the other side of the stage, does not remember any shouting. Nevertheless, he kept clear of what was evidently a heated discussion between Gary and his father by standing at the other side of the stage. 'I just walked away from it' says Mike today, adding wistfully, 'I wish I'd told Gary to walk away from it.'

The tuning problems with Gary's guitar became irrelevant, however, when, amidst the chaos, the landlord, Pat Browne, decided that the band was simply too loud and issued them with an ultimatum after a couple of numbers: turn down the volume or leave the stage. As Mike recollects: 'We just played really loud. If it wasn't distorted it didn't sound right. In those days, the only way you could get an amp to distort was to wind it right up. You had to overdrive your amp to do it.'

The audience at the Queen's Head was not a young crowd by any means. In attendance was the mayor of Haringey, a local councillor and also Paul Eddington, the actor then best known for his role as Jerry Leadbetter in the BBC sitcom, *The Good Life*, who was present as a celebrity guest. These notables, for the most part, did not appreciate the quality of Mike's expensive PA system which seemed to amplify what was already a very loud performance. Mike, who loved playing loud, would nevertheless have been happy to turn down the volume in order to placate the landlord and continue the performance but the other band members were having none of it and stormed off the stage. In his autobiography, Gary suggests that Steve Dagger was watching silently in the audience thinking that this was exactly how a proper rock gig should be but, if he was even there, he was probably cringing at the fiasco like everyone else. Nevertheless, the local newspaper, the *Weekly Herald for Tottenham and Wood Green*, was kind to the band in its report of the concert, tactfully not mentioning the sound issues in its 31 December 1976 edition, but stating instead that 'entertainment was provided by the talented "The Roots" heavy rock group, teenagers from the Alice Owen School, Potters Bar.'

On the surface, there was a definite improvement at the next gig which was also arranged by Mike Ellison. He was friends with one of Tom Robinson's roadies and, through him, had become friendly with Tom Robinson himself. The newly formed Tom Robinson Band was unsigned at the time (although Robinson was personally signed to the Konk record label established by Ray Davies of The Kinks, a contract from which he was in the painful process of extricating himself) but was already highly regarded and EMI was interested. The roadie telephoned Mike and asked if his young band fancied the support slot at a forthcoming gig by the Tom Robinson Band at the Sir George Robey public house in Finsbury Park. Mike rang up the others and, not surprisingly, they were all very keen.

This time there was no problem with their loud volume and the boys played a great set. Tom Robinson was impressed, especially with Gary who had put his problems from the Queen's Head behind him and had given a confident and assured performance. The landlord was also pleased because the band had brought about twenty or thirty pupils from Owen's with them and this had helped to fill the venue. The success of this gig meant that Roots was asked to support Tom Robinson again a few days later at the Golden Lion in Fulham, probably on Wednesday, 19 January 1977. Although Tom played every Wednesday at this venue during January, we can establish the likely date of the gig from the fact that both Tony and Gary recall Robert Plant and John Bonham of Led Zeppelin being in the audience. Led Zeppelin were rehearsing during this period at Fulham's Manticore Studios, and Plant, accompanied by Jimmy Page, was spotted by a music journalist at a gig in Covent Garden by The Damned on Monday, 17 January, with Plant returning to the same venue accompanied by Bonham a few days later. Julie Birchall also identified Robert Plant as being in the audience at the Golden Lion in her review of a Tom Robinson gig – almost certainly the one on 19 January – which appeared in the *NME*'s 29 January 1977 issue.

Before the gig, Tom had privately agreed with Mike that Roots would be the official support for the entirety of the Tom Robinson Band's forthcoming ten-date London-wide tour. Mike felt this would be an incredible once-in-a-lifetime opportunity considering that record company executives would be in attendance at the gigs and it could lead to Roots being signed, an extraordinary feat for a school band formed only a few months earlier.

Mike, however, had not told the rest of the band about his discussions with Tom Robinson. The agreement for Roots to support his band on the tour was not yet final and, understandably, Mike wanted to be able to present the others with a dramatic fait accompli once it was confirmed. He was naturally proud of what he had achieved in all but securing the support slot and was very much looking forward to breaking the good news to his band mates.

After the Golden Lion gig, which did not go terribly well – the band was asked to stop early once again by the landlord for being too loud – an angry Tom Robinson informed Mike that one of his band mates had approached him to ask when they were going to get paid for the two gigs they had done so far. Whoever it was that had pestered Tom did not know that it was unspoken practice for a support band to play for free in return for the exposure. At the time, Mike suspected it was Gary who had asked for the money, simply because he had the most front out of all of them, but Tony mentions with disgust in his autobiography that Tom Robinson offered the band no more than their tube fare home and, in return, was told what he could do with it, so it may be that it was Tony who annoyed Tom by asking for payment. Mike did not care who it was – he never asked – but he was absolutely furious, believing that no-one should have spoken to Tom directly on such a topic without checking with him first. He was the link with Tom and he naturally felt he should not have been by-passed. 'I was angry with them,' he recalls, 'they'd upset a friend of mine. I'd known Tom longer than I'd known them.' Moreover, he believed the incident had destroyed any chance of Roots being the support band on the tour.

Perhaps if the problems from the Queen's Head gig had not occurred, Mike might have reacted differently to the incident but, on top of everything else, he felt his continuing existence in Roots had become untenable. A day or two after the gig, he called John and, without giving any reason, told him he was leaving the band. A few minutes later he received a telephone call from a bewildered Gary: 'What do you mean you're leaving?' to which he replied simply, 'I don't want to do it any more.' To this day, despite Mike remaining in touch with his former band mates, none of them know the true reason for his decision to leave the band. Probably out of a desire to avoid a confrontation, and unwilling to have anyone try and talk him out of his decision, he simply did not tell them why he wanted out and kept all his feelings bottled up inside him. 'What I probably should have done,' reflects Mike, 'was go to them and say "Tom's had a go at me. What was really being planned was this [i.e. being the support band for Tom Robinson's tour] and you blew it by going up to him and asking him [for money]. Why didn't someone ask me first? Why did you just go and do it behind my back?"' But he didn't do that and the Roots split.

An almost inevitable process of ex-post facto rationalization led the other band members to come to believe that the problem was that Mike had been different in some way – he was too straight, too laid back, not punk or cool enough, *not really one of them* – but this was not what they thought at the time when they were hugely disappointed to lose their talented bass player.

Nevertheless, Mike had decided he had to go, so that was that and there was no further discussion on the subject (although, having calmed down, he did offer to perform one 'farewell gig' with the band – but this offer was declined). The name Roots had to go too, not least because it made them sound like a reggae band due to the existence of a musical sub-genre of reggae known as 'roots reggae' and it also clashed with Alex Haley's best-selling 1976 book of the same name in which Haley attempted to trace his family history back to an individual slave who was stolen from Africa. With the versatile Steve Norman on bass, they became The Cut, a name taken from a road near Waterloo station. Steve did not own a bass guitar but, thankfully, Mike Ellison was not one to bear grudges and happily lent him his, and, furthermore, allowed the band to continue using his expensive PA system for their gigs. Consequently, despite no longer being a band member, Mike attended most of The Cut's gigs and was also present when they rehearsed, as they sometimes did, upstairs at the Crown and Woolsack, a pub in St John Street, Islington. After a while, though, Mike needed his bass guitar back so someone with their own bass was required in order for the band to be able to continue.

By good fortune, another Owen's boy called Richard Miller owned such an instrument, or perhaps he was bought one specially by his parents so that he could join the group. He was certainly not known at the school as a bass guitarist before then and Mike Ellison, for one, was unaware that he could play anything. Nevertheless, Miller was accepted as a new member of the band which changed its name to The Makers, inspired, according to Gary, by the name of a leatherette store in Islington which he noticed when going past on a bus one day, although, it has to be said, no such shop name appears in *Kelly's Post Office Directory* for the period.

An early but long-forgotten gig during this transitional period was secured, according to Vicki Bird, who lived a few houses away from Tony, by Tony's mother, who was on a committee organizing a street party in Inglebert Street, off Myddleton Square, to celebrate the Queen's visit to Islington, in what was known as her 'Northern Tour', as part of the Silver Jubilee celebrations, on Wednesday, 6 July 1977. A more established band, which had been due to perform, apparently pulled out at a late stage and Mrs Hadley quickly and proudly informed the committee that her son was in a band which could step in at short notice to save the day, thus beating all other local bands to what appears to have been a quite highly prized slot in front of what was anticipated to be (and turned out to be) a reasonably large crowd of Islington residents.

Sandie Maley, then a young local resident aged seven, remembers that the gig took place in the late afternoon or early evening of a hot day, after the children had first been to school and had all then lined up along the streets to wave at the Queen in her motorcade as she returned with the Duke of Edinburgh from Highbury

Fields at shortly after four o'clock and travelled down Rosebery Avenue, passing by Finsbury Town Hall, on her way back to Buckingham Palace.

Vicki Bird, who was then aged twenty-one, four years older than Tony, who had just turned seventeen, was aware of the gig taking place outside St Mark's Church in Myddleton Square, but she did not hang around to listen. She had way cooler plans that evening which did not involve watching the band of which her rather straight young neighbour was the lead singer at what was essentially a children's street party. Instead, she was off to meet up with friends who were then going on to an ultra-trendy West End club called Louise in Poland Street. Vicki was working at the Public Record Office in Chancery Lane at the time and some of her colleagues were connected with the fashionable people who knew of, and frequented, clubs such as Louise. As Vicki recalls: 'At Louise's…you would knock on the door and a little slit would open and you would be vetted…you go to this tiny room downstairs and it's like, don't stare at the people. Act cool, act cool. It blew me away the way they looked. Like they'd come from Covent Garden or the ballet or something like that…All the time I'm thinking to myself, they couldn't have come on the train like that, they must have changed in the ladies when they got here which, of course, a lot of them did.'

Among those who did stay to watch the Silver Jubilee performance were Sonia Byrne and Liz Silvester, teenage girls who both lived in the area. Sonia remembers the street party as being 'amazing, a big celebration' with food, hats, flags, good weather and hundreds of locals in attendance. It seems that the band, on a specially built stage, played mainly cover versions, such as 'Gloria' by The Kinks, with a few of their own compositions thrown in, and the performance was enjoyed by all, or almost all. According to Liz: 'I remember a lot of people being at the front of it but I don't think it was popular with a lot of the residents because it was a noise, you know in the middle of their flats.' Another thing that Liz remembers is that Martin Kemp was there as the band's roadie or 'general setter upper' and that Richard Miller was playing bass. Sandie Maley recalls that they were 'very good, poppy' and 'everyone had a really good time and were talking about it for weeks after…how good they were'. According to Vicki Bird, the general reaction she heard from the locals was that, 'the kid's got a voice he could really sing' (referring to Tony) and it 'seemed as if they were already an established group'. It appears that their success at this street party brought about a request to play again to local residents at Bevin Court, near Tony's home in Percy Circus, shortly afterwards.

The Silver Jubilee performance was an important event in the history of the band because it brought them to the attention of the young people of Islington, outside of those who went to Owen's, for the first time. As Liz says, 'it was a nice early showcase for them' and ensured that future gigs would be attended by those who had enjoyed the show. Liz, accompanied by her younger sister, Vicki, for example, would go and follow the band whenever they played locally, or sometimes in the West End, and, encouraged by Steve Dagger, would mock scream at the front of the stage in a bid to attempt to impress watching record company executives.

Many of those who were too young to follow the band never forgot the street party gig. Sandie Maley, well remembering his performance at the same spot six years earlier, ended up being outside St Mark's Church on the day Tony married Leonie Lawson and, then aged twelve years old, she presented the bride with a horseshoe which a local journalist had given her to pass on.

As for Vicki Bird, she would shortly be romantically pursued with some vigour by Tony (before he met Leonie), and even agreed to go on a couple of dates with him, but he was a bit too young and not quite louche enough for her. Nevertheless, she did give him some firm advice to look after his voice and seek professional training which he seems to have heeded.

The Makers' first big break occurred with the help of Tony Hadley's grandfather, Bill Tee, who, according to Tony, writing in his autobiography, knew one of the owners of the recently opened home of punk, the Roxy Club in Neal Street near Covent Garden, and he used his contacts to secure the band a gig there. Unfortunately, Tony does not say in his autobiography which owner of the Roxy his grandfather knew: a shame because they were a fascinating collection of characters in the middle of a power struggle over who had control of the club.*

It was on an audition night at the Roxy on Wednesday, 20 July 1977, when The Makers were due to support a group called The Transistors. An advertisement naming them as the support band was published in the 16 July 1977 issue of the *NME*. However, when the next issue of the *NME* (dated 23 July 1977) was published on 20 July, the day of the gig, the bands advertised to perform at the Roxy that night had changed from The Transistors supported by The Makers to Stinky Toys supported by The Killjoys and the audition night had, it seems, been cancelled. The Stinky Toys were a leading new wave band from France with an attractive female lead singer, Elli Medeiros, who evidently had a gap in their schedule between playing the Vortex on 18 July and the Marquee for three nights between 21 and 23 July and could presumably only be accommodated by the Roxy on 20 July; hence other bands were squeezed out. That must have been a disappointment for The Makers but they did eventually debut at the Roxy on Tuesday, 6 September 1977, with their own support, Blue Screaming; at least there is no record of them having played at the venue before this, although, given the fact that they were listed as a headline band that night, it is quite possible that they appeared unheralded at one of the Wednesday audition nights during the summer.

Unfortunately, the only advertising The Makers' 6 September gig received was in the issue of *Sounds* dated 10 September, available in the shops from Wednesday, 7 September, the very day *after* they played at the Roxy – so not of much use – and to rub salt into the wound, the advertisement referred to them as 'The

---

* See Appendix 2.

Maker'. But still, Tony's grandfather, with his connections, had given their career a welcome, if limited, boost.

It seems that the band played at the Roxy again, a month later, on 6 October, this time supporting Gene October's Chelsea, although their appearance as the support band is not listed in the music press. Gary refers to this as Steve Dagger's 'first booking' in his autobiography, which may be correct if he attributes the previous bookings at the Roxy to Bert Tee; and both he and Tony say that Gene October attempted to poach John Keeble (although only Gary specifically says this was at the Roxy) so it is probable that The Makers did indeed play this support gig. Throughout the period of The Makers' existence, Chelsea only played at the Roxy on 6 October 1977 (and they actually broke up after the gig, only for Gene to reform the band in December) so if the Islington band supported them at that venue, as Gary recalls, it must have been on this date.

Then, a few weeks after this, there was a major breakthrough: or so the band thought. One Sunday evening in November, a rock journalist with the *NME* called Bev Briggs decided to telephone a pub/music venue in the King's Cross area of London called the Pindar of Wakefield to ask who was playing there that night. According to Gary Kemp in his autobiography, The Makers had a 'regular Sunday residency' at the Pindar of Wakefield during 1977, although listings in the music press suggest that the act with a regular Sunday residency at this venue during the period July to December 1977 was, in fact, a musical comedy duo, Thunderclap Newman & Bob Flag; subsequently, from March 1978 onwards it was a jazz-rock group called Swift. While The Makers could certainly have played at the pub without being listed, it is noteworthy that at no point in the period from October to December 1977 did *Sounds* include any bands performing at the Pindar of Wakefield on a Sunday in its 'Steppin' Out' listings section, *except* on Sunday, 20 November, when it stated that The Makers would be playing there. The exact same thing is true of *Record Mirror* in its 'Upfront' listings section. For the same entire period, *NME*'s listing page ('Nationwide Gig Guide') had 'Thunderclap Newman

& Bob Flag' playing at that venue every Sunday, including (presumably wrongly) 20 November.

So there would appear to have been something special about The Makers' gig of 20 November 1977 which merited an inclusion in both *Sounds* and *Record Mirror*. The likelihood is that this was the band's debut performance at the Pindar of Wakefield when they expected that a lot of their new Islington supporters (especially those who had discovered them at the Silver Jubilee party a few months earlier) would come and see them play properly for the first time. For sure, none of the nice girls who saw them at the summer street party would have gone anywhere near the Roxy in Covent Garden which was a trashy, unsafe place even for punks. The Pindar of Wakefield, situated within walking distance of the Angel, Islington, was a safer and much more convenient venue at which the band could present themselves to young Islingtonians. So this was probably the big one that everyone who knew the band at the time attended. Sisters Vicki and Liz Silvester certainly remember going to see The Makers play at this pub; it was the first time Vicki had ever been to see a live band. We may note that *Melody Maker* (but not *Sounds*, *Record Mirror* or *NME*) has The Makers playing at the Pindar of Wakefield again during the evening of Sunday, 11 December 1977, as included in its 'Club Calendar' advertising feature, but these two listings (i.e. 20 November and 11 December) are the only known listings for the band at the Pindar.

In any event, Bev Briggs' telephone call to the Pindar of Wakefield just happened to coincide with a Makers' warm-up session for the November gig, so the person who answered the telephone held it up for her to listen to the band. Suitably impressed by what she heard, which she later described as '3 minutes of footstomping, pogoing, singalonga-ecstasy', Briggs went along to the gig that same night, on 20 November, and wrote such a glowing review, which appeared in the *NME* of 10 December 1977, that it caused John Keeble to write in his diary 'Today the Pindar, tomorrow the world'. She said:

The Makers *are* a new band. A kick in the groin band. A needle in the arm band. An everything you've always wanted but never thought you'd hear band. An Alka Seltzer after a New Wave hangover. All this and a bunch of five fresh-faced nubiles…The Makers are the clean-cut guys who move in as the safety pin brigade move out. Musically it still bangs your head off the wall, spikes your red corpuscles, and ties your bondage strap in knots. You can gob to it, pogo to it, puke to it…but hang on…you can also sing to it! Some nice heavy bass for anarchy bit, and a nifty lead guitar for some of the prettier moments. Add some adolescent enthusiasm, harmonies and one hell of a lot of energy and you've got the makings of the 1978 era…Add splashes of Yachts/New Hearts and Noo Wave and you've got the Makers. O.K. So you've never heard of them…neither had I until I saw them…even the Beatles had to start somewhere!

Being compared to the Beatles was unquestionably a good thing and the band followed this up by supporting The Lurkers, who were then signed to the Beggars Banquet label, at the Rock Garden on 17 January 1978. Things were all going well for The Makers at this time. Tony even recalls being recognized outside the Nashville when he went to see Rich Kids perform live. This must have been on the night of Thursday, 26 January 1978, when Rich Kids and John Cooper Clarke played at that venue. Gary Kemp, incidentally, also appears to have been at the Nashville that evening: 'I remember really liking the Rich Kids which was Glen Matlock's band' he has said: 'I'll never forget coz I saw them play at the Nashville and everyone was spitting at them as punks did and Rusty Egan was the drummer and he got up off his kit and went to the front and he said "no-one fucking spits at me". Gary's and Rusty's paths were to cross again in due course but for the moment it seemed that fame was beckoning for the boys from Islington.

Shortly after this, Bev Briggs, now working for *Record Mirror*, wrote the band another glowing review when they appeared at a benefit gig in Hornsey for the threatened Other Cinema in central

London's Tottenham Street which Steve Dagger's good friend Steve Woolley was now managing. But then... nothing happened. The major record labels did not come knocking to offer a deal. A couple of good reviews changed little. The Makers were still just one of hundreds, if not thousands, of new wave power pop type bands in London playing gigs to small audiences in tiny venues hoping that something would magically happen for them.

The Makers continued to perform from February to May 1978, playing the Rock Garden again and other smaller venues, mainly pubs, such as the Hope & Anchor in Islington, Rochester Castle in Stoke Newington and the Railway Hotel in Hampstead but with no obvious signs of success. 'We played at every pub and club that would have us' recalled Tony in a 2007 interview for *Woman's Weekly*, adding, 'We'd go in pleading for a gig and be lucky if we got £25 and a pint of lager each.' Tony did manage a starring role in a *My Guy* photo-story called 'Sister Blackmail' in April 1978 (ironically playing a character called 'Gary') but this was not the type of fame he was really looking for.

By now Tony had dropped out of school and had started working for IPC – which is where he was spotted by *My Guy* – and he was followed there by Steve Norman. IPC were the publishers of *NME* and this allowed a few strings to be pulled to secure free adverts for The Makers' gigs in the *NME* – with the appearance of their own band logo – making them appear to be a much more well-known and successful band than they really were. Still, it didn't seem to attract the A&R executives to their gigs, let alone a recording contract. Tony remembers sitting on the end of his bed sobbing at the lack of a record deal. Even a further good review by Linnet Evans in *Sounds* of 13 May 1978, albeit of a clearly difficult gig, did not help:

> THE MAKERS introduced themselves before the gig as a band heavily biased into soul, reggae and Motown with a following who'd 'never go near a rock gig'. Granted they probably know their audience (young indigenous Islington – their home base)

better than I (blinkered Shoreditch gentry), but in practice the Makers appeared to have only a dot more blackness than e.g. Bernie Tormé. No they size up as a currently very typical pop/rock band, laced with statutory energy and with beautifully cut hair, who've spent their first 18 months tightening up to good effect and ought now to spend the next 18 loosening down again. Most of their material is basically quite strong and colourful and at its best carries certain traces of 'Rubber Soul', Hollies, etc. without the dinkiness of say, The Smirks. Lead singer Tony Hadley's lyrics were hard to follow, but I'd blame that and perhaps his unwitting aggression to the non-arrival of hired PA and the consequent last-minute borrowing of another, very inadequate system. This also fouled up subtleties in the vocal harmonies department. Trouble was, many of the songs were no more than airless, graceless slugs of unrelenting sound where the only thing you could pick out were some over-topical licks from the drum department (John Keeble). Against which just tiny differences could pick up something like 'Fantasy Girl' into a minor rollalong classic, and there were a couple like 'Pin Ups' with its natty bass line and others whose titles I couldn't catch which were really intriguing on the mind, and hence motivating on the body even for the stolid Grope and Spanker audience. The Makers have obviously a long way to go to keep the average punter satisfied – but they shouldn't let that worry them.

Well, in fact, The Makers did not have a terribly long way to go, only a few more weeks in fact. Richie Miller was replaced by Gary's brother, Martin, in a coup supposedly orchestrated by Steve Dagger (although Martin has said it was his mother who pressured Gary to include him!) and the band was transformed from The Makers to Gentry, a choice of name perhaps subconsciously influenced by the *Sounds* journalist's mention of being 'blinkered Shoreditch gentry'. Martin had always been slightly off the band members' radar, not only because he was younger than all the others, but also because he was the only one of them not to have gone to Owen's. Nevertheless, even though he had never played bass guitar before, albeit that he had been a guitarist in a punk band called The Defects, Martin was already a bit of a local star, having had a credited part in an episode of a major BBC2 drama, *The Glittering Prizes*, which had been broadcast on 11 February 1976. Steve Dagger had not failed to notice the 16-year-old Martin's stunning, celebrity like, good looks. According to Dagger: 'Martin Kemp was the roadie for the group. He didn't look like a roadie at all. He looked like he should be in the band. There was as much interest in him as there was some of the band members from the female members of the audience. The band was a handsome line-up but if we could get Martin in the line-up as well playing bass then it would be an extraordinarily good looking bunch of guys.' As Gary remembers it, he was in a club with Dagger one evening when Dagger said to him, '"Look, what about getting your brother in the group?" I said "Why?" He said "Well look at him". I remember looking down this bar we were in and he was surrounded by girls.... And I said "He can't play bass", he said "Well you can teach him"…I remember sitting up all night teaching him all the bass lines. He was so happy to be in this group that he learnt everything and became our new bass player.'

Martin thinks he was told by Dagger that he was in the band at Steve Norman's eighteenth birthday party but, as Steve Norman turned eighteen on 25 March 1978, it was probably Tony Hadley's party that he recalls, Tony having turned eighteen on 2 June 1978. Gentry's first gig was on 1 July 1978 at the Middlesex Polytechnic in Cockfosters and Martin had learnt his bass lines well but, despite the improved look of the band, they had equally little success as The Makers. In fact, one could say they had even less success as Gentry because they never even achieved a single review under this name. They continued to play at the same old beer stained, sweaty type venues as before, lugging their equipment around London, returning home in the early hours of the morning and sometimes not even being paid. A few days after Gentry's first gig, as an example of the stresses they were under,

Tony broke up with his then girlfriend after she criticized the band's performance at the Red Cow in Hammersmith on 6 July 1978.

Their one moment of glory – an appearance in May 1979 at the *Marquee* in support of The Showbiz Kids – turned out to be their last. They certainly did not seem to be exuding confidence according to the manager of The Showbiz Kids, Geoff Docherty, who remembers them being 'exceptionally quiet and subdued' in the dressing room (as mentioned in his 2002 book, *A Promoter's Tale*). Things looked hopeless; they could not just keep gigging forever, and the band effectively gave up. They stopped performing and wondered what else they could do.

By now they had all left school and some of them had jobs which could have provided a satisfactory living. Tony was a sales executive for an electronics publication and a trade union representative to boot. Steve Norman was a senior copy and make-up clerk in the publishing industry. John Keeble had a steady and relatively well paid job as a foreign exchange clerk in Barclays bank. Martin was an apprentice printer. Gary was less settled in employment but was undoubtedly confident he was going to be famous one way or another. However, the dreaded thought no doubt crossed all of their minds that perhaps they needed to give up the dream of being pop stars.

At exactly the same time as the members of Gentry were thinking of giving up, a new band called Spandau Ballet was optimistically playing the first of what its members hoped would be many London gigs, at the Hope & Anchor in Islington.

CHAPTER TWO

The First Spandau Ballet

THE STORY OF THE ORIGINS of the first Spandau Ballet begins in September 1971 in Bedfordshire, in the small rural town of Ampthill, when, at exactly the same time as Gary Kemp, Tony Hadley and Steve Norman were starting secondary school in Islington, two eleven-year-old boys were commencing their first year at Redborne School and quickly became best friends due to their mutual interest in art; they were the most talented artists in the school. The two boys were Michael John Austin and David Agar Wardill.

Michael, or Mick as he was known, lived in Ampthill but David, who had been born in the United States to English parents and came to England as a baby, was living further out, in a tiny village called Wharley End, near Cranfield. He had passed the eleven-plus with high marks and was destined for Bedford's grammar school but was reluctant to go there because it was an all boys' school and, moreover, pupils were required to attend on Saturday mornings, which he didn't fancy. Fortunately, his parents were sympathetic and he was allowed to go to Ampthill's Redborne Comprehensive School instead, the only other school in the vicinity, although he still had to travel about ten miles on a bus to get there, a journey that took some forty-five minutes. When he joined, he didn't know anyone at the school but, on virtually the first day, he became friends with Mick, who was in his tutor group, and, from then on, the two boys were inseparable.

For a few years, while sitting next to each other in class, Mick and David would create drawings together, usually cartoons, but, as they grew older, they both developed an interest in music. In 1974, at the age of fourteen, David read a book called *A Journey Through America With the Rolling Stones* by the American journalist Robert Greenfield who had been embedded with the Rolling Stones on their 1972 tour of the United States. According to David, Greenfield's book, 'gives you an insight into the kind of gang mentality of the band. It's a sort of beyond the law sort of lifestyle and I just read it and was like, yeah this is what I want.' Thus influenced, he decided he wanted to become a musician and took up the bass guitar, 'because I didn't know anything about music, like chords or anything, I couldn't read music, and I thought I can't do all that so I thought I'd play the bass.' It wasn't only that it was the easiest instrument to play, though, because, he says, 'I'd always been very attracted to the noise of the bass, the sound.' He borrowed a 'crappy old' bass guitar and 'a friend of my mum's had an amp, a Vox 80/30, which had been used by a mod band in the sixties, so I just practised at home playing along with records and learnt to play.'

Mick, who had not until then been especially keen on music, soon developed an interest like his friend and taught himself to play an acoustic guitar. In a short time, he and David would 'make songs and play old Elvis songs and put different lyrics to them… and have a bit of fun.' One day, while in class, the two boys solemnly agreed that they would one day definitely form a proper band and become rock stars. For the time being, however, it was all extremely informal and they 'started playing together just as you do at school you know.' Not many pupils in Redborne School at the time were interested in rock music, let alone could play instruments, so they were pretty much on their own in this respect and there was no pool of willing musicians for them to draw on in order to form a band.

At the end of their fifth year, in 1976, Mick was keen to progress his artistic skills and decided to sign up for a fine art foundation course at Barnfield College in Luton. This required him to make a journey of some eleven miles out of Ampthill every day, which was a bit of a trek but perfectly manageable, especially as he was given a lift in a car shared with another student. For David, however, the journey from Wharley End to Luton was too far to be travelled comfortably on a daily basis so he decided to stay at Redborne to continue his studies and embark on his 'A' Levels.

Although Mick and David were now at different educational establishments, they remained friends but things were not quite the same as they had been during their time at school. In the first place, Mick made a new friend at Barnfield in Mark Robinson, a talented artist and guitarist.

Having lived in Luton since the age of six, Mark Edgar Thomas Robinson, to give him his full name, had been exposed to a more musically sophisticated crowd than Mick, and was, consequently, more advanced as a musician. In contrast to Redborne School, where only a few students were interested in music, at Stopsley High School, which Mark attended, 'everyone wanted to be in a band' and there was 'a little scene going on.'

Mark had been playing guitar since the age of about twelve when, while on a family holiday in Benidorm, he had been allowed by his parents to buy himself an acoustic guitar. Once he had mastered that, his parents bought him a copy stratocaster which he learnt to play rather well and teamed up with other young local musicians. Initially he formed a band called Jade with his friends Paul Gittins and Vernon 'Tubby' Doggett. Paul's older brother, John, ran a rehearsal studio called Quest in Windmill Road, where Jethro Tull rehearsed, and, 'when the big boys were taking a break they used to let us go there and bash the hell out of everything.' Mark also fancied himself as a vocalist and was the lead singer in Jade which played at both the East Hall in Stopsley High School and the Slough Rock Concert but the band came to an end when Mark transferred from Stopsley High School to Bedford School, and, at the same time, moved from Luton to Pulloxhill, in 1975.

Mark's musical abilities certainly caught Mick's attention. He recalls, 'He was a good musician even then. I remember him with an acoustic guitar and he was just superb.' He first noticed his abilities in a college music club which they both joined and, 'the bloke with the guitar said, "Can you just go around and show us what you can do" and the guitar was passed around and we were all rubbish except when it came to Mark and he just sort of put on an impromptu little gig. He was singing and playing and he was absolutely brilliant, fantastic. He was really, really good.' Furthermore, Mark's connections with other musicians were impressive, especially as he knew some good drummers: vital if you wanted to form a band but very hard to find, whereas, as Mick says, 'there were loads of guitarists because everyone wants to play the guitar.'

Mick was certainly one of those who wanted to play the guitar. On 23 March 1977, he purchased an electric guitar – a Cimar Les Paul copy – for fifty pounds from Aflyn music shop in Luton, run by John Gittins. After getting to grips with that, through jamming with friends in the local church hall, he was allowed to play in one of Mark's bands, the one with arguably the worst name of all: Jack the Ripper, which featured a drummer called Michael Harvey.

Michael John Harvey, who had known Mark at Stopsley High School but had lost touch with him after he moved to Pulloxhill, was already a skilled drummer, having applied himself to the art since the age of eleven after becoming entranced by the drummers and drum kits of glam rock bands such as The Glitter Band, Wizzard, Sweet and Roxy Music. 'I had noticed', he says, 'that the drums were the biggest, brightest and often loudest instruments in the various groups.' He coaxed his mother into acquiring on his behalf some drums and cymbals and started practising in his lounge, before ingeniously creating his own 'home studio' with two tape recorders, recording a drum beat on one cassette then playing it back while recording a piano line on the other and subsequently adding more instruments onto additional 'tracks', although the sound quality rapidly deteriorated the more tracks he attempted.

He had teamed up briefly with a saxophone-playing neighbour to form a duo called Wild Movements and had taken weekly drumming lessons from a professional musician at the age of fourteen. He hadn't played drums in Jade due to the fact that 'Tubby' Doggett had been a more experienced and superior drummer but, when he bumped into Mark at Barnfield College while studying there for a two year Ordinary National Diploma in Business Studies, his old friend immediately suggested they form a band and introduced him to the guitar playing Mick Austin. The three of them rehearsed in a college outbuilding classroom during the spring of 1977 and decided to call themselves Jack the Ripper, blissfully unaware that this name would put off most people from seeing them play, especially girls.

A bass player called Tim Lewis was recruited and the four boys would rehearse either in a church hall in Ampthill or in Quest Studios in Luton. Their first gig was in the college refectory where Mark perfected the art of igniting flash powder on stage as a song reached a crescendo. Sometimes they would wear caps and braces on stage to capture the flavour of the Victorian East End of London and used dry ice to replicate fog. Michael Harvey managed to obtain a newspaper stand covered with a wire mesh into which the band would slip a poster saying: 'GET YOUR PAPER HERE, THE RIPPER STRIKES AGAIN!' To complete the package, some of the songs also had a Ripper theme.

At one point during 1977, Jack the Ripper played a small gig at the Ampthill Youth Centre, located next to Redborne School in Flitwick Road. The Youth Centre was a purpose built building, designed and paid for by Bedfordshire County Council, which had been opened in late 1970 and hosted the Ampthill Youth Club, so that the Youth Centre and the Youth Club were commonly regarded as the same thing. With nowhere else for young teenagers to go and nothing for them to do – there being no cinema in Ampthill and the last bus from Bedford, where there were three cinemas, left before the pictures finished – the Youth Club, which was open to kids aged fourteen plus, was a real social hub where the kids of Ampthill all hung out, chatting, watching television, listening to music on the juke box, playing table tennis, darts or table football, or drinking milk shakes or coffee (purchased from the purpose built coffee bar) with the occasional disco thrown in. There was even a small stage area and, consequently, it was the natural venue for any local band (of which there were not many) to perform at, hence the appearance in 1977 of Jack the Ripper which performed some original songs written by Mark, as well as some cover versions of classic rock songs. Pulloxhill, where Mark was now living, was only a few miles from Ampthill, so the Ampthill Youth Centre was a convenient location for both Mick and Mark. Watching the performance at the Youth Club was David Wardill who, like Mick, had found a new group of friends.

AS SOON AS HE HAD seen a photograph of the Sex Pistols in 1976, David had cut his hair, 'and I ended up with short, spikey, messy hair'. He started to go and see punk bands such as Ramones, Buzzcocks and The Clash. As he says, 'That took over. That was the thing. In my lifetime that was the cultural shift. That was different. So I did that and that was my thing then.' He had still been playing bass occasionally with Mick during jamming sessions but Mick had noted David's cool new 'punky friends' and felt that 'we'd sort of drifted apart a little bit' to the extent that it wasn't clear their friendship would survive. Mick had tentatively attempted to join in the spirit by cutting his hair short but, as he admits, 'still wasn't punked up'. He liked Led Zeppelin and hippy or heavy bands and had not been totally seduced by punk like David. Thus, when playing covers of rock songs, such as 'Hotel California', with Jack the Ripper at the Ampthill Youth Club, Mick was worried that his friend's reaction, especially to the long guitar solos, would be dismissive, even hostile.

Some of Mick's fears were realized because, in truth, David did not wholly enjoy the performance: 'They did this atrocious version of Hotel California,' he recalls, 'I was thinking this is not my cup of tea.' He didn't say this to Mick, of course, congratulating him enthusiastically after the performance, remarking that it was 'very good'. His positive comments were not entirely untrue, however. While not being keen on the songs they played, he *was* extremely impressed by the fact that Mick had become involved with a group which had been able to perform competently in public. As David explains: 'If it's friends of yours, people making music, even if you don't think it's your thing, it's kind of impressive and you get excited. I thought, what was good about it was that we, people of our age, could do this, form a band and make music. We were only sixteen or seventeen. They were very professional. Mick is a super over-achiever, if he does something he does it with phenomenal concentration. What was obvious was that he'd sat down, learnt chords, learnt how to do it, and learnt how to do things like solos, which were anathema to me in punk. He was clearly someone marking himself out to be a professional musician. And he was very good looking. In a band he'd be a definite asset: good looking, great at playing the guitar.' Furthermore:

> I remember them sounding like a proper rock band. It was very professional. It wasn't exactly my cup of tea. Especially 'Hotel California'. For young people to get something together like that, the organization and concentration and dedication to do it properly. They would pass as a tribute band today. They were good. That's impressive. I was hungry to get involved in music and I was definitely impressed…There were precious few other people I knew who could do that. I didn't know any other people who could play like that. And they took it seriously. To make music properly you have to take it very seriously and do what's necessary. That's what I got from them when they were doing it. These were people who wanted to do it. It's that gelling, how they played together…. and they played in time. When you're sixteen

[or seventeen] and you watch your mates play in time, in tune, and they played recognizable songs without making mistakes, that is bloody impressive.

There was also something about the lead vocalist. According to David, the band's singer, Mark Robinson, 'had that sort of mad, narcissistic drive that you imagine a singer should have. That kind of confidence to stand there and do the singing thing. And he had that. He did have that.' Not only that but he felt that Jack the Ripper had a very decent drummer in Michael Harvey. According to David, he was 'a great drummer, he just had that thing. Not too flashy, solid. He was definitely a professional standard drummer.'

David's brain was now working overtime. He had in no way lost his schoolboy desire to be a rock star. In fact, it was still all he wanted to be. Now that he saw that his best friend had not only developed as a guitarist but had attached himself to some serious musicians, who could potentially help him to achieve his ambition, he realized this could be his big opportunity. Before this, however, he needed to complete his 'A' Levels. Being so far out from the others in Wharley End meant it also wasn't practical for him to be part of any bands operating and rehearsing primarily in Luton.

In the meantime, there was a bit of a falling out within Jack the Ripper. Tim Lewis left the group to be replaced by a seasoned semi-professional bass player whose view was that the band was never going to achieve any success in the music industry so they should make as much money as they could by playing covers and performing as many gigs as possible at local pubs. Mick, on the other hand, wanted to perform original material and spend everything the band had on going for glory, buying equipment and recording demo tapes in professional studios. This clash led to Mick's departure from the band which did not last long without him.

IN LATE 1977, MARK AND Michael Harvey teamed up with two new Barnfield College art students – rhythm guitarist Tim Shorten and bass guitarist Neil Philips – to form a band which Mark named The Edgar Thomas Band, showing quite clearly who was in charge. By this stage, Mick Austin had left Barnfield and was working full-time, so that his mind was not directed towards music at all. The new band continued to rehearse at Quest and other places, such as Neil's home in Bedford, and recorded four original Mark Robinson composed songs at a studio in John Street, Luton, on 22 January 1978. Its first gig was a charity concert at Bedford's Bromham Hospital before an audience of special needs children. The Edgar Thomas Band also participated in the Oxford area heat of the annual *Melody Maker* rock contest in May 1978 at Oxford Polytechnic and played at various pubs, including the Unicorn in Luton on 31 March 1978 and the Tidal Basin Tavern in Canning Town on 14 April 1978 in support of a band called The Mistakes, although the latter gig, in front of a bunch of East End punks who were not terribly interested in the type of soft rock music that The Edgar Thomas Band played, might have been a mistake.

With Tim Shorten and Neil Philips due to leave Luton for college, The Edgar Thomas Band came to an abrupt end in July 1978 but Michael was introduced to Mick's friend, David Wardill, and, as Mark, Michael and David had now all finished their exams and had plenty of spare time, the boys decided that the time was right for them to form a band. By this stage they were all pretty decent musicians. Michael's drumming was tight, David had mastered his bass guitar, Mick was fast improving as a guitarist and Mark, already a proficient guitarist, was developing as a singer. One thing that these young musicians did not possess, however, was a decent band name. For a short time, they toyed with the bizarre sounding Olé Ma Rathon & the Yumettes but they knew they needed to come up something better, much better.

IT IS A REMARKABLE FACT that both Mark and Mick were fascinated by one word during 1978: Spandau. Mark had been reading a book he had borrowed from his father's private library, the recently published *Spandau: The Secret Diaries*, comprising the diaries supposedly written in Spandau prison by the Nazi war criminal Albert Speer before his release in 1966. Mark had not only enjoyed the book, which he heartily recommended to Mick, but 'Spandau', from the book's title, struck him as an interesting noun and certainly worthy of forming part of a band's name.

By pure coincidence, Mick Austin had also been conscious of the word 'Spandaü' (which he fancied contained an umlaut over the letter 'u') since the age of fourteen. He loved the way the word looked, especially with that umlaut at the end – even though there should not be one there – but he did not relate it to a book, a prison or a Nazi war criminal. Mick was intrigued by anything related to the military, especially in respect of German militaria, which seemed to him more interesting than the British variety, and he associated 'Spandaü' with a German machine gun.

Strictly speaking, a Spandau was a First World War heavy machine gun, the Maxim Maschinengewehr 08, or MG08, commonly known as the 'Spandau gun' because it was manufactured in Spandau, an industrial district of Berlin in Germany, and thus marked 'SPANDAU' on a plate on the side of the weapon. As it happens, Mick owned a prized, and much thumbed, deactivated gun catalogue featuring an illustration of a Second World War German Maschinengewehr 34, or MG34, machine gun, which at the time, like many people, including British soldiers, he wrongly believed to be the Spandau gun and which had always fascinated him. According to Mick, 'One thousand two hundred rounds per minute, I mean it's a superb gun and just looks fantastic…So I was really into that gun and I loved the word Spandau.'

At the time, as many boys did in the 1970s with Airfix and Tamiya kits, Mick had recently made a model of a German motorcycle with sidecar which had an MG34 mounted on the back, so the Spandau gun was very much in his mind. David greatly shared Mick's interest in militaria, including the Spandau machine gun. As he says, 'All the kids I knew were mad about the war. War comics were very common. Mick and I had collected soldiers, made military models and played war games as kids.' Like Mick, David had constructed a Tamiya model of a soldier on a motorbike carrying an MG42, another weapon that was sometimes known as a Spandau gun. Says Mick, 'We used to say the name [of the gun], "The Big Spandaü", and we used to put an umlaut at the top.'

Now that there was the prospect of forming a real band with some rather tasty musicians, the need to devise a good band name took on a greater urgency, especially as the boys were already booked to play a benefit gig at the Ampthill Youth Club in order to raise money for it; and it was decided that some organizational focus was required. According to Michael Harvey, the four of them met in the drawing room of Mark's home in Pulloxhill, in order to devise a name for the new line-up. As Michael remembers it:

> We were sitting in his [Mark's] parents' drawing room with books on shelves all around us and we started to discuss ideas for the name of the group. Various suggestions were made. I suggested Lemon Tree but this was unpopular. I'm sure it was Mark who was continually repeating this awful name 'Spandau' which I didn't like. Numerous words were called out at random. The conversation would drift into other areas, other names, other suggestions would be made but Mark kept on coming back to this Spandau thing which I couldn't comprehend. It just seemed so irrelevant and off the wall. And then I think it was Mick who suggested looking in the books from the bookshelves. He started pulling out books off the wall and calling out names from books, none of which seemed to be suitable. And then he had this idea, and this was Mick's idea, to make up three numbers. He said, 'you just shout out any three numbers at random, first number will be the page, second number will be the line, third number will be the word.' I don't know how many times we did that. Mick pulled a gardening book off the shelf. The numbers led to the word 'ballet', possibly because some flowers in the book were described as 'balletic'. I did not find 'Spandau' or 'Ballet' particularly attractive, even less so when combined, and for a

while we continued shouting out names in a haphazard fashion. Mark kept on about his 'Spandau' word which he seemed quite keen on and then somebody in the room put the two words together. And I didn't like that...that's not going to work. We're not an opera group or classical ballet group in any shape or form. However, Mark continued to repeat 'Spandau' and the others warmed to the idea of pairing this with 'Ballet'.

Michael thought that 'Spandau Ballet' was an 'awful' name which 'would never catch on' but, at this stage, he was anticipating that, as long as his exam results went well, he would be going off to the Chelmer Institute in Chelmsford, Essex, to study law, having been offered a provisional place there. Hence, knowing that he would not be around in Bedfordshire much longer, 'I did not protest particularly vociferously.' The justification for the name, as Michael understood it, was that, 'Some of our music was hard, heavy and dark as one would expect a German prison to be while some songs were light and lovey-dovey, like ballet can be.'

Mick Austin's memory of how the name was conjured up is rather different. He thinks that he and David jointly devised it at his parents' house. As he explains:

> I remember being on the kitchen table and the dining table. And it's quite open plan, my parents' place. Where was the eureka moment I can't remember. I remember being on the dining table with lots of bits of paper. We did the old David Bowie thing. We put them all down and Spandau was one of them. I can't actually – I remember being there and I remember I was coming up with that but it was a long time ago and I can't remember the moment we picked one out. We put loads of things together...we just thought of all good words. Spandau was one of them. And we sort of fitted them together to see what sounded good.

According to both Mick and David, in response to Mick's proposal of 'Spandau', or 'Spandaü', David immediately and instinctively replied 'ballet' and the two boys realized that the combination of 'Spandau' and 'ballet', one strong Germanic word linked with a softer, romantic word, worked very well. David says: 'I remember the duality of the name, the contrast between the two words being interesting' and he thought the whole package was 'nicely decadent'.

Although, on both accounts, the association was formed randomly, the boys had by pure chance hit on a fairly natural name. Many towns or cities in Germany, like other major towns and cities around the world, have ballets associated with them so that we find a Hamburg Ballet, a Stuttgart Ballet, a Berlin State Ballet and so on and, while Spandau is not a town or city, it was not totally implausible that it could have had a ballet company of its own, although, in actual fact, one had never been established there.

The name also had a certain resonance in the way it could be said to have conjured up an image of the four Allied powers – the United States, the Soviet Union, Great Britain and France – being engaged in a perpetual, metaphorical, dance with each other as they formally handed over responsibility for guarding the elderly Rudolph Hess in Spandau prison. By 1978, he was the only remaining prisoner held at Spandau, after six other high ranking Nazis who had been imprisoned there after the war, including Albert Speer, had been released. Monthly throughout the year without fail, a platoon of soldiers from one nation's army would hand over external guard duties to another; so the British Army would, after a month, hand over to the French Army, who would, at the end of the following month, hand over to the Soviets who would, in turn, make way for the Americans a month later before the Americans returned responsibility to the British, thus starting the cycle over again, ensuring that each nation was responsible for guarding Hess for a total of three months of the year. As Roy Bainton, author of *The Long Patrol: The British in Germany Since 1945*, said in 2003 of this constant ritualized, timetabled, almost musical, rotation of the guard: 'You cannot help calling it a "Spandau ballet"…the four powers all straining for their own particular show of intricate protocol and uniformed discipline.'

The band members, mainly sheltered art students in Ampthill, did not have ballet companies or military routines specifically in mind when they devised and/or approved the name Spandau Ballet. It was the interesting sound of that combination of words which appealed to them rather than any specific meaning. According to Mick: 'The two words coupled beautifully: one violent, deadly and Germanic, the other the essence of peace and culture. Also, the rapid fire of the gun would be inclined to make one dance quite fast!'

In contrast to Michael Harvey's memory of the name being coined at Mark's house, and Mick and David's recollection of inventing it together at the home of Mick's parents, Mark Robinson has yet another memory of events surrounding the naming of the band. According to Mark, doing his best to recall events of more than thirty-five years earlier, 'I do remember going round to his [Mick's] mum and dad's house and the cutting out of the names. We used to rehearse in my parents' house in Pulloxhill and maybe one time we cut out names in the study. I clearly remember [Spandau] and I think it was Mick saying we need the opposite of that: "So why don't we have ballet?" And I remember sort of saying, "Yeah, we could have a ballet dancer of barbed wire"...Whether I dreamt it or not I don't know.'

As Spandau Ballet, the boys prepared for their very first gig at the Ampthill Youth Centre on Wednesday, 30 August 1978, even designing their own poster to advertise it. Mark took control of the visual appearance and design of the 'Spandau Ballet' name, which probably explains why it never actually had an umlaut over the 'u' as Mick had imagined it. Making creative use of some black bin bags, sticky tape and white acrylic paint he also created a huge banner to be deployed as a backdrop during the gig, bearing the name Spandau Ballet in big letters: 'SPANDAU' appearing in large capitals with *'Ballet'* beneath it at an angle in script. Above the band name were various words cut from tabloid newspaper headlines. Those that can be read from the surviving photograph are 'FUN', 'HAPPY!' '[SCORING?] TWICE!' 'SPECIAL', 'WORLD',

'PAIN', 'CHAMPAGNE', 'FIGURE', 'BEST', 'SAVAGE', 'TO GO ON...BIGGER CROWDS', 'TENDER', 'CREDIT', 'WEDDING', 'REAL COOL', 'SPEED', 'CRASH', 'HORROR'.

There is a difference in recollection amongst the band members as to whether the Ampthill Youth Club gig actually went ahead. Michael Harvey is sure it did. He made a note in his diary that it was the third time he had played at this venue in one guise or another and he remembers the others informing him afterwards that it had been David Wardill's first ever live gig. As they could only have had a few weeks to rehearse, and no time to compose any new material, he believes that the band played a few covers, such as Led Zeppelin's 'Rosalie', and probably cobbled together some songs that Mark had originally written for The Edgar Thomas Band. In saying that the gig took place, he is supported by Gill Morris (as she was then called before she married), a former resident of Ampthill and member of the Youth Club, who recalls that, 'It was really exciting and it was noisy and it was very rocky...I just remember it being fun and it was so big for us to have our mates playing in a band...It's not a big youth club, it was only a small gig, but they did actually play a gig as Spandau Ballet; I know they did.' Mick and Dave, however, have no memory of the gig having occurred and think it was cancelled. Mick, in particular, is fairly sure that it never happened. What is certain, however, is that Mark, Mick and David all went down to live and work in London later in the year, in either September or October 1978.

As Mick explains, 'All bands went to London. We knew we had to go to London' or, as David puts it, 'We decided we were going to go to London and become rock stars and that was our plan.' Unfortunately for the plan, Michael Harvey did not want to come to London to chase the rock star dream. He preferred to go to college and study law, despite the others trying to persuade him to stay on with the band. David, for one, had no interest in going to college or university: 'I saw that as postponing real life', he says, 'I wanted to get on with real life.'

As part of his plan for getting on with real life, David had treated himself to a new guitar. 'As soon as we were eighteen and I'd finished sixth form,' he relates, 'I bought another bass guitar; a proper bass guitar. In those days you could sign on as a student in the summer and I didn't get my benefit money until – I got it in one lump sum. It was like eighty or ninety quid or something. And I went straight down to Woolworths in Bedford and bought a bass guitar. It was a fender jazz copy.'

Having arrived in London, Mick and David moved into a house at 32 Sibley Grove, East Ham, being rented by a friend of theirs, Deanne Pearson, a graduate of journalism from the London College of Printing who was then a writer/sub-editor for *Horse & Hound*, being compelled to write articles about things like the All-England Ploughing Championships when she really just wanted to be a rock music journalist. Deanne, who had also gone to Redborne School, had been spotted by David at a bus stop in Ampthill and he had fallen instantly in love with her, so his move to London might not have been exclusively to become a rock star. Mark initially lived with his sister's boyfriend in Battersea before he too moved briefly to East Ham. Initially, the three founder members of the fledgling Spandau Ballet were sleeping on the floor of the sitting room with mice running over them at night because there were no spare rooms and they had no money. Also living in the house at East Ham were Kim Bowen and Lee Sheldrick, both students of fashion at St Martin's School of Art, who were later to be regulars at a small, fashionable, wine bar-cum-nightclub in central London called Blitz. Deanne had met them at a party in Basingstoke, through a mutual friend, Elida Morris, who was also living at Sibley Grove, and became friends with them, leading them all to share the house in East Ham.

At the end of October 1978, Mick and David secured themselves jobs at Richard Branson's soon to be opened new venue in Victoria on the site of the old Metropole Cinema called, rather unimaginatively, 'The Venue'. Mick received his offer letter, which he still possesses, dated 22 October 1978, instructing him to attend The

Venue eight days later on 30 October for a brief training period, culminating in a staff Halloween party the following night, on the eve of the club's grand opening on 1 November.

The Venue had two high-minded aims. Firstly, it wanted to provide studio quality sound for its audience and, to this end, the stage was designed like a recording booth, carpeted to studio standard, with an adjustable bronze mirror to brighten or soften the sound as required and a mixing desk at the centre. Unfortunately, it did not work. As a result, The Venue was forced to close for a week before the end of its first month of operation in order to cure problems with its PA system and to make design alterations. The second, slightly more successful, aim was to provide a civilized location where people could watch and listen to bands in comfort as opposed to small, dirty, sweaty, dives which were de rigueur at the time. Thus, unusually for a music venue, one could sit, drink and eat at dining tables while watching the acts. There was a big kitchen and Branson had decided to offer an American style diner with burgers and chilli on the menu. This naturally required plenty of staff, such as chefs, waiters, waitresses, bar staff, as well as people to bring food to the tables and clear up the plates afterwards, known as 'busboys' – which is what provided employment for the boys from Bedfordshire. Mark Robinson, meanwhile, originally worked as a board marker for Ladbrokes in Whitehall but then he too obtained a job as a busboy at The Venue.

In addition to bringing food and clearing plates, the boys did other menial tasks. David recalls that his first job was to unwrap all the new chairs, 'but it was great because we were working at night and got to see all these bands for free, like brilliant bands, and we met loads of great people. It was amazing…We were thrust into the middle of this rock thing. I'd be clearing plates off Pete Townshend's table.' Basically, 'It was the best job you could have as a young man working at The Venue because you just met all these interesting people.'

For Mick too, it wasn't all work and no play. The Venue had one of the earliest Space Invader machines in the country and

Mick thinks that he and a barman called Mike must have been the first Space Invader champions of the UK due to the amount of games they were able to play when it was quiet. As he says, 'We were discovering things on Space Invaders that no-one else knew.' For a short time, he and Mark actually lived in The Venue because, having moved out of Sibley Grove, where they could not go on sleeping on the floor for ever, they were allowed to stay in the artists' bar in the backstage rooms. According to Mick, 'We used to go out there [into the main area of The Venue] at night, when there wasn't a band on, turn the music up, the whole sound system, put records on; we used to fire up the kitchen. It sounds unbelievable but we did, you know, make ourselves burgers...we weren't allowed out, we had to stay there until it opened in the morning.' However, they had a solution for this: 'We used to climb through a little window on the back staircase and climb over the security fences.'

This living arrangement could not last very long and the management eventually kicked them out so they found other digs in London. David, however, had moved in with Deanne, who had become his girlfriend, so he was living at Sibley Grove the entire time.

They hadn't forgotten about the need to progress their band and, as they obviously needed a new drummer, an advertisement was placed in *Melody Maker*. There were no replies but a soldier stationed and living at Mill Hill barracks who was moonlighting as a bouncer at The Venue had a sixteen-year-old son, Gordon, who played the drums and wanted to join a band. The soldier gave his son the contact details of the members of Spandau Ballet so that he could arrange to attend an audition.

Gordon Bowman had become interested in drumming when he saw the Beatles film *Help* at the Gaumont Cinema in North Finchley during a children's Saturday Morning Pictures presentation and was fascinated by Ringo Starr. He had two friends who owned drum kits and he started to practise at their houses, playing along to hit records. After a few years of this, his father lent him the money to buy his own drum kit from Blanks music store in Kilburn High Street. It was a red Shaftesbury and cost £250 but he had to pay his father back in weekly instalments so he took a part-time job at Tesco in Finchley to enable him to do so. For a short time, he played informally with a group of older musicians, comprising soldiers stationed at the Mill Hill barracks, before joining Spandau Ballet.

After school one evening he caught a bus to Victoria for the audition which consisted of him jamming with the others on the main Venue stage, using the club's Sonar drum kit which he enjoyed playing. Speaking to the others, he realized that he liked the same kind of punk and new wave music they did and he was invited into the band that very same evening. David wasn't entirely convinced by him though: 'He was nervous. Bands don't operate with nervous people. He had a reasonable kit and could play solid and straight but, because of that nervous thing, would make mistakes. He would falter.' But, he adds, 'he gave it a go.' Gordon himself admits he was nervous, mainly because he was so young and inexperienced but also because he felt that the others were superb musicians and he was intimidated by this. As he says, 'I think the reason why I was nervous is not so much putting myself down but these guys were good. They would blow me out the water.' Mark comments, 'We didn't have much choice. He's a really nice guy. He wasn't as good as Mick Harvey but it was right in a way because the rest of it wasn't very good either!'

As the three busboys got to know the management at The Venue, their band was allowed to rehearse in the mezzanine bar of the club, or even on the proper stage, during the day when they weren't working. According to Mick, 'We used to practise there a lot.' Indeed, they were playing so much that Spandau Ballet jokingly became known by the other staff as the house band of The Venue. Marking out their territory, Mark stencilled the name of their band, together with a logo he had devised of a ballet dancer surrounded by barbed wire, on a door in the upstairs toilet for everyone to see, having first practised his handiwork in the boiler room. He, Mick and Gordon also took the opportunity to write the band's name in felt tip pen on any other unguarded walls they could find at other pubs or venues they visited. Gordon wrote the band's name on bus stops in north-west London, around the Hendon/Mill Hill area, and, on one occasion, in large lettering with a green spray can, on the side of a garage newly built by his girlfriend's father, much to that poor man's understandable annoyance.

At the start, Spandau Ballet was quite a raw, new wave, even punk type band, although they settled down into a more melodic groove as their songwriting improved, and Mick describes their music as 'pop rock mainly, based on riffs and pretty simple melodies on the whole; quite catchy, certainly not wishy-washy or boring.' Most of the band's songs were composed by Mark on his own at home with his acoustic guitar, a tape recorder and notepad for the lyrics. He would then bring the ideas to rehearsals where the rest of the band would add their own touches, changing the initial ideas as they developed the material. 'I always had a pretty good idea of how I wanted the songs to sound,' says Mark, 'and all ideas were welcome to improve sections.' He adds that 'Mick had an abstract playing style which I think added strange key changes.' Rehearsals continued on a regular basis.

Meanwhile, Mark was offered, and accepted, a position as spot operator within the lighting crew at The Venue. As Mark explains it, 'The lighting designer asked [the busboys] if anyone wanted to do a follow spot. We sort of looked at each other and said "What the hell's that?" and I said "I'll do it". And it went from there and he started paying me a bit of money to do it as well.' In fact, he was part of the lighting crew when The Skids filmed their video for 'Into the Valley' on stage at The Venue in about February 1979.

After a few months of working at The Venue, writing songs and rehearsing in their spare time, the boys managed to secure a gig at the Hope & Anchor in Islington on Sunday, 6 May 1979, in support of The Softies, a new wave band with a rather fluid membership which had been formed in 1977 by its vocalist and guitarist, a former roadie for The Damned called Michael Smith, a.k.a. Big Mick, and was then signed to Charly records. It seems that the gig came about due to one of the waitresses at The Venue being Big Mick's girlfriend. Having heard them rehearsing, and knowing they were looking for gigs, she put in a good word.

By coincidence, on that very same evening in May 1979, Gentry were playing one of their last gigs, at the Rock Garden, so they did not get to see Spandau Ballet perform in their home borough of Islington. Just like the members of Gentry, though, the members of Spandau Ballet were dreaming of success and fame.

In front of a reasonable crowd in a small space, filled with many of their friends, Spandau Ballet used the Softies' drum kit for the night and, with Mick playing a guitar proudly marked with the name 'Spandau Ballet' on its front, gave a decent account of themselves in a half-an-hour set consisting of seven songs, despite playing through a single amp. 'I'm fairly certain I didn't forget anything and mess anything up,' says Mick modestly, 'It's a lot easier when you are playing at a high level of amplification you can get away with it. It all seemed to go alright… We made a lot of noise and people dutifully clapped.' According to David, 'I remember us being incredibly nervous. I was incredibly nervous. I looked at the floor the whole time. But that was it.' Gordon, who needed to leave the pub as soon as the performance finished because he had to go to school in the morning, was especially nervous at the start. 'I was bricking it,' he says, 'so scared…I was sweating buckets.' The first song called 'Don't Lie to Me' ended on an off-note and he hadn't always got it right in rehearsal. On the night, however, he was fine 'and after that I just relaxed'.

One of the songs Spandau Ballet played that night, with four days to go until a general election which would elect a controversial new female prime minister, was, very topically, called 'Maggie & Jimmy', referring to Margaret Thatcher and James Callaghan respectively, being a cynical track about lying politicians. Other songs performed included 'Everybody Breaks The Law', 'Too Much of A Good Thing', 'Rude Boys' and a Mick Austin composition concerning sexual noises coming out of an imagined residence called

'Number 47'. Gordon's impression of the evening was that, 'The crowd seemed enthusiastic' and it was 'really good fun'. Mark adds, 'I think it went okay'. At this point, he thought that 'it really was starting to come together' and they had written 'some good tunes'.

The Spandau boys were certainly pleased with their performance at the Hope & Anchor and someone apparently managed to wind up the Softies by saying that Spandau Ballet had blown them away on stage, a comment which could have brought the two bands to blows. It was probably lucky for the young boys that no actual fight took place considering that The Softies had the label of 'the heaviest band in Britain' with an average weight of about sixteen stone each.

After they played the Hope & Anchor, the members of Spandau Ballet believed that success was just round the corner. 'We saw it as that's it, we've made it,' says Gordon, 'gigs will start flowing in'. He assumed that David's relationship with Deanne Pearson would work to their advantage. Deanne had stopped working for *Horse & Hound* in late 1978 in order to write gig reviews for the *NME* on a freelance basis. Gordon had no doubt in his mind that she would use her connections to promote the band. 'We thought that's it, we've played the Hope & Anchor, we'll start getting more – people will start talking about us…I just naturally assumed because of Deanne and who she was, she'd be plugging us all over the place, I just naturally assumed that this is what she was doing.' However, Deanne flew to the United States for three months at the end of May to report on bands in Los Angeles for the *NME* and couldn't have done anything to help her boyfriend's band even if she had wanted to. In fact, despite the high hopes, nothing happened at all for Spandau Ballet following the successful Hope & Anchor gig. 'It was a real downer,' says Gordon, 'it was such a let-down, it really was.'

The members of Spandau Ballet continued to rehearse at The Venue hoping that Richard Branson, who often walked by and smiled in their general direction on his way to his office, would sign them. They even recorded a demo tape of three songs, newly composed by Mark Robinson, at a small eight-track studio called RMS in Crystal Palace in order to circulate to record companies, although it does not seem that much was actually done with it. Living over in Mill Hill, Gordon only spoke to the rest of the band on the few occasions in the week when he travelled over to Victoria for rehearsals at The Venue so was never fully informed as to what was going on with the demo tapes but, he says, 'I assumed that the guys were sending them off to Virgin, EMI, plugging them, giving a few to Deanne; I assumed that's what the guys were doing. When I heard it back I thought this is really good; if we don't get noticed from this something's gone wrong.' The demo tape did not, however, produce any positive results but some interest was received through the efforts of a friend of the band called Erica who mentioned to B.P. Fallon that she knew this amazing band called Spandau Ballet.

B.P. Fallon, otherwise Bernard Patrick Fallon, had been a media consultant or publicist to many well-known bands and artists, including Led Zeppelin, T-Rex, Marc Bolan, Roy Harper and King Crimson. On a day in June 1979 (the exact date is indecipherable) he sent the following handwritten note to Mick Austin, Dave Wardill, Mark Robinson and Gordon Bowman:

TO SPANDAU BALLET
I am interested in rock 'n' roll, ladies & other things.
Also v. interested in making £'s or preferably $'s.
Erica tells me you're her fave band: can I make £'s/$'s out of you therefore make you more than I'll get?
huh?
If ya wanna, send tapes,
pix to: BP FALLON
69 New Bond Street W1
Tel: 408 1606

Unfortunately, in June 1979, despite the relative success of the Hope & Anchor gig, the band was in no position to respond to this or any other communication. A number of factors conspired against them. Concentrating on his new job as a spot operator at The Venue, whilst making new friends in the lighting crew, Mark was less connected with the busboys on a daily basis, had developed new interests, and basically stopped rehearsing. At the same time, Mick had become disillusioned with London and wanted some youthful adventures in the country, so he resigned from his job as a busboy and embarked upon a road trip to Cornwall where, after one particularly drunken evening directing traffic, he ended up in a prison cell wearing only his underpants. David, on the other hand, was loving London. Deanne's new career writing for the *NME* meant she was getting into lots of venues on the guest list and David joined her whenever he could, calling in sick on nights of particularly attractive free gigs. At some point, David had started working in the store room at The Venue, which he liked because it gave him normal hours of employment, meaning that he could go out more in the evenings, providing him with the opportunity to hang out more with Deanne, go to free gigs and meet people in the music business.

As mentioned, Deanne was in Los Angeles for three months from the end of May but there were plenty of other distractions for David, meaning that his attention was not fully focused on band matters. Furthermore, as David explains, 'it was logistically very difficult functioning as a band in terms of rehearsals, equipment, storage etc.' and the band didn't have a manager to encourage, cajole and organize them. Consequently, although there was no actual break-up of the band, in the absence of any further gigs the members of Spandau Ballet rather lost heart and drifted apart during the summer of 1979.

On Sunday, 29 July 1979, one of Dave's female friends living in Clapham, called Jean, wrote him the following letter in response to one (now lost) that she had obviously received some time earlier:

Dear Dave,

    Oh yes, I do remember you, the piont (sic) is I hid your letter for safety and couldn't find it for a week. My hiding places in the house are even too good for me to find. I was looking forward to hearing from you so as to hear you rehearsing as I do not hear live music very often. Thanks for writing. It seems a shame that even before starting Spandau Ballet it ceased, but as you said your looking for other musicians, to get something together I wish you luck. Hoping that you will let me know when your playing or rehearsing anywhere so that I could come hope to see you soon.
    Love Jean.

The Spandau Ballet of Mark, Mick, David and Gordon never performed again. Says Mark, 'I don't know exactly why it fell apart. I've often thought about that. Why we decided to call it a day. I'm not sure. Perhaps to do with Dave and his girlfriend, perhaps that put a bit of pressure on him, we weren't good enough or whatever. It didn't fall apart. We hadn't said it was all over.' According to Gordon though, 'What I remember after that is Mark left. I remember coming down to The Venue and a couple of times Mark hadn't turned up and I remember Dave saying to us Mark's quit. He didn't tell me why. Mark had gone, he just went. I'm not sure if it was anything personal or if he was pee'd off with the band, because we'd put a lot of effort into it: Hope & Anchor, the demo and we just weren't being noticed.'

At the end of the summer, Mick returned from his holiday in Cornwall and resumed work at The Venue. Mick, Dave and Gordon decided to continue the band without Mark. As Gordon explains, 'After Mark had gone I thought that's it and I think we spoke about carrying on and the guys wanted to carry on and because Mark had left we had nowhere to practise. Because of where I lived there was this huge youth club [in Mill Hill] and I asked my dad if we could use one of the rooms…we had that free of charge. The guys moved their gear up and I moved my drum kit personally. A couple of hours before the guys turned up I would go and practise on my own'. A female lead singer called Maureen was recruited. 'I don't know how they met Maureen', says Gordon, 'she started singing with us and I thought this isn't going to work, it don't seem right. She was lovely but I thought she doesn't fit us.' Gordon did eventually come around to thinking that the band was 'really good' with Maureen as its vocalist but she walked out on the first occasion they played to an audience, at the Mill Hill Youth Club, complaining of sound issues, and that was the end of the band.

In the meantime, Steve Dagger and the members of Gentry had been inspired by a new club scene that had started the previous autumn at a small West End club.

CHAPTER THREE

From Gilly's to Billy's

THE BUILDING AT 69 DEAN STREET which housed the legendary Billy's nightclub has a long history. Built as a two storey house in the early part of the eighteenth century, at the corner of Dean Street and Meard Street, on a site where Nell Gwynne was once said to have lived, it was initially occupied by various people of title from 1732.

The first occupant arrived in tragic circumstances. Elizabeth Morris, only fifteen years old but described by a leading journal of the period as 'a young lady of excellent character', married a nineteen-year-old baronet, Sir John Chaplin, on 26 March 1730 but he died from smallpox less than two months later on 23 May. Elizabeth, now Lady Chaplin, had conceived during the marriage and gave birth to a girl, Ann, on 4 January 1731. Even this was not such good news because her failure to produce a male heir meant that she lost a small fortune to her late husband's relatives. In March 1732, the unfortunate young widow who, to add to her woes was embroiled in legal proceedings in the Chancery Division of the High Court regarding her late husband's estate, rented 69 Dean Street for £22 per annum from the lessee, John Meard, who had acquired a 102 year lease. Lady Chaplin resided there until 1739 and subsequently found happiness in 1750 when, quite remarkably, at the age of 35, she married Charles Gregory Wade, the younger brother of Arthur Gregory who had married her own teenage daughter, Ann, earlier in the year! Elizabeth did eventually give birth to a son, William, in 1754, subsequently living a long life before her death shortly before Christmas of 1778.

69 Dean Street continued in use as private apartments for the remainder of the life of the lease although, in the early nineteenth century, some of the building was also rented by an upholstery firm, Dawes & Newton. At the expiry of the lease in 1834, the building was acquired by the composer Vincent Novello who, with his son Joseph, established a music publishing company, J. Alfred Novello, later to become Novello & Co and then Novello, Ewer & Co. It was from '69 Dean Street, Soho-square' that the younger Novello wrote to *The Magazine of Science* on 1 October 1848 with his radical proposal for a twenty-four hour clock in railway, shipping and postage timetables. As he explained in his letter: 'The announcement, "The packet sails Sept. 16, at 14 o'clock," would completely explain the time, instead of saying 2 o'clock in the afternoon' but his far sighted proposal was not adopted and the twenty-four hour clock did not come into common use in timetables in Britain until the following century.

During the 1860s, two upper floors were added to Novello headquarters (so that the building now had four floors) and, as a printing works, the building was reinforced to cope with heavy machinery. The company remained in the building, known as the London Sacred Studio Warehouse, until 1867, returning four years later in 1871, before finally departing for good in 1898. By the early twentieth century, after Novello had moved out, the building had become rather run down and neglected.

Its fortunes changed dramatically in the 1920s, however, when David Tennant, the son of Lord Glenconner, chose it as the venue for his new social club, the Gargoyle. This club, which opened on the fourth floor of 69 Dean Street on 16 January 1925 after extensive and costly refurbishment, including the creation of a roof-top dance floor, soon became one of the most exclusive clubs in London and was widely admired for its bohemian atmosphere. Within a few years it expanded down to the third floor of the building with the opening of a stunning new dancing room. It had a reputation, according to one observer, for being 'a rendezvous of the bright young people' attracting 'a swarm of actresses, society girls and men about town' and there were said to be 'always beautiful women interestingly dressed' in the club. Its membership included Bertrand Russell, Nancy Mitford, George Orwell and John Betjeman. Surviving the German bombs which dropped in Dean Street during the Second World War, the club continued to thrive but suffered a setback in 1949 when it was refused a music and dancing licence which would have allowed it to open after midnight. Then the club's reputation took a massive knock when it was publicly disclosed in 1951 that the notorious Russian spies and defectors, Guy Burgess and Donald Maclean, had both been members.

David Tennant had now had enough and sold up in 1951 for £5,000 to a caterer called John Negus who was in partnership with a former war-time director at the Supply Ministry, Sir Duncan Campbell. The Gargoyle continued to operate as a members' club but Sir Duncan died in January 1954 and Negus evidently felt that he wasn't really cut out to run the club on his own. On 3 May 1955, making a tidy profit on his investment, he sold out for £15,000 to a consortium led by wealthy publisher and member of Lloyd's insurance syndicate, Billy Bolitho, in partnership with Rosalind Fox (who, earlier in the year, had been a witness for the plaintiff in a well publicised court case in which a 49-year-old woman called Agnes Empson had sued her former fiancé, Cecil Eales, for breach of promise after he changed his mind and broke off their engagement; Miss Empson controversially won the case and £2,000 in damages). The actual composition of the consortium which owned the club changed during the year but by November 1955 it included Michael Klinger, later to become a major film producer, and Julius 'Jimmy' Jacobs in association with Harry Roy, a well-known band leader who provided the entertainment with the Harry Roy Orchestra.

Things did not go terribly well for Harry Roy at the Gargoyle. In February 1956 he was violently attacked inside the club and, a few days later, was reported to have locked himself in his flat while police searched for an anonymous letter writer who had threatened to 'get him for good'. A few days later, police were called to the club when a man, believed to be the author of the anonymous letter, tried to force his way in to see Roy (who was now being protected by two private detectives) but fled when the police arrived. At the end of March, Roy moved on from Dean Street and subsequently took over the Hollywood Club in Clifford Street.

Meanwhile, in April 1956, the Gargoyle once again had an application for a licence to allow music and dancing to continue after midnight refused on the grounds of fire safety, which could have led to its closure, but, after making certain necessary improvements, it did manage to obtain one at the end of May, amidst allegations of corruption in the London County Council.

A few months later there was more trouble for the club when the *Daily Mail* ran a story over two days in September 1956 about a party at the Gargoyle attended by young members of the aristocracy at which, to the horror of the paper's readership and many older members of the club, rock 'n' roll music was played, men took off their ties and, even worse, women danced barefoot, having removed their stockings. The implicit message was that rock 'n' roll music had driven everyone at the Gargoyle that night into a state of sexual frenzy (although it was more likely the alcohol) and it was not good publicity for the club. Appreciating this, Jacobs offered a terse statement to the *Mail* reporter saying: 'I have given instructions that there shall be no more Rock 'n Roll sessions.'

In August 1958, the Gargoyle, now solely owned by Klinger and Jacobs, suffered another misfortune when a gang of professional thieves hid in the building overnight, blew open the club's safe with gelignite, using butter to deaden the sound of the blast, and escaped with £1,300 in cash. By this time, in order to generate more income, the new owners had turned the now vacant fourth floor into a striptease club known, after one of the site's most famous supposed residents, as the Nell Gwynne. For legal reasons it could only operate in the afternoon and early evening while the Gargoyle club on the third floor was closed. The Gargoyle itself continued as a cabaret nightclub and restaurant at which one could wine, dine and dance late at night, subsequently becoming a strip club of its own. The striptease activities soon became known to the authorities and, inevitably, in July 1960, the police raided the Gargoyle, with the owners convicted at Marlborough Street Magistrates' Court for membership irregularities and fined. Nevertheless, the Gargoyle and Nell Gwynne both continued to operate. In 1961 the Gargoyle offered a twice nightly floor show entitled 'Soho Scandals' and the club also featured as the location of a dance sequence in one of Michael Klinger's dubious early films, *Naked as Nature Intended*, in 1961.

In September 1962, Michael Klinger sold his share of the business to Julius Jacobs in order to focus on film production and went on to produce successful films starring Roger Moore and Michael Caine. Controversy continued for the club though when, in August 1966, the police raided the Nell Gwynne, having first sent in undercover officers to observe the striptease acts and purchase alcohol in order to secure a successful prosecution. Julius Jacobs was convicted for 'selling intoxicating liquor outside permitted hours' while the club was fined for 'the public performance of striptease' although, fortunately for Jacobs, the restrictive laws against public striptease were repealed in December 1966.

A couple of years later, in October 1968, Jacobs sold the Nell Gwynne to a consortium led by Ronald Ward (commonly known as Don Ward) who, at that time, owned another striptease club called the Sunset Strip in St Anne's Court. A verbal agreement was apparently made between Jacobs and Ward that Jacobs would, in due course, also sell the Gargoyle to Ward but, following redevelopment of St Anne's Court in May 1970, the Sunset Strip was forced to close and its membership transferred to the Nell Gwynne. This boosted attendance at the Gargoyle because most patrons moved on to that club at midnight when the Nell Gwynne closed. Seeing business boom, Jacobs changed his mind about selling the Gargoyle to Ward and this led to a falling out between the two owners of the clubs on the third and fourth floors of 69 Dean Street.

In October 1970, Jacobs made a formal objection to the GLC against Don Ward's proposed opening of a new strip club at 30 Dean Street. Jacobs put forward a number of rather spurious reasons why Ward should not be allowed to open his club: for example, that it was close to a synagogue at 20 Dean Street of which Jacobs was a member and also next to the house at number 28 at which Karl Marx had once lived. It was touching that the owner of one of Soho's largest striptease clubs should be concerned about such things but Ward's club was not much closer to the synagogue than 69 Dean Street and was rather less conspicuous because the large striptease sign which adorned the outer wall of the Gargyole could easily be seen from the front of the synagogue and, for that matter, from Karl Marx's old house too. Jacobs also complained that Ward's show had 'lesbian leanings' and he dropped in some prejudicial gossip that Ward had been a comedian in a notorious show at the Keyhole Club in Old Compton Street in 1961 which had led to its owner, Stanley Bloom, being jailed for three years after the prosecuting counsel at his trial had referred to the entertainment as having been 'so foul, so vile, so obscene that a more appropriate venue would have been a sewer or a cess pool rather than a club.' Jacobs' objections were not taken very seriously by the GLC, which was unable to confirm that Ward had even been involved in the show at the Keyhole Club, and Ward's new club, which he again called the Sunset Strip, and which survives to this day, was allowed to open.

In January 1971, suffering from ill health, Jacobs did end up selling the Gargoyle to Ward who continued to run both the Nell Gwynne and the Gargoyle as strip clubs; the Nell Gwynne operated up until just before midnight, with the Gargoyle offering dinner and continuing until 3:00am.

The building was also home to various other businesses during the twentieth century and, most prominently, the ground floor was occupied by an auction house, A. Stewart McCracken, until it went bust in 1975. During the latter part of the 1970s, 69 Dean Street also housed a massage parlour and sauna, originally called the Way-A-Hed Sauna but, using a combination of its address and the type of services offered, changed its name to the less subtle Sauna 69. Next door, at 2 Meard Street, was a brothel, possibly a clip joint, called the Golden Girl Club, although, to remain within the law, prospective clients were simply invited in for 'a drink and a chat' and then whatever transpired, if anything, between two consenting adults was no-one else's business.

Another component of the building at 69 Dean Street was to be found down in the basement. This was a club called the Mandrake which had been opened in 1947 by chess players Harold Lommer and Boris Watson in the basement of 4 Meard Street but which, over time, had expanded through the basement into 2 Meard Street and then into the larger basements of 69 and 70 Dean Street.

At the start, the Mandrake was a serious chess club during the day but gained a reputation as a rather more bohemian social club during the evening with a juke box, live jazz music and also, apparently, prostitutes freely available. Christine Keeler and Frank Sinatra were reputed to have visited in the 1960s. From 1969, however, the club was owned and run by a respectable husband and wife team: James and Lilian Delaney. Following refurbishment in 1971, a flyer on behalf of the Mandrake Club said:

> We feel sure that old members will be delighted with the decor and ambience of the new club which promises to be one of London's more interesting up to date members' nightspots where one can eat, drink, dance or relax with friends. An atmosphere of live music or quiet discotheque with a sunken dance floor, a large attractive bar, pleasant services with facilities for watching colour TV or playing chess.

The Mandrake at this time opened until 3:30am, Mondays to Saturdays, but, following complaints from a resident of 4 Meard

Street relating to excessive noise by patrons leaving in the early hours, the entrance to the club, originally adjacent to the residential property at 4 Meard Street, was moved a little way down the road to an entrance along the side of 69 Dean Street, albeit that this entrance was still in Meard Street. The newly refurbished club was not to everyone's taste. Benny Green in the *Spectator* complained that it was too dark and bemoaned the lack of free periodicals which the previous management had made available for patrons to read. However, as he had been banned from the Mandrake in the 1950s for disturbing the chess players by playing jazz music too loud, he was not in the best position to make a comparison. He did, however, appreciate the fact that the new management continued to cater for jazz enthusiasts, with late night, live jazz music sessions.

It was not to last, however, and, in 1973, the Delaneys sold the Mandrake to their own planning and design consultant, Richard Wofinden, in partnership with one Gordon Pearce, but it was not well run and, before the end of the year, following trouble and violence in the club due to the admittance of 'undesirable persons', they closed up and sold on to Granville Vincent Hutchinson, known simply as Vince (although, for reasons no doubt best not enquired into, he took to calling himself Vince Howard). Vince immediately decided to change the name of the club from the Mandrake to Gilly's, probably chosen in honour of his girlfriend, Gillian Roberts, with whom he was living. The club obtained a licence allowing it to open in December 1974; a sign saying 'Gilly's – Disco Dancing' was placed over the Meard Street entrance of 69 Dean Street and a notice on the wall read 'ALL NATIONALITIES WELCOMED TO GILLY'S'. By June 1975, Gilly's was describing itself as 'London's Newest and Funkiest Soul Disco'.

Vince was originally a carpenter who had been born in St Andrews, Jamaica, in October 1934 and emigrated to Britain in March 1960. He claimed to have subsequently made his money as an insurance broker and this is supposed to have financed his acquisition of the nightclub. Considering, however, that he listed his occupation as 'club manager' on an official company registration form in March 1974, some months before Gilly's had opened, it is more likely that he had been a manager at another London club, perhaps the Q Club in Praed Street owned by Count Suckle, a.k.a. Wilbert Augustus Campbell, or Gerry Bailey's Bee Club in Peckham, because Vince was associated with both men. Vince did, in fact, form a partnership with a real insurance broker called Robert Bradford and, no doubt, *his* capital was of assistance in getting Gilly's started.

The club originally specialized in soul and reggae and was said by one London guide to be 'highly popular with West Indians in London'. *Time Out* described it as 'a nondescript, dark and quite comfortable basement, with a partly underlit dance-floor and a reasonable sound system'. It attracted some big names such as Gregory Isaacs, who appeared at the club in September 1975. The *West Indian World* newspaper promoted the club on the top of its front page with an appeal to 'BROTHERS & SISTERS' to 'Please support Gilly's Club...This is a community Discotheque WE should go to'. The club's slogan at the time was 'Friends Getting Together' and its advertising claimed that it was 'London's most fashionable club. The in-place of the new Jet-Set'. Vince was not averse to branching out a little and announced in October 1975 that he was launching 'Gilly's Glamour Girl', a beauty contest, also known as 'Miss Gilly's', won in January 1976 by a suitably beautiful woman called Anne Wharton. The club had a restaurant offering three course meals and there was, of course, a disco – hosted by DJs such as Joshua J.J. Jones – and also live music, with a house band called The Funkees, which played 'dynamic Afro rock and reggae'.

However, it was not all reggae aimed at the West Indian community. One of the main difficulties for any nightclub owner is to fill up their club on weekday evenings. For any decent club, Fridays and Saturdays take care of themselves, and possibly Thursdays too, but the challenge is how to get punters in through the door on Monday, Tuesday and Wednesday nights when everyone has to get up early for work, college or even school the next day. Rising unemployment in the late 1970s might, ironically, have helped some club owners in this respect but the unemployed were hardly likely to spend much at the bar. Vince's solution was to hold gay disco nights from Monday to Wednesday when the club was otherwise empty. Listings for these nights started to appear in *Gay News* from 10 April 1975.

It was not an unmitigated success and the gay weekday nights seem to have stopped in February 1976. Changing tack, Vince then decided that gay discos might be the answer to the problem of what to do on Sundays, when the West End was dead, and Gilly's began to host what were called 'Camp One Disco' nights on Sundays from December 1976 but, again, this only appears to have lasted a few months into 1977. The reggae and soul discos, which were the real money makers, continued from Thursday to Saturday nights and by 1977, according to *Nicholson's Guide to London*, Gilly's was regarded as one of the top three reggae and soul clubs in London.

The name Gilly's was retained until June 1978 when, following some problems with Customs & Excise (then responsible for collecting V.A.T.) which forced Vince to reorganize his business affairs, it was changed to Billy's. At about the same time, Vince, having further refurbished the club, brought in new management with the aim of broadening its appeal from the West Indian community in order to attract a gay crowd during the entire (working) week and a mixed patronage at the weekend. A different type of music was introduced and DJs Nikky Price and Chris Lucas played European sounds while George Power played jazz-funk and soul. In his autobiography, Robert Elms recalls that the club was attended in 1978 by 'lotharios and nurses' while Midge Ure, on the other hand, remembers it as a transvestite club. The difference in recollection may be explained by the different target audience Billy's was aiming for on different nights of the week.

For the new gay nights, which began on Thursday, 6 July 1978, Vince placed an advertisement in the 29 June 1978 issue of *Gay News*. True to form, he attempted to lure the boys in with a male glamour contest, the prize being a holiday for two to Jamaica, the same type of prize which had been offered to 'Miss Gilly'. However, as entrants had to send in their photograph with details of their name, address and profession, not something many gay men at the time would have been comfortable doing, one is forced to wonder how successful a competition it was. In the event, the gay disco nights appear to have stopped quite quickly and *Gay News* removed them from its listing page in August 1978.

One likely effect of the *Gay News* advertisement is that Billy's came to the attention of an ambitious young gay man called Steve Harrington, who preferred to be known as Steve Strange, a former punk rocker with dreams not only of stardom, having already been in a couple of short lived bands, but also of creating a new club scene. He and his friend, Rich Kids drummer Rusty Egan, decided to pay a visit to Billy's one Tuesday night and, finding the place virtually empty – which probably provides a good clue as to why the gay discos were stopped – offered to take over Tuesdays themselves with their so-called Bowie Nights, aimed at both straight and gay clubbers. Vince, sensing an opportunity for profit, readily agreed and the Bowie Nights started in September 1978. They involved Rusty Egan as DJ, playing glam-rock by David Bowie, Roxy Music and Brian Eno as well as new electronic synthesizer based music from the likes of Kraftwerk, Ultravox and a then little known band called Human League, all of which Steve Strange liked to call 'electro diskow', while the audience posed, if not danced, in striking costumes.

Many of these costumes were purchased at a clothes shop in James Street, Covent Garden, called PX, run by Stephane Raynor and Helen Robinson. Most sources state that PX was opened in the autumn of 1978 but this is not the case because it was mentioned in the January 1978 issue of the fashion and gossip publication, *Ritz*, and was thus probably opened in late 1977. In this January 1978 issue, *Ritz* columnist Stephen Lavers, in the context of noting the recent appearance of 'futuristic fashion stores', explained that PX sold 'paramilitary and post-war chic' with a 'specialised appeal'. Rather prophetically he added, 'It should become a cult shop' and said that Nicky Haslam, the well-known interior designer, had been 'raving' about it. Steve Strange worked at the shop as a sales assistant and took advantage of his daily contact with the trendy young people who shopped there to invite them along to Billy's; Robert Elms, for example, recalls in his autobiography being recruited in PX. In a 1981 interview, Strange spoke of visiting other London nightclubs to hand out cards printed with Billy's' address and the tag line 'Fame, fame, fame. What's your name? A Club for Heroes' to suitably attired individuals. Billy's on Tuesdays was, according to Stephen Lavers in the October 1978 issue of *Ritz,* 'frequented by ex-punks and David Bowie clones...one or two of [whom] have developed an interesting 'new' style...the neat, but camp paramilitary look.'

The early paramilitary look quickly evolved into a somewhat more flamboyant style as Billy's regulars, usually declining to sport the same costume twice, competed with each other to wear something more outlandish every week. This was noticed in December 1978 by the *Daily Mail* which ran a feature on the Bowie Nights in which it was stated that:

> Bowie Night at Billy's is an elite, with its own club rules. You don't have to dance. Music is important – it sets a mood – but dancing is not as imperative as posing. Every carefully contrived new outfit is under close scrutiny by the rest of the in-crowd.

The girls, said the newspaper, would 'dress up like a fashion plate and go to be admired' and they would display their personality 'by their peacock clothes' with faces 'heavily made up, in a mask almost' and hair 'dyed, greased, swept up, swathed'. It was, in short, a 'mecca for the poseurs, the peacocks, the kids who're trying to bring a little bezazz and brightness to their lives.' It didn't really matter what one was wearing as long as it was fairly outrageous and drew attention to oneself. Consequently, although not everyone at Billy's dressed up, the hardcore regulars tended to look more like they were on their way to a fancy dress party, or actors in a period play who had just come off stage, than ordinary young people out for a night of clubbing. The limelight is exactly what they wanted and the publicity provided by the *Daily Mail's* feature was secretly very welcome to these attention seekers who nevertheless pretended they were not seeking any attention.

Strange and Egan did not stay long at Billy's, moving out before Christmas and re-opening at Blitz in February 1979. According to Elms, both Strange and Egan were evicted from the club by Vince because there were no more than seventy regulars and they were not making any money. In his autobiography, Steve Strange tells the direct opposite story that the club was so popular that they had to move on because bigger premises were required. In fact, although it is often said that Blitz was a larger venue than Billy's, that is a myth. The capacity of Billy's was officially set at 190 persons, according to its music and dancing licence, while the equivalent capacity of Blitz was a mere 175 people. So there is no question of Strange and Egan moving to bigger premises. At the same time, the *Daily Mail* of 11 December 1978, whose reporters attended the club, noted that, 'By 1am the dance floor at Billy's is packed with 200 kids' so that is reasonable evidence of its popularity at the time.

Nevertheless, Strange told a *Daily Express* reporter in December 1981 a rather different story when he was quoted as saying that, 'the management [of Billy's] felt that they had lost control and were annoyed even though it was successful. So we had to move.' To Ian Birch, for the 1984 *Smash Hits Yearbook*, he said that 'the kids started coming but the owners got greedy and so we went on to Blitz.' That is certainly a plausible reason for the departure, with Vince wanting a bigger slice of the financial action and Strange refusing to hand it over. Strange is quoted in *We Can Be Heroes* as saying that Vince wanted to double the price of both admission and drinks but that he, Strange, was opposed to this. This account was confirmed by Rusty Egan in an interview for a Sky Arts programme, *Trailblazers of the New Romantics*, first broadcast on 12 August 2016. In that interview, he explained that Vince, sensing he could make a nice profit out of the large numbers attending the Bowie nights, had, without asking him or Steve, not only increased the entry fee from fifty pence to a pound but put up the price of the drinks which, until then, had been cheap for the Tuesday night crowd. Furthermore, he said that Vince started to print his own flyers to attract a wider audience which was totally at odds with the Strange/Egan philosophy of exclusivity. Strange says in his book that Egan went into hiding out of fear that Vince, supposedly a black belt in judo, might take retribution due to his anger at the loss of business caused by the move. Egan, however, says it was the doorman of the club who wanted to kill him – on Vince's behalf.

Other reasons have been put forward to explain the move to Blitz. In his autobiography, Gary Kemp suggests that Strange and Egan were forced out of Billy's by Dean Street's pimps who were unhappy that the Tuesday night visitors to Billy's were not using their prostitutes, something which sounds like an urban myth type story that Gary probably heard from someone, who heard it from someone else, a number of years later. Much earlier, in a 1984 interview, he had told Ian Birch: 'Blitz came about because Billy's was too small and became a bit predictable.' Yet another reason for the departure, which has the benefit of being rather more contemporary, was put forward in the November 1979 issue of *Tatler* by Ted Polhemus who said that the management of Billy's 'let in hordes of unstylish types' which Strange was powerless to prevent and the move to Blitz was because it 'offered Steve control of the door'. This matches what Strange told Chris Sullivan over thirty years later for the 2012 book *We Can Be Heroes*, in which he referred disparagingly to 'pimps and prostitutes' being allowed entry into the club.

In an article written by Rusty Egan for *New Sounds, New Styles* in 1981, Egan said that he asked the manager of Billy's to let Steve stand on the door and 'sort people out' and, although he does not record the response, implies that the manager refused the request. This does not mean that Strange did not stand outside for other reasons; he told the *Daily Express* in 1981 that Egan 'persuaded the manager [of Billy's] to let me stand on the door', not in order to sort people out but rather because 'I represented an attractive visual image', drawing people into the club. Egan also stated in his 1981 article that the management of Blitz agreed to give them 'a lot more money' which probably helped.

Whatever the truth of the matter, we may note that for £5 one could become a member of Billy's in 1978 and, in theory, gain free admission every night from Monday to Thursday. Considering that Strange and Egan made their money from people paying to enter the club (while Vince made his money from the bar) there must have been some tension between the membership system, allowing free entry on a Tuesday night, and the desire by Strange/Egan to collect an entry fee. In fact, it would appear that, contrary to the terms of membership, a charge of 50p *was* imposed for members on Tuesday nights but this would not have provided much profit for the hosts. One thing is for sure: the Tuesday Bowie Nights at Billy's hosted by Strange and Egan came to an early end only three months after they had begun.

Gary describes 'the whole band' of which he was a member as 'Billy's regulars' in his autobiography but did all the members of Gentry go to any of the Strange/Egan club nights at Billy's during those three months of 1978? Well, this is a bit of a mystery and difficult to confirm one way or the other. The band members certainly don't appear in any photographs taken in the club in 1978, although one can see other well-known regulars in snaps by photographer Nicola Tyson such as George O'Dowd (Boy George), Peter Robinson (Marilyn), Martin Degville, Julia Foder (Princess Julia), Siobhan Fahey and, of course, Steve Strange. In an early interview published in *Record Mirror* in November 1980, Gary Kemp said, 'We used to go to Billy's long before Rusty Egan started his Tuesday nights' and there is no particular reason to doubt this. Gary, Steve and John in particular were lovers of soul music and might well have gone down to Billy's at the weekends. The mystery is whether the members of the band were regulars, or even just occasional attendees, at Billy's on Tuesday nights with the more exotic crowd.

Steve Strange has said in one interview, for a TV programme called *Smash*, that the members of Gentry 'originally started coming to the first club that we did and it was called Billy's.' However, in his autobiography, in which he listed those who attended Billy's, he did not include any of the Gentry. He did, however, include Simon Withers, a friend of the band and former pupil at Owen's from the same year as John Keeble and someone who Martin Kemp rightly describes in his book as 'a New Romantic through and through.' Robert Elms, who was one of the originals at Billy's, also does not appear, from the evidence of his book, to recall the members of the band being there from the early days (although in another context he does mention having spoken to Gary at Billy's, and Gary also recalls having met Elms at that club in his own autobiography). Elms also knew Steve Dagger, because Dagger attended a course at the London School of Economics where he (Elms) was studying political science, and in one interview he has said that he invited Dagger to Billy's one Tuesday night in 1978 and Gary came along with him. This matches an account given by Gary in his autobiography.

It is notable, however, that Martin Kemp does not mention Billy's at all in his autobiography, nor does Tony Hadley in his. Of the band members, it is only Gary who claims to have been to any Steve Strange/Rusty Egan club nights at Billy's and, while this is certainly not impossible, especially with the Elms/Withers connection, it is curious that, until he came to write his autobiography, he almost always said that he first went to Billy's in *1979*. Thus, in a Radio 2 interview broadcast on 2 June 2001 he said:

> And one day *I walked into a club called Billy's in 1979*. I was taken down by Steve Dagger. And on this Tuesday night it was being run by a couple of guys called Steve Strange and Rusty Egan – very hedonistic. People dancing to this strange electronic music that I'd never heard before.

Writing in the Reformation CD sleeve booklet in 2002, Gary said:

> *In 1979*, when all in London seemed bored and grey, drawn by the moment, we walked down the steps of a small Soho night club called Billy's.

Similarly, in an interview for T5M in January 2009, Gary said:

> ...we gave up after a while because there wasn't the kind of market for us *and it wasn't until 1979* when Steve Dagger said, "Look you know we've got to go to this thing called a Bowie night which is at this little club called Billy's in Soho", and I remember going there and that changed my life, that's what made Spandau and that's what was the next step for me.

It is quite possible that Gary was simply confused about the year and we may note that, in his autobiography, he offers a story of one occasion in 1978 when he went to Billy's with Steve Dagger and was accosted by Stephen Linard who informed him (wrongly) that Billy's used to be the Gargoyle club. He also says that he met Chris Sullivan and Bob Elms while he was there. Curiously, however, soon after the publication of his autobiography, Gary was back to identifying 1979 as the year he went to Billy's and met Elms. Thus, in an interview in the *Independent on Sunday* published on 27 September 2009, he said:

> I walked into this place and it was full of the most exotic-looking people I'd ever seen. *It was 1979* and we were still in that never-ending winter of discontent so we felt we were kind of dancing on the deck of the Titanic. I saw Bob and he was wearing this kind of sci-fi, am-dram kit with padded shoulders and he had this geometric haircut that fell over one eye that I'd never seen on anyone.

The problem here, of course, is that Steve Strange and Rusty Egan both started and stopped putting on club nights at Billy's in Dean Street at the end of 1978. If Gary was right in his interviews about the year being 1979, and about Strange and Egan being there, then (despite his apparent recollection of going down some steps to enter the club which fits Billy's in the basement of 69 Dean Street but not Blitz on the ground floor of 4 Great Queen Street) he can only be thinking of Blitz. Indeed, it is interesting that, in one of the aforementioned interviews, Gary recalls first going to Billy's after the band 'gave up'. This can only be a reference to some point after May 1979 when Gentry stopped performing. By this time, Steve Strange and Rusty Egan had long since left Billy's. So if he first went to a Steve Strange/Rusty Egan club night after Gentry had disbanded he must certainly be thinking of Blitz.

In addition, when Gary refers to the band as 'Billy's regulars' in his book, he also makes the claim that, at the same time, the Gentry seemed like 'yesterday's men', which is historically impossible because, when Steve Strange started his club nights at Billy's, the Gentry had only recently been formed and were gigging regularly and optimistically. It may even be that Gary, or his publishers, recognized this problem; the hardback edition of his autobiography was entitled 'I Know This Much: From Soho To Spandau' but, when the paperback version was published, the second half of the title had mysteriously vanished and was now simply: 'I Know This Much'. Perhaps the change reflected a subconscious awareness that the band simply did not have its true origins in Soho and that Gary has muddled both Billy's and Blitz and the years 1978 and 1979 in his mind.

There is, however, one way that it is possible for Gary and the rest of the band to have gone to a Strange/Egan club night at Billy's in 1979. It is a little known and certainly long forgotten fact that, in some circles at least, 'Billy's' was believed to be the name of the Tuesday club night at Blitz, as distinct from the Soho club called Billy's; or, as it might be promoted today, Billy's@Blitz. This may seem odd to anyone familiar with the Blitz story but it is certainly the case. For example, a photograph by Sandra Tiffin in *Ritz*'s June 1979 issue was captioned: 'Steve Strange at Billy's (Blitz)' while Francis Lynn, in the September 1979 issue, referred to 'Billy's (Tuesday nights at Blitz)'. So it may be that Gary does have a genuine memory of going to 'Billy's' on a Tuesday night in 1979, except that it was to Billy's at Blitz.

At the same time, even if Gary's autobiography is correct in saying that he went to Billy's in 1978, it is by no means clear from his account whether this was a one-off visit or if he ever went back again. The story he tells in his book is that he and Dagger immediately recognized that Billy's indicated the way forward for the band, which must have been no later than December 1978, but this does not seem to square with Gentry continuing to plug away with the same songs at the same types of venues until May 1979, nor with the concept of them 'giving up' at that time. Furthermore, even if Gary did make one or two visits to Billy's in 1978, one thing that seems to stand out is that no other members of Gentry went with him.

CHAPTER FOUR

—◄o►—

From Holborn to Halligan's

BLITZ WINE BAR AND RESTAURANT was opened in early 1976 by an employment consultant and, according to *Ritz* newspaper, former male model, called Michael Brown (who was later to run a law recruitment company from 4 Great Queen Street alongside Blitz) and a congenial Irishman called Brendan Connelly, who was the manager of the venue, which was situated on the site of a former office furniture warehouse known as Pooley's. Although commonly referred to as being in Covent Garden, this is misleading because the actual location of 4 Great Queen Street is just off Kingsway, closer to Holborn.

Decorated with a Second World War theme, there were posters and newspaper cuttings from the 1940s on the walls along with advertisements for Bovril and the like. There was also an old train station waiting-room clock and a London Midland station sign as decoration. The bar, with a dance floor and stage, was on the ground floor while a restaurant (with 'Blitzburgers' on the menu), where one could eat lunch and dinner, was upstairs in a gallery overlooking the dance floor where one sat in old railway carriages. The venue had a staircase but that only took customers up to the gallery, not down into a basement. In 1977, it was opening until 3:00am and thus, while officially called Blitz Wine Bar and Restaurant, it was to all intents and purposes a nightclub.

During 1977 there was live music by the resident band Propaganda on Thursday evenings, and Forties themed cabaret nights at the weekends. Initially, the club's main cabaret attraction was The Busby Berkleys, a two man song and dance team, described by *Ritz* as 'so decadent. So Berlin. So Cabaret'. Also on the bill in 1977 was Blitz's resident singer, James Biddlecome, known as Biddie, and a 'banana strewn giantess', as *Ritz* described her, called Eve Ferret, known as 'Big Eve', the two of whom eventually paired up to become Biddie & Eve. Their act was described by Steven Lavers in *Ritz* as 'a hilarious pastiche of '40s cabaret kitsch, Carmen Miranda Rhumba fillies and a Teddy Boy tribute to the '50s which features everything imaginable including a nude scene in a kitchen sink! Well almost.' The cabaret nights proved so popular they were extended into Thursdays and Fridays; and Biddie & Eve were the headline attraction when Blitz re-opened on 22 August 1978 after refurbishment with a new stage, sound and lighting system. By this time, the venue was calling itself 'Blitz Bar and Restaurant' in its advertising, having dropped the 'Wine Bar' element of its name as presumably too limiting.

One of the main publications in which Blitz advertised during 1978 was *Gay News* and, while not actually a gay bar as such, it certainly targeted the gay market with a line-up which featured drag artists and 'camp cabaret' including, for example, a barber shop quartet called The Gay Blades. The club evidently gained a rather outlandish reputation and, following a robbery of £700 one Thursday night in early 1979, during which the night manager was tied to a post, the *Ritz* newspaper commented, rather unkindly, that most passers-by would probably have thought it was just the club hosting another bondage party! However, although the weekends and Thursday-Friday nights were popular, there was still a problem filling the club during the rest of the week and, of course, this is where Rusty Egan and Steve Strange came in on Tuesday nights from 6 February 1979, having evacuated from Billy's.

Admission prices on Tuesday nights in 1979 were £1 for club members and £2 for guests. Everyone supposedly had to pay although, no doubt, there were some exceptions. A rarely mentioned fact in connection with the Bowie Nights is that you could go upstairs for a lavish selection of food, including salads, roast beef, roast turkey, boiled ham, various cheeses, paté, cold quiches and gateaux, with the buffet open until 1:00am.

Steve Strange stood at the door to vet potential recruits and one of the most famous incidents connected with Blitz occurred when Mick Jagger apparently had some difficulty getting into the venue. The earliest known mention of this incident, albeit an oblique one, appeared in the gossip column of the July 1979 issue of *Ritz*. As Jagger was living abroad as a tax exile at the start of 1979, and only flew back to London in May – to contest his divorce proceedings with Bianca – any attempt by him to visit Blitz must have taken place sometime between May and July 1979. But what actually happened?

Tony Hadley was curious about it at the time but, as he notes in his autobiography, was never able to establish the facts. Steve Strange gave various different accounts of the incident at different times. The earliest known version of the story was related by Ted Polhemus (evidently based on what he had been told by Steve Strange) and appeared in the November 1979 edition of *Tatler*. According to this version, Mick Jagger got into Blitz without any difficulty but only after having queued up like everyone else and paid his entrance fee, the point being that Jagger was treated just like an ordinary punter. Thus, said Polhemus:

> He [Steve Strange] maintains that even Mick Jagger had to queue up, pass inspection and pay his money.

In the next version of the story, this time told directly by Steve Strange, Jagger was initially turned away only to be allowed in later the same evening. Thus, an article by Christena Appleyard published in the *Daily Mirror* of 3 March 1980 quoted Steve Strange as saying:

> Mick Jagger turned up once. I had to explain he couldn't come in, just because he was Mick Jagger...Frankly his clothes sense wasn't

going to get him in. In the end he came back with a member and got in as a guest. But he's never forgiven me for making him pay the £2 entrance fee.

Over time the story grew and became more colourful. An interview given by Steve Strange to Nick Monson which appeared in the December 1980 issue of *Ritz* included the following exchange:

Nick Monson: Tell me about the time you chucked Mick Jagger out of Blitz?

Steve Strange: Oh God! Here we go again. One night he came to the club. He was drunk and shouting his mouth off. Neither me nor any of the kids were really into the Rolling Stones. He was very tiresome so I asked his entourage to take him away and they did. There was some reporter or photographer from the Daily Mirror there. And the whole story was blown up out of proportion but that's the press for you.

The questioner here assumed that Jagger had been allowed into Blitz and was thrown out, an assumption that Steve Strange did not contradict. As far as can be established, it was not until an interview by Strange published in *Rolling Stone's* 23 July 1981 edition that it was first claimed that Jagger was totally refused entry:

He came to the club and was *completely* pissed out of his head. He was shouting over the queue, "You don't know who the fuck I am!" "I don't know why I should bother to queue up for this place – I should just walk in through the door!" The people he was with were so embarrassed. I said "Look Mick, you're just making a fool of yourself. I think you shouldn't bother to come in, you should go home".

In his autobiography, Steve Strange says pretty much the same thing as he told *Rolling Stone* in 1981, adding that the real reason he didn't let Jagger in was because he had recently been told by the fire brigade that, if they were caught over capacity, the club would lose its licence and Jagger showed up at a time when the club was full. Strange again remembers Jagger becoming annoyed and saying, in time-honoured tradition: 'Don't you know who I am?' before storming off to another nightspot. He adds that the story would not have become known had not a tabloid journalist been present.

So when we look at the reasons for Jagger's supposed failure to enter Blitz we find the story changes regularly. In the version of the story told to Ted Polhemus, in which account Jagger did get inside, there appears to have been an issue over the fact that he had to pay to gain access like everyone else. In the *Daily Mirror* story, it was his 'clothes sense' which led to the refusal (although he managed to enter in the end) but, in the *Ritz* and *Rolling Stone* interviews, it was because he was drunk whereas, in Steve Strange's autobiography, the reason was simply because the club was too full. The tabloid journalist Strange refers to in his book must be Christena Appleyard of the *Daily Mirror*, only she was not there and did not witness the alleged incident; she simply reported what Strange told her some months later which is why the story was told in a tabloid newspaper.

If we look at the earliest known reference to the incident, by Barbara Brownfield in the July 1979 issue of *Ritz*, we find this:

> You can never tell who you might bump into on a Bowie night at Blitz. ZANDRA RHODES finds it fascinating, so does MICK JAGGER (when he's allowed in).

It will be noted that the suggestion here is that Mick Jagger *has* got into Blitz on a Tuesday, and finds it fascinating, but there was clearly a story in circulation as at July 1979 that he had had some difficulty getting in on at least one occasion. However, as far as it is possible to ascertain, this story had not appeared in any major daily newspaper. It may be that there was a mention somewhere in an obscure publication but it is just as likely that the story was originally told by Steve Strange himself, and circulated by word of mouth, or was a rumour which he ended up confirming. Although the *Ritz* mention appears to suggest that the reader would know all about this story, that particular publication was not averse to in-jokes or stories that only a select few people would know about so it does not necessarily mean it had been reported elsewhere. In any event, it does not appear that any such incident was independently witnessed by a tabloid journalist, or anyone else for that matter, and there is certainly no known photograph of it. Although Strange is quoted in *We Can Be Heroes* as saying that the next morning's headlines were that he had turned Jagger away, this is wishful thinking many years later and there were no such headlines, or even small reports of the incident, at the time.

We may also note that, in its 14 July 1979 edition, the now defunct weekly music paper, *Superpop*, referred to Steve Strange's door entry policy at Blitz and identified Gary Numan and John Lydon as having been refused admittance but made no mention of any failure by the more famous Mick Jagger to gain entry, as one assumes it would have done had there been such a story in circulation at the time.

In any event, if there is one fact that does emerge from a review of all the different stories involving Mick Jagger, it is that, if Jagger *was* refused entry to Blitz by Steve Strange, it was almost certainly not as a result of anything he was *wearing*. The only version of the story to suggest this is the one told by the *Daily Mirror,* which also says that in the end he did gain admittance as a guest, yet the reason the story is most commonly cited is as an example of the strict sartorial policy of the club. For example, Jason Cowley in the *New Statesman* of 6 May 1982 said that, 'he [Strange] once correctly turned away the ridiculous Mick Jagger for arriving in a baseball cap and trainers', while Judith Frankland, a former Blitz Kid, told the *Sunday Sun* of 5 May 2006: 'The Blitz was the place to be seen. It wasn't big and could only hold 200 people, but I don't know a club as exclusive. You could never be too outrageous and only the wildly dressed got in. Mick Jagger was famously turned away because Steve didn't like what he was wearing.' According to the *Sunday Times* of 7 January 2007, 'Steve Strange once knocked back Mick Jagger at the door of the new-romantic club Blitz – he just didn't look the part.'

But the truth would appear to be that either the incident never occurred at all or, if it did, Jagger was refused entry because he was drunk or the club was too full or perhaps simply because he refused to pay to get in. It had nothing to do with Blitz being an exclusive club to which only the outrageously or trendily dressed could gain access. However, the story in the *Daily Mirror* had mentioned Jagger's 'clothes sense' as the reason for the refusal and this was the story that made its way around the world in March 1980, some eight months or so after any actual or imagined incident, via the Associated Press.

Interestingly, there is a similar myth about Mick Jagger which relates to the famous New York Club Studio 54, although this story says not that Jagger was refused entry but that he physically could not get into the club on its opening night in April 1977 because of the massive crowd in the street outside which was blocking the entrance. However, while there is a contemporaneous record of a frustrated Frank Sinatra sitting in his car outside the club unable to get near the venue – and, indeed, the story of Sinatra giving up after seeing the crush was reported in the *Washington Post* of 28 April 1977 (which also said that Warren Beatty was in a similar position) – there does not appear to be any similar documented evidence of Jagger's inability to gain access.

There was, however, one nightclub which Mick Jagger admitted to being turned away from in 1979. This was a New York nightclub called Hurrah. In an interview given to Liz Derringer in New York on 31 December 1979 (but published six months later in *High Times* of June 1980), Jagger was asked about his beard, which he had first revealed in public while in London in the first week of July 1979. He told Ms Derringer that his beard got him 'thrown out of all the best discos' and that, 'I couldn't get into Hurrah's one night'. So that appears to be the only venue that we can reliably say turned away Mick Jagger.

In any event, one cannot help but wonder if Steve Strange, who certainly knew of Marc Benecke's strict door policy at Studio 54 (in March 1979 for example he was quoted in a short lived publication called *Pop Star Weekly* as saying of Blitz, 'I suppose it's like Studio 54 in a vague sort of way in that if I don't like the look of somebody then I won't let them in') was attempting to emulate the New York club in deliberately spreading a story about Jagger being unable to get into Blitz, thus creating the illusion of extreme exclusivity.

Whatever the truth of the Mick Jagger story, there is, as mentioned in the *Superpop* article of July 1979, a much lesser known, but more plausible, example of Steve Strange refusing entry into Blitz to a pop star, and one whose music was played at Blitz to boot. The following story was told by Paula Yates in her 'Natural Blonde' column in *Record Mirror*'s 13 October 1979 edition:

> The other day I was talking to the delightful Steve Strange (friend of the stars and anyone who makes trousers) and was bewailing the Gary Numan lig, that epic orgy of haute cuisine you may recall from last week. Apparently Steve once made the tragic error of not allowing Gary into Blitz (this was probably due to the fact that as Blitz DJ Rusty Egan forced everyone to listen to Tubeway Army, Steve didn't want them to have to look at his eye make-up as well). Anyway, when he and Rusty swaggered in, Gary promptly told a bouncer to throw them out immediately. You're not coming to my party yaboo sucks.

So it would seem that Gary Numan was denied entry to Blitz and partial corroboration of this story is to be found in Numan's autobiography in which he explains that, following a successful television appearance by Tubeway Army to perform 'Are Friends Electric?', he went to the club to celebrate with the four other 'members' of the group who, although they did not play on the record, were used for cosmetic purposes on television to give the appearance of being a proper band. These would have been Paul Gardiner (bass), Chris Payne and Billy Currie (both synths and keyboards) and Chris Sharpley (drums). Numan says that Strange actually allowed him and Currie to enter the club but refused entry to the others so that Numan and Currie could not go in without breaking up the group, which they refused to do, thus leaving them all standing in Great Queen Street in the rain. His recollection is that this was immediately after Tubeway Army's first *Top of the Pops* appearance but he can't be right about this because that would have been on a Wednesday night (23 May 1979) when the show was pre-recorded before being broadcast the following evening. It would almost certainly have been after Tubeway Army's performance on a live broadcast of *The Old Grey Whistle Test* at 11pm on Tuesday, 22 May 1979, being their debut television appearance. In any event, Numan recalls that he was 'very angry' that Strange had spoilt what should have been a major celebration. Indeed, in a 2001 book by Graham Vickers, he is quoted as describing Strange as 'a prima donna tossbag'. At the same time, Billy Currie does not seem to have been quite so affected by the incident and he later teamed up with Strange on his Visage project.

As a final word on this, we may note that the story could have been even better than Gary Numan or Mick Jagger not getting into Blitz. The gossip column of *Frizz* magazine's November 1979 issue reported the following:

> An amusing vignette outside BLITZ on a BOWIE night. A tall emaciated individual is trying to get in, but when asked by the ever vigilant STEVE STRANGE whether he has a membership card he replies rather ironically: 'I only have Access'. After a few minutes STEVE relents and allows DAVID BOWIE (for it is he) to enter. At the sight of their hero the clones go berserk, emptying the dance floor in a matter of minutes.

So it seems we nearly had an incident of David Bowie being refused entry to a Bowie night! One might, incidentally, question the veracity of *this* story but there is some corroboration that Bowie did at least visit Blitz in the latter half of 1979; Paula Yates reported in her *Record Mirror* column of 29 September 1979 that Bowie had telephoned her then boyfriend, Bob Geldof, one Tuesday night and invited him to Blitz (with Paula going along too). She reported that, while she personally didn't enjoy the evening because it was very hot in the club, 'Bowie likes Blitz because he thinks it's like a Berlin club...He also thinks it's a place Marc Bolan would have loved' and Bowie and Bob spent the evening 'wedged in the corner together'. So Bowie at least could get in – and he would return to the venue to collect extras for his 'Ashes to Ashes' video in 1980 – along with perhaps, even then, the scruffiest man in England, Bob Geldof, suggesting that Blitz was not quite as exclusive as the myth would have us believe!

Indeed, despite Steve Strange vetting guests at the door, on most nights anyone young and good looking was likely to gain access regardless of what they were wearing. As Strange told music journalist Huw Collingbourne in a revealing moment in 1982: 'It's true that I did vet people at the door but it really wasn't that heavy. The barrier was because we didn't want people who were out to get pissed and violent, or skinheads or football supporters.' He also said something similar to music journalist Steve Sutherland in late 1980, as reported in *Melody Maker's* 27 December 1980 issue. However, this was not quite the message Strange wanted to convey to the general public at the time he was running the club and he was quoted in the 14 July 1979 issue of *Superpop* as saying, 'We don't allow anyone who's not dressed outrageously', with the journalist who secured the quote adding that anyone under or over weight should 'forget it' because 'Steve doesn't let fat or thin people in either.' In any event, weight issues aside, it is fair to say that quite a few people did come extravagantly dressed, even if large numbers were nevertheless allowed in wearing normal clothes.

The Bowie Nights at Blitz soon became well known and, indeed, the first issue of *Pop Star Weekly* in March 1979 commented that 'Blitz is the name of a disco which seems to be on everybody's lips, especially on Tuesday nights', adding that, 'they have their own scene going – a scene which isn't quite like anywhere else.' Writing in the March 1979 issue of *Ritz*, Barbara Brownfield advised a certain Wilf Butler, who can 'now be seen lurking at reggae round-ups in search of new beauties to grace the books of his new model agency', to 'try Blitz on Tuesdays'. At the same time, even though it had only just begun, it was thought by some to be 'passé' but, in a perceptive piece in the July/August 1979 issue of *Ritz*, Stephen Lavers wrote:

> Although the people who frequent Bowie night at Blitz have already become ultra-passé to many sections of the media, particularly the music press, I still feel that they are the only grouping at the moment with any potential for positive development. The elements of a successful youth culture are an identifiable genre of music, a distinctive look and, if possible, a radical ideology or mode of behaviour. Well the music is already there...The style too exists if in embryonic form. It has developed from a straight clone approach (trying to look as much like DAVID BOWIE or BRYAN FERRY as possible) into a synthesis of the PX 'Extraterrestrial Uniform' the ROLF and FLORIAN 'Extremist Normality' look and a plain monochrome minimalism. The only eccentric aspect of this desire to go boldly where no man has been before seems to be an almost unhealthy preoccupation with cross-dressing.

Interestingly, Lavers added that Gary Numan's then current look was 'largely derivative' of the sound and look at Blitz. In the next issue, Lavers' colleague, Francis Lynn, mentioned the 'weirdly dressed teenagers' who hung around at Blitz on Tuesday nights. And it was not only on Tuesdays that one would find them. On Sunday, 1 July 1979, for example, Blitz was the venue for a 'Come

As Your Favourite Blonde' fancy dress party featuring an electronic disco by Rusty Egan, with appearances by Steve Strange dressed as the Milky Bar Kid and Peter Robinson ('Marilyn') as Marilyn Monroe, naturally. Footage shot of the evening by Lyndall Hobbs for a short documentary called *Steppin' Out* shows a heaving dance floor, highlighting the popularity of Blitz at this time. Strange is also filmed hamming it up at the door, refusing certain people entry for being too square, thus helping to perpetuate the myth of total exclusivity.

Blitz was referred to in the (circa) July 1979 issue of *Frizz* which described Steve Strange as 'a very interesting young man who can be seen lounging decoratively at Legends on most nights except Tuesdays when he plays host at Blitz' and pointed out that he works 'in the futuristic clothes shop PX whose clothes he wears so stylishly'. Paula Yates, after a visit to the club in September 1979, reported, rather more cynically, in her 'Natural Blonde' column in *Record Mirror* of 29 September 1979: 'Blitz is a club where the motto should be "The only thing worth living for is style". In the morning I'm sure most of the clientele go off to work at dentists and the supermarkets. But on Tuesday night they put their hair up in bouffants, wedge themselves into their lame space suits and set off to wow the dental nurse of their dreams. It's a little like an extremely decadent hairdressers convention.' Ouch!

In the same issue of *Record Mirror*, a review of a gig attended by a mainstream audience at Blitz in September 1979 by the *Rocky Horror Picture Show* actress turned recording artist, Laura Campbell, better known as Little Nell, led the reviewer, Mike Nicholls, to ask: 'What was she doing there and why this exclusive wine bar, generally the domain of synthesiser freaks and Gary Numan lookalikes…?'

In November 1979, a curious *Melody Maker* journalist, Steve Taylor, paid a visit to Blitz's 'electronic disco' one Tuesday evening. He described Steve Strange as looking like an Elizabethan courtier wearing 'clumpy, painfully pointed shoes, aerosolled-on black tights, topped by a matching collarless frock-coat framed in a white frilly ruff and cuffs.' He noted that the dominant style of dress of 'the extravagantly dressed and coiffured post-punk hangers-out' in the club could be described as 'science fiction cowboy, a marriage of the two classic movie/comicstrip myths: like many a supposedly "new" or future-oriented style, it's very much a cocktail of past elements.' Taylor continued:

> Bandanas are almost mandatory, double breasted shirts (preferably taken to the extreme of running the line of buttons to the point of the shoulder) are common, and trousers should be baggy around the crotch and thighs and taper precariously to the ankle. Bouffants are popular with the girls, coal-black or henna-red, and anything monochromatic or just downright ungainly...It would be wrong, though, to give an impression of dominance by any particular style, as one of the more refreshing things about the place is that it clearly provides a platform for the satisfaction of the peacock instincts of those who don't happen to be blessed with colour-magazine outlines.

As for the music played at the club, Taylor reported that 'the ingredients of synthetic style boil down to pretty simple basics: much electronics and distorted/treated vocals, a bass sound flattened to the point of bursting, and that ubiquitous disco hi-hat.'

We know that by the autumn of 1979, the members of Gentry, or at least some of them, were certainly going to Blitz on Tuesday nights but we need to bear in mind that when Steve Strange began his club nights there in February of that year, the Gentry were performing at standard sweaty rock venues such as the Rock Garden, the Hope & Anchor and the Marquee. There is no reason to believe that they dressed out of the ordinary at this time or that they were attracted by the weird and outrageous outfits of the period. Certainly, their early fans like Liz and Vicki Silvester do not recall anything unusual about what the band were wearing and, says Vicki, 'they were just like some blokes on stage who were quite good but they could have been any band.'

Photographs of the band members from early 1979 are hard, if not impossible, to find and, although Tony does mention in his autobiography that he managed to shock his grandfather one day in about 1978 by wearing an embroidered shirt with a mandarin collar, there is no evidence that any of them were dressing up as dandies and popping down to Blitz on Tuesday evenings during that early stage in the life of Bowie Nights at that venue. A photograph which appears in Gary's book of Gentry performing at Camden Girls' School on 12 December 1978 – a gig which was attended by Liz Silvester, a pupil of the school, who had suggested the idea of the band performing there to Tony's younger sister, Lee – shows them to be very conventionally dressed.

In his autobiography, Martin Kemp says that his print job 'at the end of 1978' was providing him with enough money to get into Blitz every Tuesday night. However, as the Tuesday club nights at Blitz hosted by Steve Strange and Rusty Egan did not begin until February 1979, this cannot be right and Martin would appear to be recalling the end of 1979, not 1978. This is supported by the fact that he also says in the same paragraph of his book that it was at about the same time that he gave up his job in a print shop which would not have been until December 1979 at the earliest, when the band were offered a recording contract by Island's Chris Blackwell (and more likely in early 1980). It is certainly the case that Martin was captured on film outside Sloane Square tube station with other Blitz-goers before an unconventional party on the Circle Line, as featured in the 2014 documentary film, *Soul Boys of the Western World*, but this was to celebrate Steve Strange's twenty-first birthday party at the end of May 1980.

Martin also includes in his book a photograph of himself, looking quite young and dressed in typical 'New Romantic' style, captioned: 'At home before the battle of the Blitz'. As he explains in the text of his book, this refers to a fight he remembers between Blitz regular Chris Sullivan and 'the local hooligan' which developed into an all-out attack on the Blitz's patrons in Great Queen

Street. If the fight could be dated to early 1979, this might show that Martin Kemp at least was a visitor to Blitz at this time.

Martin, who anachronistically calls it a fight between 'The New Romantics' and 'The Hooligans', says in his autobiography that it started when the 'local hooligan' had talked his way into the club and was given a smack by the mountainous Chris Sullivan. The hooligan swore to come back mob handed and did so at 3:00am when everyone was leaving. However, to his surprise, 'the trendies' fought back and actually won the fight, sending the hooligans packing 'with their tails between their legs.'

Gary Kemp, who provides a similar account of the origins of the fight in his autobiography, has even offered up the identity of one of the 'hooligans': only he wasn't a hooligan at all, according to Gary, he was 'a Futurist' and the fight was really between New Romantics and Futurists. Thus, said Gary in a Radio London interview with Gary Crowley in 2002: 'We weren't really Futurists but the Futurists were happening at the same time. I remember Jock McDonald had a Futurist club not far down the road. I remember one terrible night there was a fight between the Futurists and the New Romantics in the middle of Soho in the Blitz. I remember Chris Sullivan chasing Jock McDonald down the street. I have no idea who won.'

Jock McDonald was a boisterous Glaswegian former DJ and punk rock concert promoter who had assisted club owner Kevin St John in running the Roxy in early 1978 (after another Glaswegian friend of St John's, Kenny MacDonald, had been sent to prison for stealing a purse). When the Roxy was forced to close in March 1978, Jock carried out a number of stunts to try and save it, including a threat to stage a march of six hundred punks in full bondage regalia from the Roxy to County Hall to hand in a petition against its closure, mystifying attempts to surround and invade the offices of *Sounds* and *Melody Maker* respectively and a forced entry into the locked club to try and start it up again.

After these protests failed to achieve their intended purpose, Jock returned to live band promotion and was soon embroiled in controversy when an Adam & The Ants gig he was promoting at the Rainbow Theatre in December 1978 was cancelled at the last minute while the band was on stage doing a sound check, with hundreds of fans turned away from the venue. The Rainbow's management explained that the reason for the cancellation was that Jock had failed to make an agreed payment for the hire of the hall. Adam & The Ants went public about the shambolic way the matter had been handled and this may help to explain a later incident in which Adam Ant was physically attacked by Jock (and his band 4 Be 2) at the BBC Television Centre studios in Shepherd's Bush, where Adam & The Ants were recording a performance of 'Dog Eat Dog' for *Top of the Pops*, although Jock was to claim at the time that it was a fight over a girl. Jock also co-promoted (with the band) a Christmas Day 1978 debut gig by now ex-Sex Pistol Johnny (Rotten) Lydon's newly formed Public Image Limited, a gig which the reviewer of the following week's *Sounds* described as 'horrible from beginning to end. A bloody disaster. Just a bad gig, organized by and starring a group you didn't think could ever be bad. No magic. No spirit...Did you ever get the feeling you've been conned...?'

During 1978, Jock was also running a record stall in the Beaufort Market, off the King's Road, which was home to a number of punk fashion stalls, and he was absolutely furious when the leaseholders served all stall holders with notices to quit. He devised the idea of a protest gig against the closure, headlined by Public Image Limited, upon the roof of the Arts & Crafts Studio building which housed the Beaufort Market, on 25 November 1978, along with a number of other punk bands in support. However, Lydon pulled out the day before the 'gig' and, in any case, the police prevented it going ahead, arresting the bassist of support band, The Pack, after he played a few bars.

Undeterred, Jock arranged another, identical rooftop gig on Saturday, 31 March 1979, the day of the closure of the Market, which was pre-announced in *Melody Maker*, with Jock promising that 'one major band will play'. Jock spread the word that this was to be The Clash, leading to a couple of thousand punks and skinheads turning up in the King's Road. Perhaps surprisingly for one of Jock's stunts, The Clash had actually agreed to appear, and the band made a brief but silent appearance as, once again, the police prevented the gig going ahead, this time by ensuring that the van carrying the sound system was unable to get anywhere near the King's Road. Instead of a gig, there was a mini riot in the street with fighting between punks and police, resulting in many arrests. Jock, not apparently learning any lessons, optimistically promised a further benefit gig by The Clash in support of those arrested, as well as yet another protest gig against the closure of Beaufort Market, supposedly to occur outside Buckingham Palace. Neither event ever took place and Jock, finally giving up on Beaufort Market as a lost cause, turned his attention to club promotion.

In April, Jock was behind a plan for Billy's in Dean Street to host a brand new London disco 'primarily for punks' (as announced in the *Superpop* music paper of 14 April 1979) with Tuesdays and Thursdays dedicated to David Bowie, in direct competition with Blitz; records to be played by an enthusiastic teenage DJ called David Elton Archer. The idea was for Monday nights to be dedicated to the Sex Pistols, with Johnny Lydon optimistically said to be the DJ, while Wednesdays were to be general punk nights. This rather confused concept never seems to have got off the ground and, having second thoughts, Jock decided to attempt to directly recreate the Roxy at Billy's by turning it into a live punk venue, booking The Psychedelic Furs to headline the opening session. He also intended to record a live album at the club (similar to a top twenty live album which had been recorded at the Roxy) to be produced by Johnny Lydon. However, on the day of the big opening, the police were called to Dean Street following complaints from local residents about the noise generated in the afternoon by the rehearsals. The police refused to allow the gig to go ahead and McDonald was forced to abandon the whole idea.

For the Bank Holiday Monday at the end of May, Jock claimed to be organizing a one thousand-a-side football match in Brighton between Glasgow punks on one side and 'Johnny Lydon's London punks' on the other but that bizarre, and clearly impractical, game never kicked off, with a large police turnout preventing anything of the sort, although the *Sun* imaginatively reported that a smaller game of two hundred-a-side was played before police stopped it. Nothing could stop Jock though. At the end of June he planned another one thousand-a-side football match in Hyde Park on a Sunday which he designated 'Punk Sports Day' but all that happened was a fight in the park between punks and members of the Household Cavalry while the police prevented any actual sporting, or other, activity occurring. The following month, Jock announced that he was organizing the recording of a special benefit album, to be released by Hammer Records, in order to raise funds for punks hospitalized after being assaulted in a King's Cross squat. The album was to include contributions from Public Image Limited, The Skids and The Psychedelic Furs but the Furs immediately denied that they would be contributing to any such album and stated that they 'no longer had any connections with McDonald'.

In August, the irrepressible Jock, who seems to have appointed himself as leader of the punk movement, was reported to be 'representing London' at a so-called International Punk Conference in Brussels but it was never explained what this actually meant and certainly nothing was achieved. Then, in early September, he took over the Apple Club off Wardour Street on Friday and Saturday nights to host punk, mod and reggae concerts. Later in the same month, along with his best friend Jimmy Lydon, the brother of the Sex Pistols' John, and with David Archer as co-DJ, he started a Saturday club night at the newly opened Studio 21 in Oxford Street. This was the so-called 'Futurist' club which Gary referred to, albeit that it was a bit further away from Blitz than 'not far down the road'. However, the club was basically an attempt to imitate Blitz in its Tuesday night form on a Saturday night and the fight had nothing to do with Futurism versus New Romanticism. It also did not take place in Soho (a slip by Gary which confirms that he confuses Blitz with Billy's on occasion).

The Kemps' recollection about the details of the origins of the fight also does not appear to be quite accurate, although it is possible that Chris Sullivan was involved in a dispute with Jock at some point which led to some simmering resentment. As far as it is possible to establish from clues in contemporary published reports, the fight was actually caused by guest DJ Rusty Egan refusing to play the debut single of Jock McDonald's new band, 4 Be 2, at a launch party for a new teen magazine called *Midnight* at the Embassy Club in Old Bond Street in October 1979. His refusal was hardly surprising because the song, entitled 'One of the Lads', was nothing like the type of dance-based electronic music that Egan played at the time and, indeed, McDonald himself described it as 'Irish Gaelic disco for building site workers'. However, *Melody Maker* of 3 November 1979 reported that Egan's refusal caused a 'considerable fracas' at the club, which, like *Ritz* Magazine of November 1979, it identified as the Embassy (although a report of what appears to be the same event, by Paula Yates in *Record Mirror* of 13 October 1979, seems to place the launch party at a nearby venue but not in the Embassy itself, while Midge Ure in his autobiography says the altercation was at the Blitz). According to *Melody Maker*, the fracas involved the violent McDonald 'tearing Egan's clothes off'. The 4 be 2 record was, it seems, played by Egan in the end (under duress) but McDonald had taken offence at the initial refusal and paid a visit to Blitz with some punk friends on a subsequent Tuesday night, leading to a fight kicking off either in Blitz or out in Great Queen Street which, as we know, Jock and company ended up losing.

There may have been some additional history between Jock and the Blitz club. The October 1979 issue of the *Ritz* Newspaper, which appears to have pre-dated the incident at the Embassy club, reported in respect of Steve Strange:

STEVE'S been staying with OLIVER TOBIAS and JOHNNY STEWART recently with the excuse that a character called JOCK MACDONALD is out to get him.

It is not known what this was about but it is interesting to recall the claim made by *Popstar* magazine in April 1979 that Steve Strange had apparently denied Johnny Lydon, a great friend of Jock's, entry to Blitz one Tuesday night. We know that Jock was very quick to take offence at insults against himself or his friends and this just might explain Jock's strange announcement in April that he was going to host Bowie nights at Billy's on Tuesdays and Thursdays. Was he sending out a message to Steve Strange that he was going to destroy his business? And did his complete failure to do so lead him to make threats against Strange, followed up by his attack on Egan and then his assault on the Blitz itself?

An alternative cause of the fight is suggested by Ted Polhemus in the May 1980 issue of *Tatler*. He reported that the 'punch-up at Blitz' was due to Steve Strange saying to the *Evening Standard* in late January 1980 that there was nothing to do on a Saturday night, a comment to which Jock McDonald, who ran the Saturday night club at Studio 21, supposedly interpreted as a personal attack. Jock was certainly offended by Strange's comments; his response to them appeared in the *Evening Standard* of 31 January 1980 when he said of Strange, 'If he wants war, fine'. In any event, the fight in Great Queen Street appears to have occurred in either October/November 1979 or January/February 1980, neither of which helps to place Martin and Gary Kemp at Blitz in early 1979.

Without doubt, the members of the band must have started to visit Blitz on a regular basis at some point in 1979, almost certainly from the late summer or early autumn of that year. Gary's consistent memory is that it was Steve Dagger who introduced him to Steve Strange's Tuesday club nights in 1979 (e.g. 'I was taken down by Steve Dagger', 'Steve Dagger said, 'Look you've got to go to this thing called a Bowie night'). Was this a skilful attempt by manager Dagger to influence Gary to write more electronic based dance songs in order to sell the band? At times, Gary appears to be quite open that it was all a marketing ploy. In a filmed interview broadcast on the internet in January 2009 he said that he noticed that the crowd at Blitz 'didn't have as the Sex Pistols punk did a band that represented them', adding with a wry smile and knowing look, 'I saw there might be a gap in the market...So we got our little group back together and I wrote an entire new bunch of songs based on the synthesizer and four-on-the-floor drum beat.'

Gary was certainly right about there being a gap in the market for a new band playing electronic dance music aimed at, and representing, the Blitz party crowd, despite some preliminary efforts to fill it. Tubeway Army had been one of the first out of the blocks in May 1979 with a massive hit single, 'Are 'Friends' Electric?', although this was really a solo project by Gary Numan, who *Record Mirror* of 9 June 1979 described as looking 'rather starkly romantic...He steals his music from Ultravox, his image from David Bowie.' A weird looking synth pop band called Classix Nouveaux appeared in August 1979 and were to release a Kraftwerk influenced track called 'The Robots Dance' a year later, without any chart success. Steve Strange and Rusty Egan had already formed a 'Gary Numan type band' (according to their producer Martin Rushent, quoted in *Record Mirror* of 19 September 1979) called Visage, with Midge Ure and Billy Currie of Ultravox, plus a few musicians from the band Magazine, and released a single, 'Tar', in November but this failed to make any impression upon the charts although it was, not surprisingly, regularly played at Blitz on Tuesday nights. Some existing bands, such as David Sylvian's Japan, were just starting to introduce synthesizers into their music but, as yet, no-one had grabbed the imagination or attention to become the sound of the young Blitz crowd let alone incorporated its fashion to become its public face.

In his autobiography, Gary Kemp recalls Steve Dagger, recognizing the need for Gentry to find an audience, recounting the story of Peter Meaden's redesign of The Who to suit a mod audience. This had occurred in 1964 when Meaden, then a publicist, became co-manager of The Who and promptly changed the band's name to The High Numbers: not, in hindsight, his best decision. He was very familiar with the mod scene and, despite the fact that none of the members of the band were mods, altered their image so that they looked and dressed like mods. In addition, he wrote two new songs with obvious mod references, 'I'm The Face' and 'Zoot Suit', which were recorded and released (as the A and B side respectively) by The High Numbers as their debut (and only) single on the Fontana label. Meaden's press release for the record claimed that 'I'm The Face' was to be 'the first authentic mod record' and that The High Numbers were 'drawn from this facet of society in which they are totally immersed'. This was not true but it was the transformation of the band into mods, thus appealing to a large record buying audience, which was the central feature of the Meaden masterplan. Unfortunately for the sake of the masterplan, neither of the songs on the record were very good and it sank without trace. New management followed, and the band's name reverted to The Who, but the mod image and direction was retained and the Meaden plan eventually bore fruit. So Dagger and Kemp had the examples of both The Who and the Sex Pistols to guide them and, having found the scene at Blitz, the future direction of their band was clear to both.

Thus, Gentry deliberately ditched all their old songs (bar one), wrote some new dance based material, acquired on hire purchase a Yamaha CS10 synthesizer – available to buy for under £300 at the time – started to wear more flamboyant and stylish clothes and transformed themselves into what was eventually to become known as a New Romantic group. In a moment of pure genius, Gary devised a simple but effective fourteen note sequence for the new synthesizer which would come to define the group, and indeed the era, comprising the intro and theme of a song entitled 'To Cut A Long Story Short'. With their new focus established, and now wearing the sort of flamboyant clothes seen every Tuesday at Blitz, the band rehearsed furiously, but secretly, and, in November 1979, Steve Dagger decided it was time to invite a carefully selected group of somewhere between thirty and fifty friends and Blitz regulars to a grubby rehearsal studio at 103 Holloway Road called Halligan's Band Centre.

So it was that a small group of oddly dressed, and no doubt rather tired (despite the amphetamine pills that they may have taken), men and women were gathered together at about eleven o'clock in the morning of Saturday, 17 November 1979, immediately after a Friday night of clubbing. Although they all knew, or knew of, the band members individually, most had never seen them play. It had been six months since Gentry's last public appearance and that had been a completely different collection of songs played to a completely different group of people. What the crowd at Halligan's heard that morning was a bit more like the type of music Rusty Egan was spinning every Tuesday night. The boys could all play their instruments, including the synthesizer, Tony could certainly sing in his very distinctive style and they all looked good.

In many ways, the event at Halligan's was less of a gig and more of an audition by the members of Gentry to the Blitz regulars. The Gentry were, in effect, saying to the crowd, 'Look at how good we are, don't you want to be associated with us and help us?' Virtually everyone in the crowd that morning could indeed help the band and, in the process, themselves by furthering their own careers. Those who were journalists could write about the band. Those who were artists could design posters and invitations. Those who were fashion designers could design outfits. If you knew even a little bit about lighting you could be in charge of lighting the band on stage. Most importantly, those who were not musically or artistically talented but were well connected could use those connections to promote the band. It was to be a joint enterprise and the Halligan's performance seemed to do the trick. As Gary has said: 'We did a gig in Holloway Road studios to test out this sound with a bunch of these people who'd come and watch and it was during the middle of the day we did it and it went down very well.'

After the performance, everyone went for a drink at a local pub, possibly the Lord Nelson at 100 Holloway Road, just across the road from Halligan's. It was clear that the band needed a better name than Gentry if they were to succeed in their aim of world domination. Robert Elms had the answer: Spandau Ballet. He did not at the time, it seems, mention to anyone where he had got the idea from but it was immediately recognized as a great name – a High Court judge, no less, would many years later describe it as 'an inspired name…a wonderful name' – and it was adopted by a grateful Steve Dagger so that Gentry shed its dull two syllable name and became the far more majestic and mysterious four syllable Spandau Ballet.

CHAPTER FIVE

The Second Spandau Ballet

> '...the date, time and place are not advertised on radio, television, or in newspapers: the tradition is passed from generation by word of mouth....Beneath the beauty of costume and liturgy....is an inward journey, a journey to something beyond oneself – a journey to glory.'
> —From *Journeys to Glory* by Marjorie B. Young and Adam Bujak, Harper & Row, 1976
> (referring to Christian pilgrimages in remote Polish villages)

THE FIRST PUBLIC APPEARANCE OF the new Spandau Ballet was, suitably enough, at a Blitz Christmas party, held not on a Tuesday on this occasion but on Wednesday, 5 December 1979. A number of famous guests are recorded as having attended, such as fashion designer Zandra Rhodes, journalist Emma Soames and interior designer Nicky Haslam. The head of Island Records, Chris Blackwell, also came along that night, having been specifically invited to see the freshly named Spandau Ballet by a friend of the band. He liked what he saw and immediately offered them a record deal. In response, Steve Dagger hired solicitor Brian Carr, who had recently represented John Lydon/Rotten against Malcolm McLaren, to represent the band in negotiations.

At first, it looked like Dagger was going to accept the offer – there didn't seem to be any reason why he would not – and John Keeble gave up his job at Barclays Bank in anticipation of becoming a signed artist. Keeble was not amused therefore when, after further negotiations, Carr advised the band not to sign the contract with Island because the terms were not good enough and there was, according to Tony, an 'almighty row' within the band about this decision.

Meanwhile, the band was continuing to make use of the connections formed at Blitz. Steve Strange ensured a mention in *Melody Maker*'s 8 December 1979 issue which reported that he was trying to break into personal management 'of a young band ominously titled Spandau Ballet'. Shortly afterwards there was another mention by Francis Lynn, in *Ritz*'s December 1979 issue, who wrote: 'Singer STEVE STRANGE has paid me an enormous amount to say he is managing a group called "Spandau Ballet".' Although Strange was not, of course, managing the band, there was a small element of truth in these comments because he was doing some managerial type tasks; both Steve Strange and Chris Sullivan had been asked after the Halligan's performance to help the band obtain gigs. Further assistance from another Halligan's attendee came when Graham Smith designed the posters for what Robert Elms has described as the band's 'official début performance' at a warehouse party organized by Chris Sullivan (yet another Halligan's attendee) at Mayhem Studios in Battersea on 22 December where there was no stage and the band had to play on the floor. Gary remembers this because, 'I had condensation on my head and a skinhead staring me in the face for the whole gig.'

In January 1980, Steve Strange took the decision to host Thursday evenings at Blitz, in addition to Tuesdays, which would have more of an alternative cabaret theme, with fire-eaters, jugglers, strippers, posing bodybuilders, poetry readers, alternative plays as well as bands. His plan was for Spandau Ballet to perform at the opening night and possibly every subsequent Thursday too. He initially attempted to publicize this innovation through John Blake of the London evening newspaper, the *Evening News*, but Blake clearly misunderstood what he had been told which is why his 'Ad Lib' column reported on 10 January 1980: 'If you breathe fire, put ferrets down your trousers or like taking your clothes off in public the very odd Steve Strange would love you to take part in the regular Spandau ballet he is holding at The Blitz wine bar every Thursday from January 24.' So Blake appears to have thought that Strange was hosting some kind of bizarre ballet dance event every Thursday night!

Strange then turned his attention to David Johnson at the London *Evening Standard*. The editor of that newspaper, Charles Wintour, had decided in October 1979 to include a weekly page for young adult readers, and in David Johnson, who was particularly interested in new angles on London life and youth culture, had found the ideal person to run it. Johnson christened his page, 'On The Line', a name inspired by Eddy Grant's song, 'On The Frontline', intended to indicate a certain street edginess. The page included items of alternative news which would have appealed to those who went to Blitz, such as stories about Andrew Logan's film, *The Alternative Miss World*, which previewed at Leicester Square in a private screening in November 1979, and, according to Johnson, 'the page was getting a reputation for being trendy'. Johnson himself was very much a man with his finger on the pulse, having a good knowledge of London's nightlife, and had not only been turned away from Blitz on one occasion by Strange but had been distinctly underwhelmed by the Blitz experience when he *had* got in with friends on a Tuesday night.

In the fourth week of January 1980, having recently returned from a holiday in Greece, Johnson had been discussing with Emma Soames, the *Standard's* society columnist, how there was absolutely nothing going on in London at the time and was desperate for something interesting to write about. When, out of the blue, Steve Strange telephoned him to say that he would be starting a second club night at Blitz, involving a new and exotic sounding band called Spandau Ballet, Johnson, despite his previous experiences at that venue, thought it all 'sounded fabulous', so he included it in 'On The Line' at the first opportunity.

It is sometimes said that Spandau Ballet's gigs were by invitation only and known only to an exclusive few but if you were a reader of the *Evening Standard* on Thursday, 24 January 1980, as many normal Londoners were, you would have known that Spandau Ballet was playing at Blitz that evening because Johnson reported this fact with the comment: 'the band Spandau Ballet will attempt to combine vocals akin to Sinatra with "dance music for the future"'.

One of the readers of the *Evening Standard* that day was a barman at Richard Branson's The Venue called Steve. He was a mate of Mark Robinson, Mick Austin and David Wardill and thus knew about their band. As Mark remembers it, he, Mick and David were all at The Venue when Steve called them over and asked, 'What are you doing here?' The band members looked at him blankly. 'You're playing at the Blitz club tonight aren't you?' The boys were nonplussed. Steve showed them Johnson's piece in the *Evening Standard* with its mention of Spandau Ballet appearing at Blitz, which, according to Mark, is how the boys were alerted to the surprising existence of another band with an identical name to their own. Mark reflects: 'We were young, angry, hadn't a clue what to do. We thought it would go away but how wrong can you be? If we had had any brains we would have protected the name but, hey, that's rock 'n' roll.'

One can speculate as to what would have happened if Mark, Mick, David and Gordon had contacted lawyers at this point but it is unlikely that they could have forced Steve Dagger's Spandau Ballet to change their name. The original Spandau Ballet had only performed two unreviewed gigs at the most, notice of which had not even appeared in the listings of any music paper, so there was no published documentary evidence that they had ever existed. No doubt they could have gathered together sufficient witness evidence to prove that they did play a gig at the Hope & Anchor under the name of Spandau Ballet on 6 May 1979 (and, if they did actually perform there, at the Ampthill Youth Centre in August 1978) but this is unlikely to have been enough to stake a claim to that name. The courts will only protect a band's name if the band has built up a reputation under that name so that anyone else who uses it is, in effect, trading on that reputation. The original Spandau Ballet had not built up any meaningful reputation under the Spandau Ballet name. Aside from their possible brief appearance in Ampthill, they had only played one, unadvertised, support gig, and, in any event, by January 1980 had effectively given up and stopped rehearsing or performing, thus rendering any claim to the name obsolete. There is no copyright in a band's name so they would have had very little chance of success. If they had filed a legal action they might have become enough of an irritant to Steve Dagger to secure a payoff of some sort, at least once the band were signed and had some money, but it is very unlikely that they would have been able to force them to use a different name.

Steve Dagger had learnt a lesson from the years of fruitless slogging around the circuit hoping for a good review in the music press followed by a visit from a record company A&R executive. This time the band was going to do it differently and perform at more unusual, and rather more exclusive, venues. The unsigned Spandau Ballet would only play gigs not advertised in advance in the music press. Dagger wasn't going to try and book Spandau into the familiar tired old locations which advertised in *Sounds*, *Melody Maker*, *Record Mirror* and *NME* every week, or were featured in the listings pages of these publications, like the Marquee and the Rock Garden, where most other unsigned bands aspired to play. He no doubt hoped that such exclusivity would give the band an edge over the hundreds, if not thousands, of others playing the circuit, desperately crying out for attention. In forming this strategy, such as it was, he might well have had in mind a short 'secret tour' of the UK by the Sex Pistols, masterminded by Malcolm McLaren a few years earlier.

That idea seems to have originated in March 1977 when, as the result of a London-wide ban on them performing, issued by the Greater London Council, the Pistols played in secret at the Notre Dame Hall in Leicester Square, having booked a private party, and allowed fifty fans in for free, in order to get round the ban. A few months later they continued the secret gig concept when they went on tour, playing under various different aliases such as 'A Mystery Band of International Repute' and 'Spots' which, as music journalist, David Hepworth, explained in 1979: 'was in accord with the idea that few people should get to see them.' Indeed, the script for the 1980 film *The Great Rock 'n' Roll Swindle*, which had been previewed in the *NME* of 17 February 1979, set out McLaren's supposed master plan as follows: 'We must cultivate the curiosity of the Press and media but minimize the possibility of them seeing the group...Don't take any calls from venues that want the band to play...Keep a low profile and play gigs where no-one can turn up.' While the concept of a 'secret tour' might have been forced on McLaren because the Sex Pistols had quickly become so notorious that no respectable venues would take them and many of their advertised gigs were cancelled (perhaps deliberately to create the impression that the band was banned), it helped cement an aura of mystique around the Pistols and it became a mark of extreme coolness to have seen them play live, of which the observant student of the music industry, Steve Dagger, would have been very well aware.

At the same time, it would be fair to say that Dagger had no option but to book Spandau into small venues because his new band had no following to speak of – the old Islington crowd had largely moved on, with most of them not even aware of the band's new image, sound and name – and would not have filled even moderately sized venues in early 1980. Indeed, according to Dagger, speaking in a 1985 BBC Radio 1 documentary, 'We could only see one conceivable audience for Spandau Ballet at the time [i.e. Blitz Kids] and there weren't very many of them believe me. This whole business that the band only played "secret gigs", but there was no point playing anywhere else other than to an extremely small group of people in London....At the time we could only see the audience for the band being a couple of hundred people.' Still, if he had been so minded, he could have booked his band into small pubs like the Hope & Anchor and the fact that he made no attempt to do so, but went for more exclusive venues, suggests that he was indeed thinking of a new strategy or, as Gary points out in his book, appreciated that the superior and more discerning Blitz crowd would simply not deign to visit the standard, grotty music venues but needed to be tempted by something better.

Whether it was the Sex Pistols' secret tour, the lack of an audience or the fussiness of the small audience that they did possess which was the inspiration behind his new strategy, Dagger was still faced with the tricky problem of finding a trendy, exclusive venue or two where people would not normally expect to see live bands but which would indulge the still unknown Spandau Ballet by allowing them to perform in front of a small audience for little or no financial gain. In this respect, ex-Owen's boy, Steve Woolley, now managing the Scala Cinema on the site of the old Other Cinema in Tottenham Street (The Makers' benefit gig in 1978 having failed to save it), again features in the story because, with his help, Spandau Ballet played their fourth gig at that venue, at around midnight on Friday, 7 March 1980.

On the Monday before this gig, Dagger had visited David Johnson at his *Evening Standard* office in Shoe Lane, off Fleet Street, and arranged to meet him for a chat over a beer-and-sandwich lunch the following afternoon at a pub called Ye Old Mitre near Hatton Garden. Dagger had approved of Johnson's article about Steve Strange's Thursday Blitz nights and evidently thought that here was a journalist worth cultivating. Having satisfied himself that he was not a blue jeans wearing, rockist type journalist of the old school, he told him, as Johnson reported in 'On The Line' two days later, that the sound of the band he was managing was 'white European dance music', and he invited him to the Scala Cinema to see and hear Spandau Ballet for himself.

This was even more of a masterstroke than Dagger was aware of at the time because, unknown to him, Johnson also edited the pop music page of the *Daily Star* on a freelance basis, meaning that, when he came to the Scala on the Friday, he brought along with him the music journalist Barry Cain who wrote for the *Star* under the name 'Andy John' as well as for *Record Mirror* under his own name. A consequence of this was that, from a single meeting, Dagger would benefit from three articles about Spandau Ballet in influential media publications over the following few weeks which strongly contributed to the creation of a precious 'buzz' around the band.

Another consequence of the meeting at Ye Old Mitre was that David Johnson reported in 'On The Line' of 6 March 1980 that 'The Now Crowd will be out in force tomorrow at the Scala cinema where romance will be making a momentary comeback' and that, 'the extremely Now band is Spandau Ballet whose wing collars give them a distinctly Edwardian appearance'. Thus it was that another Spandau Ballet gig was advertised in advance to the whole of London, or at least those who read the *Evening Standard*, and Johnson even informed his readers that the cost of admittance would be £2, that there would also be films shown (including Jean Genet's controversial *Un Chant d'Amour*) and that the proceedings would commence at 11:15pm.

According to David Johnson, the Scala gig was 'a sensational evening in the sense that all the decorative children were there dressed to the hilt.' He had been told by Dagger at their meeting that it was a fast-changing scene with everyone dressed differently and weirdly but, until he saw the large crowd at the Scala, he hadn't fully appreciated quite how visually striking the Blitz-goers 'in their battalion' could be. All around him, he saw 'colourful people looking ridiculous, preposterous, wonderful, fascinating.' That in itself was a surprise; what he certainly wasn't expecting from this bunch of strange dressers was that they would produce a decent sounding band. Even Steve Dagger had told him (as Johnson reported in the *Evening Standard* of 6 March 1980) that 'our crowd is more into fashion than music.' However, as soon as Spandau Ballet began their first song, Johnson was amazed; 'Barry and I both turned to each other' he recalls, 'and said, "My God they can play!"'. As he explains:

This was a dress-up scene, it wasn't a music scene as far as we knew; it was a showy-off scene. One went with a lot of scepticism. And then suddenly this band could play their instruments and had a lot of style. They could play their instruments. Tony Hadley had a brilliant voice and smoked as he sang. He chain smoked as he sang….and it was new, it was conspicuously new. We both knew that this was something massive and we had it to ourselves, *it was ours*. We had to get it into print as quickly as we could.

However, although Johnson and Cain were the only professional journalists in attendance at the Scala gig, they were beaten into print by one of Johnson's colleagues at the *Evening Standard*, the newspaper's fashion editor, Liz Smith, on 17 March 1980, despite the fact that she had never seen Spandau Ballet herself. Headlined 'Dandies in hand-me-downs' and accompanied by photographs of 'this dandified crowd arriving at the Scala Cinema to hear the Spandau Ballet – and be seen', her article was based on a report of the gig by a young student of fashion journalism called Perry Haines, a member of both the exclusive crowd at Halligan's and the audience at the Scala Cinema, who had previously assisted Ms Smith with an article on modern fashion in December 1979 and who had already described Spandau Ballet in the low circulation fashion magazine *Viz* as 'the most exciting sound in London'. He now told the readers of the *Evening Standard* that they were the 'most exciting new band in town' whose music was 'brilliant applause for an amazing audience of 100 per cent individualists.'

Then, in a moment of pure genius, Steve Dagger frog-marched Robert Elms into the offices of the *NME* with a review of the Scala gig which Dagger had literally forced Elms to write, standing over his shoulder while he did so, offering suggestions and amendments. Quite incredibly, despite being an unknown politics student who had walked in off the street, the *NME* published the review of the gig after Elms persuaded them that they were missing out on the hip London scene that 'everyone' was talking about; and it appeared in the *NME*'s 29 March 1980 edition. Not surprisingly, considering its provenance, it was a very positive review! Not many bands can boast that they effectively wrote their own first review in the music press. In passing, we may note that the review included reference to a lost Spandau Ballet song, never recorded, called 'Pink Room', a song about sexual bondage which may explain why it was ditched.

On 8 April, through the connection made with David Johnson, Spandau Ballet had a positive article about themselves by Barry Cain (writing as 'Andy John') published on David Johnson's pop music page in the *Daily Star*. Barry Cain had spoken to Gary Kemp following the Scala gig and his article carried a quote from Gary protesting, 'We don't want to be a rock band'. His article was sub-headed 'Ballet stay in top gear' and would certainly have pleased Steve Dagger by including the information that, so far, 'the band has refused to sign a record contract'. Immediately after this, *Record Mirror* of 12 April (on sale from 9 April) had a full page article on the band by Barry Cain (although it only contained quotes from Gary Kemp) which helpfully referred to Spandau Ballet as 'The Next Big Thing'. In the article, Tony Hadley was mistakenly, and rather amusingly, referred to as Anthony Holden, an alias he had been using to pretend to be a journalist to gain V.I.P. access to various venues.

David Johnson was again involved in an important breakthrough event for Spandau Ballet after David Thomas, a young researcher for London Weekend Television, read the 'Andy John' article about Spandau Ballet in the *Daily Star*. As LWT was, at this time, planning a documentary series on London youth culture to be called 'Twentieth Century Box', he became interested in including Spandau Ballet in one of the episodes. On the same day as the article appeared, Thomas tracked down the pop music editor of the *Star*, David Johnson, at his *Evening Standard* office to ask if he could be put in touch with the band's management, and Johnson willingly gave him Steve Dagger's contact details. An alternative version of the genesis of Spandau's appearance on this programme has been told by the *Twentieth Century Box* producer,

Janet Street-Porter, who has said that her hairdresser, Ollie O'Donnell, another member of the Halligan's audience, mentioned a wonderful unsigned band he knew to her while she was having her hair cut and it is perfectly possible that both events happened in parallel.

On 13 May 1980, the band recreated their gig at the Scala for the London Weekend Television cameras. Interestingly, considering that we have already seen that David Johnson's 'On The Line' column in the *Evening Standard* advertised Spandau's second appearance at Blitz in advance, as well as the first performance at the Scala Cinema, it did the same thing for a third time on 8 May by informing the readers of the *Standard* that, 'Next Tuesday Spandau Ballet give their W.E.D. [White European Dance] a rare airing at the Scala Cinema' so that a significant number of people in London knew about this 'secret' gig a week before it was filmed, even if most of them would not have been in the slightest bit interested.

When the resulting documentary was broadcast by LWT a couple of months later, on Sunday, 13 July, it caused a stampede from the record companies. They were now falling over themselves to find out more about the band, the members of which, at the time of the broadcast, were about to make their way back from St Tropez, where they had played an enjoyable and lucrative fortnight's residency at the Papagayo Club. In securing this residency, they had again been unknowingly assisted by David Johnson who, on 19 April, had passed on Steve Dagger's details to his friend, the agent Phil Symes, also a publicist for Chrysalis, who was responsible for the entertainment at the Papagayo and who had needed British acts to fill slots there during the summer season.

The importance of the LWT documentary cannot be overstated because, despite all the media mentions that Dagger had brilliantly (or, as the case may be, fortuitously) conjured up until this point, there had still been no record company interest. Indeed, the only concrete achievement from all the publicity had been the St Tropez residency. The television appearance did the trick, though, and the band were able to enjoy another masterstroke by Dagger when, by pretending to book a coming-down party for a bunch of students from Oxford University, with a gentle sounding 'quintet' to provide the musical entertainment, he wangled permission for Spandau to perform on HMS Belfast, moored on the River Thames, on 26 July, echoing a notorious 1977 performance by the Sex Pistols on the Queen Elizabeth river-boat to celebrate the release of their single 'God Save the Queen'.

It is often said that Spandau did not allow record company A&R types to their gigs but the main purpose of Dagger booking the Belfast in 1980 was to allow interested record company executives to see the band live. It may be recalled that Chris Blackwell of Island Records had been invited to the first show at Blitz, albeit by a friend of the band rather than by the band itself, and it is clear that Spandau Ballet had no objection whatsoever to A&R types coming to see them; the primary objective was a record deal after all.

The final PR coup before being signed was a major interview with *Sounds* journalist Betty Page who had been vetted by Steve Dagger as someone he would allow Gary Kemp to speak to, but only on condition that he, Dagger, was present to ensure that Gary remained on message. The heretical point that Dagger wanted Gary to convey to Betty, and for Betty and *Sounds* to publish, was that fashion, looking good and posing was more important to Spandau Ballet than music: the so-called Spandau Ballet Manifesto.

At the same time, Gary attempted to convey to Betty the impression that the band members had met at Billy's and that, as a bunch of trendy young fashion loving clubbers, they had spontaneously, and very much organically, decided to form a band to play the sort of music that they were dancing to. Thus, Kemp was quoted by Betty in *Sounds* of 13 September 1980 as saying: 'The group started last November when we did our first gig. But it really started when we were all friends from clubs like Billy's, about two years ago.' We now know that this was not true but the grim reality of an ordinary band forming at school and slogging away in pubs and other minor venues for three years without any notable success was not the image Gary Kemp and Steve Dagger wanted to present to the world when they spoke to Betty Page in 1980. Thus, as Tony Hadley complains in his autobiography, the band gave the puzzling appearance of having had no past.

However, the myth of Spandau as the band from nowhere was instantly exploded by an alert *Sounds* reader who had recognized them from their photographs as formerly having been The Makers and Gentry. Under the headline 'Spandau Ballet 'were Power Pop shock' claim', the reader's letter in *Sounds* of 11 October 1980 said:

> After all, after the initial 'mystery' you published pictures of them. And I remember how they used to be a poxy old R'nB group back in 1977 called the Makers, and how they later changed their collective name to Gentry, then tried and failed (who didn't fail?) to cash in on the Power Pop explosion. Humble beginnings in sweaty dumps like Upstairs at Ronnie's. I remember.

The letter appears not to have attracted any attention whatsoever, probably because no-one really cared. No doubt most people assumed that the band members must have learnt their craft somehow and no-one would have been surprised to find that they had started out in other bands. The issue of Spandau Ballet being a band without a past was probably more important to the band members themselves, and to their manager, than to anyone else.

A few weeks after the *Sounds* exposure, Paul Rambali in the *NME* was nevertheless saying that 'Spandau Ballet have come out of nowhere'. An unabashed Gary added a twist to the myth, telling Daniela Soave of *Record Mirror* in November 1980, 'There was nothing to listen to and we thought we might as well play the music we wanted to hear', so, 'I suppose we thought we should form a group', thus further annoying the traditionalist music press, and fans of most other bands, by suggesting that there was no music worth listening to before Spandau.

Yet again, though, this line was quickly contradicted by a member of the public. 'Candy' from Islington had a letter published in the 13

December 1980 issue of the *NME* in which she said that she remembered that Spandau Ballet used to be called The Makers, a band she saw in the Hope & Anchor and that, 'They never had a synthesizer then and they used to play jolly pop songs.' Augmenting this observation, Paul Morley of the *NME* referred to the band's 'ignoble power-pop past' and added that they had also been called 'The Gentry', playing 'dirty rock 'n' roll gigs like The Rock Garden.' The theme was picked up a few months later by Sal Solo of Classix Nouveaux who said of Spandau Ballet in *Zigzag*, a small circulation music magazine, that, 'The fact of the matter is, apparently, that they've tried everything. They were a power pop band, a Punk band and now this "we don't want to play gigs".'

Despite all this chatter about the origins of Spandau Ballet, the official history of the band, as it appeared in a publicity handout from their record company in March 1981, simply stated that, 'The group emerged from an underground scene centered around a handful of clubs' and that, 'They began performing in November 1979', with no mention made of anything at all before this. A review in *Sounds* of 28 March 1981 by Chris Burkham of an early (unadvertised) gig at Sundown innocently followed this line by observing that Spandau had 'successfully by-passed the 'slow rise to obscurity', 'paying your dues' syndrome.'

Perhaps surprisingly, in light of comments in his autobiography regarding his frustration about the misleading stories of the band's history being promoted, Tony remained dutifully on message at the time, regularly repeating the fiction about the band's origins. In a 1981 interview published in *International Musician and Recording World* (April edition), for example, he was asked: 'Can you say something about the history of Spandau Ballet?' to which he replied, 'We started about 18 months ago, out of a group of friends.' Strictly speaking, one could say this was true in that a band with the name 'Spandau Ballet' did come into existence in November 1979, about 18 months before April 1981, but it ignores the fact that this 'group of friends' all happened to be in another band for a year before that and most of them had been together in other bands for two years before that. And when Tony answered the next question, 'Did any of your members play in other groups before Spandau Ballet?' his answer 'No' could only make sense if he was extending the group's formation to 1976 which is precisely what he had not done in his previous answer. Even then, it would have ignored Gary's membership of The Same Band (and Martin's membership of The Defects).

Other band members told the same tale. In a group interview broadcast on Australian television in May 1981, Gary explained the origins of the band by saying, 'We felt that there wasn't really a band that we could relate to in London so the five of us got together and Spandau Ballet was created.' He couldn't always carry this story off convincingly, though, and his discomfort was plain to see when he was asked directly by Pat Wardsley, who interviewed the band on camera in New York in May 1981, 'Had you written songs before? Had you grown up writing songs?' to which he sheepishly replied, 'Not particularly, not really, I never felt that influenced to write songs until things got exciting about two years ago' and then claimed not to be able to remember the first song he had written. He certainly wasn't about to destroy his street cred by confessing that it was a child-like, quasi-religious song written while he was at junior school called 'Jesus Rode Through Jericho'! Later in the same interview, when Ms Wardsley inquired into the musical background of the individual band members, she was told by everyone that they were 'all the same'. No details were forthcoming but, in order to reinforce the idea that they had simply picked up instruments and formed a rock group, the boys were happy to inform her, truthfully, that Martin had never played bass guitar before he joined the band. By way of highlighting all their musical inexperience, Gary stated, 'The band's been going two years', in other words, only since 1979.

At around the same time, Tony was telling television presenter Sally James that 'we evolved from the club scene' and, in response to a comment by Martin that in the clubs 'all you could hear over the Tannoy was music by old people like David Bowie and Brian

Ferry', claimed that 'it seemed a natural thing to form a group to fill that gap.' John Keeble made similar comments in the 6 June 1981 issue of *Look-in*, saying that the band was formed 'about six months' before their first performance in November 1979, 'because there were no bands who reflected the image and the atmosphere of the clubs', adding that, 'None of us had been in a band before, but a few of us had dabbled with instruments.'

Some of the truth crept out in an article by Adrian Thrills in an *NME* issue of 1 August 1981 which said that Gary had 'played in a half-hearted classroom combo called The Makers' and that Spandau Ballet called themselves the Gentry 'in the rehearsal stage' but there was no explanation that The Makers had included four of the five members of Spandau Ballet or that they and Gentry had been proper bands, playing regular gigs to paying audiences. Moreover, the article said that, 'it wasn't until the advent of a new club scene that Kemp began to think seriously about forming a group' and that, 'the thought that inspired Kemp to persuade some of his pals to pick up instruments and form Spandau…was that no British soul band had ever got on stage and truly represented their audience, attitude and dress-wise', thus continuing to give the misleading impression that the five of them only formed a band, indeed only picked up instruments, in 1979.

In a 1981 book, *New Wave Explosion*, the author and Spandau critic, Myles Palmer, observed that, 'it is popularly assumed that Spandau dropped out of the sky wearing kilts and table cloths' but noted – in similar fashion to the *Sounds* reader from October 1980 and the *Melody Maker* reader from December 1980 – that 'they used to be a powerpop group called The Makers who played scruffy pubs like The Brecknock and The Hope before it dawned on them that the pub-rock circuit is a loser scene.' However, like the readers' letters in *Sounds* and *Melody Maker*, Palmer's book made little impact on the general awareness of Spandau's origins. An article by Paul Simper on the band in *Melody Maker* of 17 April 1982 claimed that 'Spandau were just beginning to come together in 1979', at which time Martin 'couldn't play an instrument'. As late as 1983, Gary Kemp was still spinning the yarn about the band forming at Billy's. 'The only creative thing going on was Billy's', he told *Melody Maker* (4 June 1983), 'That's when we decided to form a band, most of us were already musicians anyway and that was something we all wanted to do.'

When Spandau returned to Islington to perform at Sadler's Wells in May 1983, the *Islington Gazette* ran a short piece by Keith Archer which mentioned in the sub-heading that not so long ago, 'they were an unknown band called the Makers, playing to small audiences in the cellar of the Hope & Anchor, Upper Street.' This information appears not to have come from the band but to have been within the personal knowledge of the local journalist or editor; it is not mentioned in the article itself.

In a series of interviews with the band members by Paul Simper, published in *No. 1* magazine in the summer of 1983, Tony said that when he left school he was going to get a job in a nightclub but, 'I decided I didn't want to be a cabaret singer so I just waited 'til the band came together in 79', as if he had never been in any bands prior to Spandau Ballet. Gary, on the other hand, mentioned that he, John, Tony and Steve had been in 'a school band' called The Makers but such a description was misleading considering that John and Tony had left school for much of the band's life and, in any event, The Makers were playing at proper grown-up venues for money, which is not what one would normally associate with a school band.

Not every account of the story of Spandau Ballet written at this time even included a mention of the early bands. A Flexipop publication, *Journeys To Glory: The Spandau Story* by Huw Collingbourne, for example, which was published in the early summer of 1983, contained a quotation from John Keeble that, 'None of us had been in a band before.' The fact that Martin Kemp had not played bass guitar prior to joining the band was again offered up as an example of the fact that Spandau Ballet was a band comprised of non-musicians, with Gary Kemp quoted as saying that, when he joined the group, Martin 'couldn't play a note'. The fact that Martin had been a guitar player in a band called The Defects was not mentioned.

Meanwhile, the *NME* of 11 June 1983 had obtained a publicity photograph of The Makers taken in February 1978 by Gill Davies and published it beneath a short article entitled 'Archive Fun'. The article not only mentioned that Spandau Ballet minus Martin Kemp had once been called The Makers but also that they then became the Gentry in the summer of 1978 when 'it was the Rochester Castle rather than the Royal Albert Hall where you would have caught Islington's soul-boy visionaries strutting their funky(?) stuff'. Nevertheless, even after this mini exposé, a special *Melody Maker* supplement devoted to Spandau Ballet in September 1983 only noted that Gary Kemp had played at school in 'a powerpop band called the Makers with John Keeble, Tony Hadley, Steve Norman and another school friend called Richard Miller' and of Gentry there was no mention.

Despite all these public references to Spandau's past, when Tony and Steve were asked by Mark Curry: 'How was Spandau born? How was the group born?' in a televised June 1984 interview on *The Saturday Picture Show*, Tony answered: 'Oh God, it's a long story...I'm trying to think back, the band has actually been together now for about four, four and a half years and, I mean, we knew each other for quite a long time and the thing that really prompted us to get together, I'm sure everybody's heard a million times before, is kind of the whole thing, the whole London thing at the time, the Blitz, and things like that, and it was just a very happening thing, and we just thought it was time for some kind of music to come from that and that was basically it really.'

In the 1985 authorized biography of the band, John Travis was allowed to state that Gary, Steve, Tony, John and Richard Miller had 'experimented with playing their own music' at school and had 'formed their own pop group, The Makers' but this was glossed over very quickly with no indication that they had ever played any gigs. The only mention of the Gentry in Travis' book was that it was the name they had used 'in rehearsal'. A *Smash Hits* article in September 1986 entitled 'The Spandau Ballet Story' noted that the idea to form a band had emerged at Dame Alice

Owen's in 1976 with the formation of The Makers (although Richard Miller was said to have been the bass player, with Roots and Mike Ellison's contribution forgotten) but wrongly said that the band 'split up' and that it was only in 1979 that they 'decided to try again', having become regulars of Billy's and Blitz. In this version of the story, they 'rehearsed away under the name The Gentry' before becoming Spandau Ballet.

Alvin Gray's 1987 *Story of Success* also mentioned The Makers but said that this band was formed 'primarily for their own enjoyment' and stated, quite wrongly, that, 'They never took their sound out in public', while Gentry was not referred to at all. An article (about Gary Kemp) by Chris Heath in Q magazine's February 1987 issue claimed that 'the original quartet (sic) began playing together after school in 1979', some three years later than was the case and, like Travis, stated that 'they rehearsed under the name of The Gentry' but did not mention The Makers.

The early bands did get an occasional mention in subsequent interviews by the band members and, for example, in a 1990 interview with Paul Simper, Martin said that 'the other four had been playing for years as The Makers and The Gentry' (accidentally omitting to mention that he had been in the Gentry). The entry for Spandau Ballet in *The Faber Companion to 20th Century Popular Music*, published in 1990, ignored The Makers completely (not to mention Roots and The Cut) and stated incorrectly that, 'The band grew out of a schoolboy group, the Gentry.' By the time Gentry was formed, its members had, of course, all left school. It was probably not until the courtroom appearance of Spandau Ballet in January 1999, when the history of the band was outlined in detail by lawyers for the benefit of the trial judge, that the full story was told in public for the first time.

BACK IN THE SUMMER OF 1980, Phil Symes, the agent and publicist for Chrysalis Records who had booked Spandau Ballet to play at the Papagayo Club had been urging his colleagues at Chrysalis, such as Stuart Slater, head of A&R, to sign them up. Symes had been instantly impressed when he had auditioned Spandau for St

Tropez and he ensured that Slater saw an LWT preview of the Twentieth Century Box episode six days before it was broadcast. Although, as he recalls in his autobiography, the head of Chrysalis, Chris Wright, initially thought the band's name was 'pretty awful', Slater did not take much convincing and, following the successful performance on HMS Belfast, negotiations began in earnest between the band and Chrysalis for a record deal.

In preparation for this, an already incorporated company called Marbelow Limited was acquired on 29 September 1980 and each of the five band members and Steve Dagger was allocated sixteen shares in the company, out of a total of ninety-six, with all of the company's profits to be divided equally between the six of them. Spandau Ballet signed to Chrysalis Records on 10 October 1980 with a reported £85,000 advance on royalties, although the actual figure, as revealed in later legal proceedings, appears to have been a rather more modest £40,000, with an extra £15,000 on delivery of their first album. The chairman of Chrysalis, Chris Wright, proudly announced to the press: 'They're undoubtedly one of the most original and innovative bands to emerge in the UK over the last few years.' According to Tony, looking back, 'We were over the moon that we were going to engage on this wonderful dream. For us it was a dream come true and we were very lucky and we were going to sign a record deal and wow.'

The band members contracted with Marbelow to provide recording services in return for salaries and bonuses, with Marbelow contracting separately with Chrysalis. There was much fuss made in the initial publicity that the band had set up their own record label called Reformation, named after one of the band's songs, and there was a vague intention that they would use it to release songs by other bands. However, they never did this and the Reformation label was no more than a vanity name on a record sleeve, serving no practical purpose, with the records being manufactured by Chrysalis and bearing Chrysalis catalogue numbers. In the end, the Reformation name was adopted by Gary Kemp as the publishing company for his songs.

Almost immediately, as if to signal the end of an era, or perhaps now that the job was done and Spandau was signed, Steve Strange and Rusty Egan stopped their club nights at Blitz. The 'futurist' Tuesday night events apparently carried on for a few months, administered by a woman known as 'Geno', but without the original hosts they were not the same and the Blitz eventually ran out of steam, closing a year later when it transformed into a live jazz venue called the Canteen.

On their own initiative, being confident that they would be signed, the band had already recorded the backing track for 'To Cut A Long Story Short' at Islington's Jam Studios – Peter Powell having created demand for it by playing an earlier recorded demo on Radio 1 for some time before they signed to Chrysalis – and, once Tony had added his vocals (which he says in his book he did on the same day as the signing), it was ready to be rushed out as a single at the end of October. They used one of their friends from Blitz, Richard James Burgess, to produce the track. Burgess was a member of Landscape whose single, 'European Man', released in March 1980, was later claimed (by *Record Mirror* in its 18 April 1981 edition) to have been 'the first electro-disco 12 incher specifically for Blitz kids' and Burgess subsequently wrote and produced another electro track with Rusty Egan for Shock called 'Angel Face' (although this would not be released until mid-November). He had impressed Gary Kemp and Steve Dagger with his technical knowledge and familiarity with the band's sound and was thus chosen over other more experienced producers.

Within a couple of weeks, on 13 November 1980, Spandau Ballet were on *Top of The Pops*, dressed in tartan and living the dream. According to Martin, speaking to Paul Simper in 1990, the reason for the choice of tartan was that 'the week before, the club Le Kilt, which our mates did, had opened.' It was not a totally original choice of outfit. An *NME* review of a Siouxsie and the Banshees gig in April 1979 had been headlined 'Tartan terror for the 80s' due to Siouxsie Sioux's outfit. This inspired the music paper's 28 April 1979 issue to include a lighthearted 'Tartan Chic' fashion feature with photographs of Adam Ant, Rezillo and others (including, with tongue in cheek, the Prince of Wales) wearing kilts or tartan. 'We're not sure who started it,' said the accompanying text in the *NME*, 'Some say it was Lydon and his tartan suit. Some say it was MacLaren and Seditionaries. Others yet claim it originated in an obscure Scottish cult.' So it was not the most novel piece of kit and it wasn't even terribly new romantic at the time (although a Jacobite theme was consistent with the type of outfits worn at Blitz) but it quickly became identified as a quintessential new romantic costume.

Squeezed in between Liquid Gold's now long-forgotten 'The Night The Wine and The Roses' and Abba's more memorable 'Supertrouper', the band was announced by Simon Bates with the words, 'There are five young guys from Islington who are causing a real buzz in the music industry and we've got them on *Top of the Pops* tonight, their names collectively are Spandau Ballet and the single title is "To Cut A Long Story Short", have a listen to this…'

There was apparently some anxiety within the band that the *Top of the Pops* performance had been affected by sound issues and Martin recalls that he was 'so disappointed because there were certain frequencies on the record that affected how it sounded on TV and radio.' He feared it sounded quiet compared to other records on the show – which it did – and, 'We thought, that's it – we're dead.' Such fears were groundless and viewers probably just turned up the volume of their televisions. The Spandau/Burgess partnership was a commercial success as 'To Cut A Long Story Short' hit the top ten and sold 250,000 copies by December.

However, Spandau Ballet and their debut single were not welcomed in all quarters. There was a feeling amongst certain music journalists that the band had not paid its dues or served its apprenticeship, namely by playing for years in the standard music venues and being respectful to the serious music press. Ironically, as The Makers and Gentry, the band had certainly paid its dues but, as we have seen, they did not want this widely known. However, in adopting the route of unadvertised gigs, attempting to bypass publications like the *NME* and *Melody Maker* (but see Appendix 3) and declaring, provocatively, that fashion was more important to them than music, Spandau Ballet had already made a number of enemies amongst journalists in the serious rock music press.

For some, of course, it may just be that they genuinely did not like their songs. Ian Pye, reviewing 'To Cut A Long Story Short' for *Melody Maker*, commented, 'Now we all know why this band of posers hold their gigs in secret with an audience of specially vetted friends and cognescenti – they're plain boring. Desperately trying to sound moderne, they overstay their welcome on this forgettable piece of self-regarding fluff', Mark Cooper in the *Record Mirror* called it 'an ordinary short story trying to become a novel' while Roy Carr of the *NME* was even more cutting, rounding off his review with a comment John Keeble still remembers more than thirty years later: 'Top five by Christmas and obscurity by the following yule-tide.' As it happens, Mr Carr's first prediction was spot on – 'To Cut A Long Story Short' reached number five exactly – but his second would have been closer to the truth had he only predicted obscurity for himself.

Not everyone in the music press was hostile and Alan Lewis, the editor of *Sounds*, gave the single a very good review in his publication, calling it 'a massively competent record'. In the end, no-one could argue with a top five debut single, and an album was quickly recorded at a variety of different recording studios, including Trident in Soho, Utopia in Primrose Hill and The Manor in Oxfordshire. (At about the same time, a Canadian rock band called April Wine was recording an album at The Manor which was released as 'The Nature of the Beast' in January 1981, perhaps providing Gary with inspiration for a song of that name which was to appear on a later album.)

During one recording session for their debut album, Burgess mentioned to Gary that, from his experience as songwriter for Landscape, if Gary kept all the songwriting royalties to himself this could be a potential source of friction within the band.

Consequently, when Gary later set up his own company called Reformation Publishing Company Limited to receive the publishing income for his songs, he arranged that half of the net profit of Reformation would be transferred to Marbelow and this would be shared equally between all six shareholders of Marbelow, including Steve Dagger. Over the next seven years each of the shareholders would receive about £300,000 by this route.

Clearly, Spandau Ballet had entered into a new world of business, as well as a new world of music and fashion, but their original audience, or at least some of them, had not been entirely forgotten. At one of Gentry's gigs, Vicki Silvester, the sister of Liz (one of those schoolgirls from Islington who had originally seen the band at the Queen's Silver Jubilee street party performance back in 1977) had jokingly suggested to Steve Dagger that his band were becoming so popular that they needed a fan club. Now that they were signed and a fan club really was needed, Dagger asked her if she fancied running it. Vicki agreed, and with her sister's help, ran the fan club from her home on a part-time basis, being paid for two days a week. It wasn't, it has to be said, the most professionally run of operations. As Liz explains, 'My sister used to go to Steve Dagger's office in Wigmore Street and pick up a sackload of post and bring it home and look through it. We weren't very organised at all. I think we had a few signed photos that we'd send out to people and just generally kind of read the letters and have a bit of a laugh at how much these girls were swooning over them.' This only lasted a few months before the girls became so overwhelmed by the volume of mail that they had to give it up but it was perhaps the one single aspect of Spandau Ballet that had resisted a takeover by the fashionable Blitz set and was, for a while, in the control of the Islington crowd, perhaps, one might say unkindly, because this element of the operation required hard work behind the scenes.

CHAPTER SIX

What's In A Name?

ONE OF THE THINGS PEOPLE wanted to know about the newly signed band was how they got their name and what did it mean. It was even the subject of a quiz question (set by David Johnson) in the *Evening Standard* as early as 9 October 1980 which asked if Spandau Ballet's name was 'inspired by (a) Serge Diaghilev (b) A man made stretch fabric (c) A German prison'. At this stage, an educated guess would have been necessary because no-one could possibly have known for certain the correct answer (although one of the prize winners of the competition was one 'M. Caplan NW4' – presumably Melissa Caplan who designed the band's outfits and who might therefore have had some inside information) – but the answer provided by the *Evening Standard* on 23 October, which had almost certainly come from Robert Elms, was that the name was inspired by 'Spandau, the Berlin prison'.

This was not the message coming from the band members themselves though. Asked in a *Record Mirror* interview of 29 November 1980, Gary Kemp, while admitting that a friend (i.e. Elms) came up with the name, said: 'We liked the idea of ballet, it fitted in with what we meant. There's no real point to Spandau.' Martin added: 'It's the name of a gun. The two names fitted together. We wanted something that had a sound to it like the way Bolshoi Ballet does.' No mention here of Spandau prison.

By contrast, in an issue of the *NME* published on the very same day as the interview with the Kemps was published in *Record*

Mirror, Robert Elms, taking credit for the creation of the name, was quoted as saying: 'we were in Berlin, and we saw the prison, and I just thought, what do they do for Entertainment? Ballet? Spandau Ballet!' Now, it is certainly true that Elms had been in Berlin in the summer of 1979, shortly before he offered the name Spandau Ballet to Steve Dagger. He, Chris Sullivan, Graham Smith, Ollie O'Donnell and others (but not any of the band members) had been on a football tour, representing the London School of Economics, and it is quite possible that they passed Spandau prison at some point as they travelled round Berlin and its suburbs. However, it was a rather odd thought process offered up by Elms in that interview. Assuming he did not know that there was only one 84-year-old prisoner in there at the time, he might perhaps have wondered what prisoners inside Spandau prison did for entertainment (although why it would be different from any other prison is not clear) but there does not appear to be any obvious reason to have come up with the answer of ballet.

Could it have been a journalistic error? Could Elms have been misquoted by the *NME*? It appears not. In the sleeve notes to the *Gold* compilation CD composed by Elms in 2000, he wrote almost exactly the same thing as he had told the *NME* some twenty years earlier, at least in the sense that he claimed the name Spandau Ballet was created by him when considering the type of entertainment suitable for Spandau prison:

> A name and a platform were now needed. I, as an aspiring man of words provided the moniker. Berlin was then the cool city where Bowie and Iggy hung out, and its infamous castle prison seemed like a good name for a venue for a decadent dance. Hence Spandau Ballet, a name guaranteed to grab a few headlines and imply a certain arty arrogance.

Elms' comments in the *NME* in November 1980 caught the attention of Mick Austin, now back at home in Ampthill. He was not happy. As far as he was concerned, Elms must have seen the name 'Spandau Ballet' stencilled on a toilet door in The Venue at some point during 1979. He thus dashed off a furious letter to the *NME* in December, written in the third person, which was published in its 3 January 1981 issue as follows:

> There were once two boys called Michael and David and they went to school together. One Geography lesson, whilst not learning about rain forests in equatorial regions, they decided to make a band. 'I'll play guitar' said Michael, to which David replied, 'I'll play bass then!' These two chappies grew up together and enjoyed themselves. One day our two friends were sitting together and thinking when suddenly one exclaimed 'Spandau!' This sounded so good they thought until they came up with a 'Ballet!' The boys moved to London and wrote the name everywhere. Now Michael and David are grown up, and extremely strong and are puzzled why a chap called Robert Elms says he thought of their name, and used it for his band. Michael and David would like to meet Robert one day.

The letter was signed 'Michael Austin, Ampthill, Bedford'. There was no response to it.

Mick also wrote to Radio 1's Peter Powell. A copy of the letter as sent is not in Mick's possession but a surviving undated draft is, and reads as follows:

> Dear Mr Powell,
> I thought I had better say a few words about the band 'SPANDAU BALLET' before they become too successful.
> Much as I have tried to dislike their music, I find it quite pleasing, despite their slightly 'avant guard' (sic) image. The whole point being almost three years ago my friend, a certain Mr David Agar [Wardill], & myself sat in my dining room for hours on end until we finally came upon a name for our band that we thought catchy, to the point, forcefully attractive etc. We came up with SPANDAU BALLET.
> We only did one London gig, at the 'Hope & Anchor' supporting the Softies last year.

Although our name was 'displayed' all around London on various walls and w/c's (as any self respecting band would) so before anyone else asks me, it's not Dave & Mick's band anymore, its Steve Strange's, whom I would very much like to meet in a dark alley.

Yours sincerely,
Mick Austin

Peter Powell mentioned this letter on air but did not appear sympathetic to Mick's complaint that he and his friend, not Robert Elms, had created the name 'Spandau Ballet' (although Mick's venom appears to have been directed towards Steve Strange on this occasion). On the contrary, as Mick, who had been waiting patiently, listening to Radio 1 for a number of evenings, to hear his letter read out, recalls, Powell just said something like, 'Well I guess the guys have a lot to thank you for...'

Meanwhile, David Wardill had been sacked from his position in the store room at The Venue. As he explains:

> I hadn't had any training. I was nineteen years old and had no training. A beer delivery [arrived], I hadn't checked it properly. I didn't realize. I just took it on faith. I thought it was fine. Of course, they knew that there was this kid not checking properly and they nicked – they didn't deliver a lot of the beer – they withheld ten of the big sixty gallons things. It was quite a lot of money and they [The Venue] sacked me. I was pissed off because I said, "I didn't know, you didn't train me."

He took his employers to an industrial tribunal and the case was settled with David being awarded about £700 in compensation, which he then regarded as a large and very welcome sum of money. At the same time, as a result of the employment dispute, he was banned from entering The Venue and, thus, could not see any gigs at the club, a punishment which rankled with him.

On the dole in the early summer of 1980, and now living in Finsbury Park with Deanne, David heard some interesting news from a friend about a rock group called The Passions which led to him joining the band and, very soon afterwards, performing with them in a state of some terror in front of eighty thousand people at the New Pop Festival in Holland before returning with them to The Venue in triumph, on 23 April 1981, to play a gig, about which he says, 'They couldn't stop me…the same manager was there [as when I was sacked]. Sweet revenge!'

The Passions had been formed in 1978 by singer Mitch Barker, bass player Claire Bidwell, guitarist Clive Temperley, formerly of the 101-ers, and two former members of The Derelicts, singer/guitarist Barbara Gogan and drummer Richard Williams, but Barker left the band after breaking his leg in early 1979, allowing Gogan to take over on lead vocals. Having released a single on an independent record label in January 1979, the band signed to Fiction Records and, in April 1980, released an album, which did not chart, called *Michael and Miranda*. Shortly before The Passions were due to headline at De Grey Rooms in York on Friday, 11 July 1980, for a gig to raise money on behalf of Rock Against Sexism, Claire Bidwell informed her bandmates that she had had enough of the music business and walked out, forcing the three remaining Passions to cancel the gig at virtually the last minute, albeit before they had travelled to York. At a loose end that Friday night, and desirous of drowning their sorrows in a bar, the remaining Passions went for an evening out in London at the Y-Studios in Great Russell Street to watch The Monochrome Set who were playing there that night.

A former *NME* journalist, Adele-Marie Cherreson, who already knew the Passions, was at this gig in order to review it on behalf of *Sounds*. There was plenty of spare time that evening because a fire officer initially deemed the venue to be overcrowded, which caused a brief initial hold-up, and there was an additional delay while arguments raged between the members of The Monochrome Set and the management of the Y-Studios about the appropriate use of side lighting and back projection, with technical problems meaning that it wasn't possible to turn down the bright lights in the venue which ruined the band's stage effects. Chatting to the Passions in the bar during the evening, Adele-Marie discovered that they urgently needed a new bass guitarist. As it happened, she lived near David and Deanne, with whom she was friends, in Finsbury Park; indeed, the three of them had come to the gig together (along with another one of their mutual friends, the *Sounds* journalist Robbi Millar). Consequently, Adele-Marie was not only able to inform the Passions that she knew a suitable bass guitarist but was able to introduce David to them that very evening. At this time, the Passions were naturally at a low ebb, and in a rather bad mood, but David's charm won them round and he was invited to an audition to be held a few days later. Being happily familiar with *Michael and Miranda*, which Deanne owned, David further impressed the Passions by having learnt all of their songs in the few days before the audition and was quickly accepted into the band.

Things did not immediately improve for The Passions because, despite having quickly replaced Claire Bidwell, they were unexpectedly dropped by their record label. Nevertheless, with their new, young, good looking and personable bass player who decided to use his middle name as his surname and call himself David Agar – quite possibly because he was still signing-on for unemployment benefit under his real surname – The Passions were snapped up by Polydor (the parent company of Fiction Records) and, on the basis of information that David provided to Bill McAllister, the record company's press officer, a press release was issued by Polydor in either late July or early August 1980 stating that David Agar had been 'bassist with the original Spandau Ballet' and this was duly reported in *Smash Hits* of 21 August 1980. Not surprisingly, it was incorrectly taken by many to mean that he had been a bassist in the group called Spandau Ballet managed by Steve Dagger. Even today it confuses people. The authoritative *Encyclopedia of Popular Music* for example, includes in its entry for The Passions that David Agar was 'once a member of the fledgling Spandau Ballet'.

This was not the impression that David had been trying to convey and, indeed, he had tried to correct it. During publicity interviews for The Passions' subsequent hit single, 'I'm In Love With a German Film Star', which David had helped to compose, he was asked by *NME* journalist Paul Du Noyer if he had played with 'the original Spandau Ballet'. His reply, published in the *NME* of 21 February 1981, was: 'No, I didn't. It was a different band. The Spandau Ballet that's going now, they ripped the name off from us. They probably didn't even realise they did because it was suggested to them by someone I used to live with.'

The housemate David was referring to was Kim Bowen, a well-known Blitz regular who, as we have seen, had lived in the same house as David in East Ham before moving to a property in Turnpike Lane in May 1979 and, from there, to a squat in Warren Street in July of the same year. He has a vivid memory of her confessing to him apologetically that she had suggested the name 'Spandau Ballet' to one of her friends who was forming a band because, as she explained to him, she (correctly) did not think that it was being used any more. Kim, however, speaking to the author in 2014, can recall nothing of this and does not even remember being aware that David was in a band called 'Spandau Ballet'.

IRONICALLY, THE SPANDAU BALLET NAME nearly helped bring the band to a premature end. Almost from the start there was a belief that it was a fascist right wing, even Nazi, band. In an interview in May 1980, Gary Kemp echoed Steve Dagger in describing Spandau's music as 'White European Dance Music', which created obvious suspicion coming from a group of five muscular white men in a band with a Germanic name.

The mood of Blitz, with its focus on German electronic dance music, could sometimes resemble 'Berlin in the Thirties' according to Jon Moss (later of Culture Club) or 'Germany between the wars' as Gary Kemp has put it (i.e. the period when Hitler came to power). Steve Strange used to walk around in what he called 'my leather Gestapo coat' while another Blitz regular and close friend of the band, Chris Sullivan, is said (by Martin Kemp) to have dressed up in full SS uniform on at least one occasion. As Tony explains in his autobiography, this all created gossip in London about the band being a neo-Nazi group and one or two of them did not help matters by dressing up (quite innocently) to resemble storm troopers for outdoor photographs in St Tropez. There were even rumours in circulation that 'a Spandau ballet' was the name given to the contortions and spasms exhibited by dying victims of gas in Spandau prison during the Second World War: nonsense for many reasons, not least of which being that there were never any gas chambers at Spandau. Other suggestions, which still seem to survive to this day, that a Spandau ballet referred to the kicking or twitching of the legs of dying victims hanged at Spandau prison during the Second World War (despite the fact that hundreds of thousands of people were hanged throughout Europe during that war and the prison had a more remarkable form of execution in a working guillotine), or the gruesome way a soldier was spun round by the force of the bullets from a Spandau machine gun, or the equally gruesome way a corpse would twitch when hit with such bullets, or an aerial dogfight with a German fighter equipped with such a machine gun, are equally preposterous and undoubtedly ex post facto inventions.

Following the release of the band's first album, *Journeys To Glory*, in March 1981, the criticism came out into the open and in print. The reviewer in *Record Mirror* described the album as both 'disturbing' and 'threatening', pointing to the sleeve's 'white-on-white' cover with the image of a 'noble and muscular' naked male form. Robert Elms' inside sleeve notes, with their reference to 'the sublime glow of music for heroes', were cited as were some of Gary's lyrics, such as the ideal of 'beautiful and clean' and 'muscle bound'. The implication of all this, said the reviewer, was that Spandau appeared to be linking themselves 'with some sort of Ayran Youth ideal, smacking hideously of Hitlerian master-race notions.' A review in *Melody Maker* headlined 'The Aryan Freeze Out' made similar points, querying whether the album had 'Fascist overtones' and suggested that Muscle Bound was 'a kind of Nazi sea shanty'.

The band members took this criticism very seriously indeed. If they were widely believed to be a fascist group it could have destroyed them at birth. To counter these notions, the band wrote angry letters to both *Melody Maker* and *Record Mirror* (signed 'Spandau Ballet') which were published the following week headlined (by *Melody Maker*) 'Spandau: We Are Not Fascists' and (by *Record Mirror*) 'Nazis? Not Us: say Spandau Ballet'. To *Melody Maker* they wrote:

> Without boring anyone with lists of Labour Party membership and past political activity, let's make it quite clear: WE ARE NOT FASCISTS AND WE ARE NOT TORIES…Nobody is claiming that we are starting a new movement…your attempts to link the artwork to Nazism are ludicrous. Heroic and classical imagery have been used in many contexts (for example, Russian Collectivist posters) all of which you have conveniently ignored in a bid to secure a conviction.

To *Record Mirror*:

> …thanks very much indeed for nothing, for just stopping short of calling us Nazis in your review of our album last week, that was really wonderful of you. We aren't Nazis, fascists or Tories, and we are not stupid either…We are all quite conversant with the political history of the 20th century and we don't need lectures from you or anyone else. Yours is the ignorance of not realizing that heroic and classical imagery has been used in many other contexts, too numerous and varied to mention.

Robert Elms also wrote letters to each publication – which were published alongside Spandau's – stating to *Melody Maker*: 'I resent wholeheartedly the accusation that either myself or the group are fascists or fascist sympathizers…the accusation of Nazism is simply a damning lie' and to *Record Mirror*: 'The suggestion that either myself, or the band, are fascists – or that we are toying with pseudo-fascist imagery – is so unfounded that it is almost fraudulently laughable.' Despite this, *Melody Maker* took pleasure in publishing a reader's letter in the following week's issue in which it was stated that, 'A Nazi chic is penetrating fashion and music, originating from the Covent Garden Blitz scene' and which said that Spandau's was 'a dangerous philosophy…they are very dumb dandies indeed if they think they can control Nazism.' *Melody Maker* mischievously headlined this letter 'Nazis and Spandau'. *Record Mirror* also kept the issue alive by publishing a letter from a reader which began, 'I am writing to say how much I agree with the comments about fascism and Hitler you made in the 'Spandau Ballet' album review.'

Even more worryingly, the extreme right wing organization, the National Front, latched onto the controversy and, having been told by *Record Mirror* that Spandau Ballet was a Nazi band, suddenly developed a liking for them. 'Muscle Bound' was featured as a recommended track in Issue 22 of *Bulldog*, the paper of the young National Front, beneath an ironic headline: 'They're playing White music so they must be Nazis' and a photograph of the band captioned 'Ex-members of the Hitler Youth?'. The paper claimed that Spandau Ballet were 'hated by the communists in the music papers because they are proud to be white.' Recalling Gary Kemp's rather careless phrase from the previous year, it was stated that 'Spandau's album Journeys To Glory, is also worth listening to for further examples of "White electronic dance music"'. Issue 25 of *Bulldog* returned to the topic under a headline 'White European Dance Music', the exact phrase used by Gary (and Dagger) in 1980, claiming that Spandau's music 'is the direct opposite of the Marxist understanding of what rock music should be' and that 'it is no wonder that Spandau Ballet are derided by Red journalists for being Nazis.' It was said that Spandau looked 'towards their racial and cultural roots for musical inspiration' and like 'most of the new wave futurist bands also use Nordic imagery in their music.' According to *Bulldog*, the tracks on *Journeys To Glory*, 'propagate cultural awareness and the warrior ethic...White European Dance Music is here to stay'. The band was in real and serious danger of becoming poster boys for the extreme right in Britain.

Gary Kemp immediately took great pains in interviews to stress that Spandau Ballet was, in fact, a left wing band, telling Mike Nicholls of *Record Mirror* for its 11 April 1981 issue: 'I think everyone in the band is a socialist and a couple are even members of the Labour party.' He also made clear that the band no longer described themselves as playing 'white European disco'. Despite this, the rumours would not die. When the band went to the United States in May 1981 they were hassled by journalists over the issue. Gary and Steve Dagger became involved in a heated argument with one particular journalist who asked about 'the fascist undertones I hear on songs like Muscle Bound' and who queried why there were no black members in the band. A letter in *Melody Maker* of 23 May 1981 from Jeanne Ward of Hanover, West Germany, kept the controversy alive in the British music press by claiming, quite wrongly, that 'Muscle Bound' 'bears a speeded up resemblance to a song called "Die Moorsoldaten" (Soldiers of the Moor)' which, she noted, 'was sung by the Jews in the German concentration camps during the Second World War'. Her letter concluded darkly, 'Make of that what you will.'

The controversy only really started to fade in June 1981 when Steve, Gary and Martin joined the black funk musicians of Light Of the World on the stage of the Hammersmith Odeon for a jam session along to 'London Town', at which time news also emerged of the forthcoming release of 'Chant No.1' (in July 1981) on which Light Of The World's horn section, Beggar & Co, had been asked to play, a helpful collaboration which finally killed off the fascism allegations.

Even so, in an interview with Chris Salewicz, conducted on 23 June 1981, which appeared in the August 1981 issue of *The Face*, Gary wanted to make clear that he had run the Socialist group at school and, like Steve Dagger, was a card-carrying member of the

Labour party. He also pointed out that the band name on the cover of *Journeys To Glory* 'was written on it in Russian lettering' and emphasized that the video of 'Muscle Bound' was 'very Russian' and featured the anarchist black flag. At the same time, he denied that the album cover art was 'Fascist imagery' and said that he was 'both amused and irritated by the constant suggestions that Spandau is in some way a neo-fascist organization.'

It was in this context that the name 'Spandau Ballet' presented enormous danger for the band. If they continued to put forward the story that it was connected with Spandau prison in Berlin, as Elms had originally done, this would link the band with Hitler's deputy, Rudolph Hess, who was then incarcerated in Spandau prison. In this regard, it should be noted that one tactic adopted by the British Movement, another extreme right wing political party, was to put up stickers in the street urging the release of Hess from Spandau (a fact pointed out with some force by the *NME*'s reviewer of *Journeys To Glory*). The 'Spandau' machine gun link was also dangerous, considering that a similar weapon was still being used by the Nazis during the Second World War, and it was never repeated by Martin. The whole thing was a hot potato, an extremely sensitive issue, which had potential to seriously harm the band and distance needed to be put between Spandau Ballet and anything to do with Nazism.

Consequently, the band members became reluctant to discuss the origins of their name. During a filmed interview on 5 May 1981, Gary, having been asked whether the band had been to Germany, defensively anticipated what he must have believed the inevitable follow-up question would be by saying, 'We wanted a name that no-one really knew much about to fit with ballet and Hackney Ballet didn't sound as good.' While being interviewed by Ian 'Molly' Meldrum for an Australian television music show called *Countdown*, broadcast on 24 May 1981, Steve Norman responded to the question of where the name Spandau Ballet came from by saying: 'There's no relevance to it really, it's just a good sounding name, I mean, a friend of ours thought it up actually' and he was at pains to stress that, 'Spandau doesn't mean that we come from Spandau, we worship Germany or anything like that.' In similar vein, during a July 1981 interview for the Spanish television station TVE 50, Tony Hadley, having been asked the same question, responded: 'It's just a good sounding name. It's got no particular significance.'

Martin became even vaguer as time went on. For example, in a German radio interview on RTL in July 1983, when he was asked about the meaning of the name, he said: 'It's just ah, you know, it's something that we are asked all the time and it just came about and you lose track of it. I wish I knew.' Asked by his interviewer if it was connected with Spandau [prison] in Germany he replied: 'Nothing to do with that. It's just a matter of it sounds good. The ballet part of it came about because there was more than just the group involved in getting the group off the ground, it was a whole lot of people in the clubs and all our friends and everything so it was rather like a company so we called it something ballet and Spandau Ballet sounds nice.'

A few months later, during a television interview on the American late night talk show *Thicke of the Night* in December 1983, Tony was asked by the show's host, Alan Thicke, where the band's name had come from and he replied, 'That's a very long story.…..That was God: he blessed us with that name. It's a long story.' But he did not tell the story. Pressed to elaborate, he stonewalled uncomfortably by spouting some nonsense about having had a telephone line to God installed, presumably to discuss things like band names: 'We can talk to Him any time we want' he muttered inanely. Steve Norman was similarly reluctant to discuss the subject. In a feature published in *Look In* magazine in 1983, he said that his main dislike was, 'Journalists asking me where the group got its name!'

The notion that Spandau Ballet derived its name from graffiti seen by Robert Elms on a toilet wall in Berlin appears to have entered the public domain in the summer of 1983. According to Gary Kemp, in an interview published in the Irish music paper

Hot Press, on 24 June 1983, 'Bob Elms actually got the name from a trip to Berlin, he saw it written on a toilet wall.' This information, in what was a relatively obscure publication, evidently did not make its way to the editorial team of *No.1* magazine because its 'What's in a name' feature in its 6 August 1983 issue explained that, 'Spandau Ballet got half their name from a fortress in Berlin…and they tagged Ballet on the end 'cos it looked like a place where there should be a ballet (apparently)', thus echoing Robert Elms' original story from 1981.

When the story of Spandau Ballet was told by *Melody Maker* of 24 September 1983, clearly sourced directly from Steve Dagger, and thus the official line, it was simply stated that the name Spandau Ballet was 'discovered on a Berlin wall by…Robert Elms', with no mention being made of a toilet wall on this occasion. Appearing on BBC1's *Saturday Superstore* in February 1984, however, Tony, Steve and Martin were asked by a young phone-in caller: 'Why did you call yourself Spandau Ballet?' and Tony answered: 'God, that's the most asked question, we still get asked that abroad in certain countries that we've only just broken. We discovered it on a bathroom wall or one of our friends did in Berlin about four years ago now and we liked the name so much we stuck with it…Spandau was just a name, even if you can't pronounce it, it's memorable.' This prompted host Mike Read to ask, 'I wonder how many groups found their name on walls, because Sham 69 found their name on a wall' to which Martin responded pointedly, 'I think all that shows is you've just most probably stolen it from someone else less famous.'

Steve Norman overcame his dislike of discussing the band's name in a Radio Luxemburg interview in June 1984, confirming, like Gary and Tony had done earlier, that it was not just any old wall but a toilet wall. 'The name itself, a friend of ours he came up with it', he said, 'he went to Berlin for a holiday and it's not very exotic but he actually saw it written on a toilet wall so there's a group called Spandau Ballet who are a bit upset!' This comment by Steve, although echoing Martin's lighthearted comment on

Saturday Superstore, is still curious because there was no real reason for him to believe that the words 'Spandau Ballet' on a toilet wall indicated the existence of another band with that name – it could have meant absolutely anything – and his apparent awareness that there *was* another Spandau Ballet might have come from the media comments of Mick Austin and David Agar Wardill to that effect in 1981.

That Martin was wracked with guilt about the band having stolen another band's name is evident from an unbroadcast segment of an interview he gave, with Gary, in December 1984 for an MTV documentary called *Rock Influences*. Asked how the name Spandau Ballet came about, he replied: 'I think we stole it from another group. One of our friends went to Berlin and it was just at the time we were looking for a name and he came back and said, "I've seen this name Spandau Ballet and it was written on a toilet wall." I dare say it was another group who wrote it on the toilet wall and we stole it, I think.' Gary then cut in, trying to improve upon this rather unedifying answer. 'To intellectualize about it,' he said, 'Ballet, we did like the idea of Ballet - ' but, before he could develop his theme, Martin cut him short, shouting, 'Yeah, but we stole the bloody name!' 'Well,' Gary admitted sheepishly, '*Spandau Ballet* we stole.' Martin, irritated by the attempted intellectualization, wasn't brooking any further discussion on the subject and stated firmly to his brother, 'You guys make it [sound] really clever but *we stole the name from another group*.' Gary, visibly annoyed, lifted a cup of tea to his mouth and muttered, 'Cheers Mart.'

Another aspect to the story told by the band at this time was that Spandau Ballet was a pre-existing name for an old German ballet company. To *Hot Press* in June 1983, Gary had said, 'There was in fact a ballet in Spandau called Spandau Ballet, in the 19th Century. Basically we used the name Spandau Ballet because it had a lot more mystery than, say, Neasden Ballet.' A year later, in July 1984, Steve said in a radio interview while in the United States: 'A friend of ours called Robert Elms who is a very successful journalist nowadays, he went to Berlin and there is a province in Berlin called Spandau...and he actually saw it written up on a bathroom wall. I think there used to be an actual Spandau ballet company hundreds of years ago but they're not formed any more.' The truth is that there never was a real ballet company called 'Spandau Ballet' but it was a good way of deflecting interest in the origins of the name. The toilet wall story was also very convenient and meant that the band could say that the name was, in effect, meaningless, just a strange combination of words scrawled by some drunken German in a Berlin nightclub or wherever the toilet was supposed to be. It is by no means clear if the band members themselves knew what Spandau Ballet meant or how it was supposedly devised by Robert Elms. They probably just thought the name sounded good and were taken by surprise when they were originally asked in interviews where it came from. It's possible that Elms told them he saw the name on a wall, or a toilet wall, in order to make life easier for them in the light of the public allegations of both fascism and plagiarism.

Despite the simple explanation of the toilet wall having now emerged, the band still seemed unwilling to discuss the subject of their name during interviews. For example, in a Spanish radio interview by Fernando Martinez in October 1986, Gary Kemp was asked, 'Why did you choose the name of Spandau Ballet?' to which he replied: 'Oh no! We've been coming to Spain for six years and six years ago we answered that question a million times and I think anyone in this country who likes Spandau Ballet has heard that question answered so we're not going to answer it again.' This strange answer produced the following response from Martinez's co-presenter: 'Six years coming to Spain and six years hearing the same question but they don't tell us the meaning in the end. Do you know it Fernando?' to which Martinez said: 'I have no idea. I know it must be 'ballet of Spandau' but I can't think how they got the inspiration to choose that name. It's curious and atypical. Let's get them to say the reason...'. But the boys simply refused to speak, and their translator said, 'Sorry they don't want to answer and I can't point a gun at their head to get it ha ha.' In the same month they were asked the same question in Holland by an interviewer for the station TROS and Gary replied: 'I can't believe it. For six years we've been asked that question. Everyone knows the answer.' Well perhaps the band were fed up giving the same answer to the question that they had answered previously but, as can be seen, it was actually rare for them ever to have provided an answer to the question and the answers they had provided in the past had been contradictory and, on occasions, incriminating.

These days, the Berlin nightclub toilet wall story is the 'standard' version told by all band members. According to Martin Kemp in his autobiography, Bob Elms had seen the name 'scrawled on a toilet wall in a nightclub' and, Martin concluded, as he had done back in 1984, 'The name must have belonged to another band at some point, but now it belonged to us.' Once again, there is no reason to believe that the words 'Spandau Ballet' written on a toilet wall could indicate the existence of another band with that name but Martin said it 'must' have belonged to another band. Tony told Danny Baker in a 2004 radio interview: 'He [Elms] had been to Berlin and he'd been having a leak in the toilet and saw it graffitied over the wall, you always look at the wall when you're having a leak…this was a crappy club in Berlin…graffitied across the wall was Spandau Ballet' and he says the same type of thing in his autobiography although, unlike Martin, does not suggest that the name came from another band.

Gary, however, nowadays freely admits that they 'stole' the name from someone else. Thus, in a January 2001 interview on getmusic.com, Gary said: 'Robert Elms…had just come back from a trip to Berlin clubbing and said "I've got a great name – Spandau Ballet". Spandau was a place in Berlin and we thought it sounded incredibly exotic and we took it but it wasn't until a few years later that he actually admitted to us that he had seen it written on a toilet wall in a Berlin club so I guess the truth is we stole it from another band.' Gary's comment that it wasn't until a few years later that Elms admitted he had taken the name from some graffiti seems to confirm that the band members themselves did not know where he had got the name from until 1983. This would explain why they could not answer the question of the meaning of their name in the early days. Then, when they found out the answer, perhaps they did not like it much, especially with the Nazi connection, or simply found it a dull story which is why they preferred not to talk about it. However, in a radio interview in 2002, Gary made an astonishing revelation:

> The very first time we played we didn't have a name, Bob had just come back from a club tour of Berlin….he said "how about Spandau Ballet?" which is a name of a place in Berlin, we thought "that sounds exotic"….we found out later it was actually written on a toilet wall and Bob had seen it *and this German group wrote to us saying "you've stolen our name"* (emphasis added).

If Gary is right about this, then it must mean that there was a band in Germany claiming to have been called Spandau Ballet before November 1979 as well as a band in London with exactly the same claim. The chances of there having been two bands in existence called Spandau Ballet before Gentry adopted the name are remote to say the least and Gary probably had in mind the comments in the media of Mick Austin and David Agar Wardill, having confused himself into thinking they had been made by members of a German band because Elms had told him the graffiti had been seen in Berlin. Gary's story on this aspect of Spandau's history certainly seems to have become more colourful at every telling. In January 2009, he told the internet site T5M about the Halligan's gig and said:

> I think we were still called the Gentry. We went to the pub for a drink afterwards and Robert Elms, who is a broadcaster now and book writer, he said I've got a name 'Spandau Ballet'. "Where do you get that?" And they'd all just come back from Berlin on some

sort of club trip to Berlin. He said. "Spandau's a place in Berlin I think it's a great name" and we thought "yeah like Cabaret Voltaire we don't really know what it means, great name – sounds mysterious, sounds sexy", we never thought we were going to be on *Top of the Pops* it just sounded interesting and arty. Spandau Ballet: we're not a ballet but that's good, that's funny and it wasn't until a few years later that I said to Bob, "That name's amazing how did you…?" – "I saw it written on a toilet wall in a club in Berlin; I think it might belong to another group". And in about 1990 this guy stopped his car, I was in London he stopped his car, and he went: [thick German accent] "I must speak to you, I must speak to you. I used to be in a group called Spandau Ballet, you stole our name!" Bad luck!

This is a quite extraordinary yarn by Gary, not repeated in his autobiography (although he did repeat it on an ITV special, *True Gold*, broadcast on 14 October 2014, when he dated the incident to 1984, and again on a BBC show, *Sounds of the 80s*, broadcast on 18 October 2014, when he dated it to 1986) and is most unlikely to have occurred. It may be that something got lost in the translation and that a German man did accost Gary but only to mention that he was from Spandau in Berlin and that Spandau Ballet had taken the name of his home town, a comment which Gary, having wrongly got the idea into his head that the name had been taken from a German band, misunderstood.

However, it is certainly interesting that Gary remembers Robert Elms admitting that the name 'might belong to another group' because Deanne Pearson, who was employed by the *NME* on a full-time basis from December 1979 and then wrote for *The Face* from the summer of 1980 onwards, personally chided Elms for having taken the name of her boyfriend's band. As she says: 'I knew Bob Elms for years, you know, we were sort of in the same circles from the early days really. As soon as I got to London I met him on the club scene at gigs and stuff and we worked for some of the same papers and magazines. So I did know him well. And I did ask him about it because I must have read something that he'd said he'd come up with the name. And I asked him about it and I can't remember what he told me. He did say that he'd come up with the name. And I can't remember whether he told me the story about the graffiti on the wall or whether it was when he was in Germany and came up with the name because I'd heard both stories and I can't remember which one he told me. And I remember on two or three occasions sort of saying to him, "Oh come on for god's sake you're not telling me you came up with the name completely coincidentally when another band already existed, it's a brilliant name!" and he said, "It's my name, I came up with it".

The final twist in the story is that, when Robert Elms came to publish his autobiography in 2005, he did not claim to have invented the name Spandau Ballet while thinking about what the inmates of Spandau prison did for entertainment nor did he claim to have seen the name on a toilet wall in Berlin. Instead, he said that, when he was in Berlin during the summer of 1979, he went to look at Spandau prison and 'on a nearby wall' he saw the words 'Spandau Ballet'.* This was the first time that Elms, or indeed anyone connected with Spandau Ballet, had claimed that the graffiti had been on a wall near Spandau prison. Most recently, in the sleeve notes accompanying the 2014 album, *True Gold*, he said, 'I nicked a name from a Berlin wall'. Given that Elms' story has changed dramatically from its original telling, it is hard to know what to make of it. We cannot say it is impossible that some unknown person saw the name 'Spandau Ballet' in the toilet of The Venue, or somewhere else in London, and then, having

---

* An internet myth was born on Wikipedia on 6 August 2010 when someone inserted a sentence in Spandau Ballet's Wiki entry which stated that Elms had been inspired by graffiti 'along the lines of: "Rudolf Hess, all by himself, dancing the Spandau Ballet"'. This was amended on 16 December 2010 to say that the graffiti read "Rudolf Hess, all alone, dancing the Spandau Ballet". The claim was deleted on 1 December 2011 but not before it was repeated on numerous websites and forums and ended up being stated as fact in a 2012 book by Tom Bromley entitled *Wired For Sound: Now That's What I Call An 80s Music Childhood*.

travelled to Germany, chalked it on a wall in Berlin near the prison: perhaps one of the British soldiers who, along with the Americans, French and Russians, took turns to guard Hess. Or perhaps someone independently thought up the name in Berlin and decided to write it on the wall – but this would seem to be highly improbable. Moreover, had it been a German speaker it would presumably have been transcribed as 'Spandau Ballett', or 'Das Spandauer Ballett' which Elms makes no mention of.

In considering whether Elms saw the name in Berlin, we should note that, in the 2011 book *We Can Be Heroes,* Chris Sullivan, apparently for the first time ever in print, claimed that, with Elms, he also saw the name 'Spandau Ballet' on a toilet wall in Berlin but it is difficult to know how much weight can be placed on such a belated claim, especially in view of Elms' account in his autobiography that he saw the name on a wall near Spandau prison which was not (apparently) a toilet wall. Furthermore, by the time Sullivan made this claim, Mick Austin had added to Spandau Ballet's Wikipedia entry the fact that he had been in a band called Spandau Ballet prior to November 1979, also making the suggestion that someone connected with Dagger's band had seen the name written in the toilet of The Venue in London. It is possible, therefore, that Sullivan was responding to this suggestion in order to defend his friend from the charge of having taken another band's name.

The most likely explanation of events is that Elms' memory after all these years has let him down and that he actually saw the name 'Spandau Ballet' written or stencilled by Mick Austin, Gordon Bowman or Mark Robinson on a wall, or perhaps a toilet door, somewhere in London but that, looking back after all these years (or even looking back in 1983), he has muddled it all up in his mind and connected this sighting with his visit to Berlin and thus thinks he saw it there. In this respect, we may note that, perhaps revealingly, Gary said during a radio documentary broadcast in November 2009: 'We thought he'd pulled it from the ether. But he [Elms] said "no I actually saw it written on a toilet wall". In this version of the story, Elms did not apparently mention

Berlin in his conversation with Gary and perhaps that is the way it happened, with Berlin being a later addition to the toilet wall story, despite Spandau prison having been included in Elms' original explanation to the *NME*.

Either way, as Gary Kemp freely admitted to Sara Cox on the BBC's *Sounds of the 80s* in October 2014, Spandau Ballet in its original form 'was actually a band, another band.'

CHAPTER SEVEN

Hopeless Romantics

THE ORIGINAL 'ROMANTICS' WERE A group of late eighteenth/early nineteenth century English poets, primarily Wordsworth, Keats, Coleridge, Shelley, Blake and Byron, so called because of the emotional, suggestive and aspirational nature of their poetry, although the term has also been applied to a number of European artists, authors, composers and painters of the period. The word 'romantic' in this literary/artistic context was associated not with love specifically but with general and somewhat intangible feelings of yearning, longing and desire: a wish to escape from dull, humdrum reality. The Romantics were also associated, through their chosen mode of attire, with ruffled collars and cuffs and frilly shirts.

Separately, there was also an American Romantic movement in the nineteenth century comprised solely of writers, such as Walt Whitman, Ralph Waldo Emerson, James Fenimore Cooper, Edgar Allan Poe and Henry David Thoreau, who were considered 'romantic' because they were said to be optimistic non-conformists, suspicious of logic and reason, who believed in the power of imagination and in getting closer to nature.

A number of groups of romantic poets, writers or artists who continued the tradition of the original Romantics have been called 'New Romantics'. However, it should be noted that, confusingly, the original English romantic poets and artists have, on occasion, been designated as 'New Romantics' in the sense that they were a fresh change from what had been before. Colwyn Vulliamy, in his 1948 book, *Byron*, for example, included a chapter entitled 'The New Romantics', following on from a chapter entitled 'The Kingdom of Cant'. For Vulliamy, the new school of romanticism replaced a period in English society of false opinions and hypocrisy; thus Byron was not merely a romantic but one of the *new* romantics.

That was in 1948 though; more commonly, it has been subsequent groups of poets, writers, artists and musicians – those who existed *after* the Romantics – who have been labelled as 'New Romantics'. According to the *Oxford English Dictionary*, Dante Gabriel Rossetti was one of the first to be specifically linked to new romanticism for his poetry in 1885, something he was never personally aware of, having died three years earlier. However, the expression actually appears to have been coined almost twenty years before this by Cyrus Redding, writing about the poet and novelist Victor Hugo in the September 1866 edition of *The New Monthly Magazine*. Redding's precise meaning in the following passage is somewhat impenetrable but he wrote of Hugo:

> With his power it is lamentable to see that he has no idea there can be an extravagance which he may not essay and sanction, no by-road out of the highway of nature that he may not travel, and shield under the term "romantic" to which we must beg to prefix the title of "new" – "new romantic" not that of Shakespeare, but of Dumas and Hugo.

This may well be the first appearance ever in print in the English language of the 'new romantic' term in the sense of being used to describe a person or style of art, although the *Oxford English Dictionary* suggests the phrase was derived from the German words 'neuromantik' and 'neuromantisch' of some thirty years or so earlier.

In 1930, the French painter Jean Fautrier was said in an exhibition catalogue for the New York Museum of Modern Art to be unique 'among the new romantics'. A headline in the book review section of the *Times* newspaper in 1938 branded a random group of British and American authors (James M. Cain, Alison Uttley, Kate O'Brien, Naomi Royde-Smith and D. Wilson MacArthur) as 'The New Romantics' while, later in the same year, Pierre Jeaneerat, the art critic of the Daily Mail, wrote of 'the new romanticism of Matisse, Derain, Segonzac'. More importantly, a group of British poets from the 1940s including Denise Levertov, Dylan Thomas, George Barker and Kathleen Raine also became known as 'New Romantics' following the 1949 publication of an anthology of poetry edited by Kenneth Rexroth entitled 'The New British Poets'. For Rexroth, it was the 'typically British virtues' of 'moral earnestness and personal integrity' which marked what he referred to as 'the New Romanticism'. However, the term was not only applied in a literary context but seeped into popular culture. Thus, a photograph of Richard Walker and Judy Garland in the *Montreal Gazette* of 20 July 1945 to publicize their new film *The Clock*, a romantic wartime drama, was headlined simply 'NEW ROMANTICS'.

The fashion world soon adopted the label: usually, but not always, in respect of any clothes incorporating ruffles, especially with lace, or large collars & cuffs. The US edition of the fashion magazine, *Vogue,* of 15 October 1949, carried a six page feature entitled 'The New Romantics' with a photograph of a model wearing a Christian Dior dress captioned: 'A new romanticism: the nearly shoulderless dinner dress of crinkled black velvet and chiffon', the accompanying article describing this as evidence that, 'as far as fashion goes, 1950 can be as romantic as 1850.' A couple of weeks later, the same magazine carried another article headlined 'The New Romantics' accompanied by the image of a woman wearing an outfit of ivory rayon brocade and fur.

Back in the literary world: in 1961, the architect Edward Durell Stone was said to stand 'in the vanguard of the New Romantics' while, in 1962, a group of poetry critics including John Crowe Ransom, Allen Tate, R.P. Blackmur and Cleanth Brooks, were described as 'New Romantics' in a book by Richard Foster entitled

The New Romantics: A Reappraisal of the New Criticism, supposedly because of the way they contrasted poetry to science in the manner of the Romantic poets and the way they promoted a doctrine that poetry was a high form of knowledge.

In the April 1962 issue of the American magazine *Glamour* a new spring collection was labelled 'the new romantics', said to be 'fresh and feminine as ruffle'. The US edition of *Vogue*, dated August 1966, featured a series of articles and photo shoots on new romantic fashion. The front cover announced: '1966 FASHION FOR THE NEW ROMANTICS'. The feature included one model wearing 'ruffles and pompons', another wearing 'Dandy pants – and...lace ruffled shirt' and a 'girl in lace ruffles and the Dandy tailleur.' The main article was entitled simply 'the new Romantics' and Vanessa Redgrave was featured in 'lace frills and pants', while Jane Birkin, described as a 'young heroine for the new romantic evenings', was also captured wearing 'a cage of white silk chiffon with a cut-velvet pattern over pink taffeta.' The reader was told: 'You know them – by the spring of their hair and the most optimistic spring of their walk: by their charm and gaiety and bone-deep attractiveness. They're the girls of today and...they're the prettiest girls in the world', so it seems that only beautiful women could properly be described as new romantics at this stage, at least according to *Vogue*.

The following year, the British edition of *Vogue*, dated December 1967, featured a collection described as 'THE NEW RAVES' incorporating a sub-collection called 'New Romantics', as featured on the front cover, although the article itself did not use the term, preferring 'Modern Romantics'. Dresses featured in the collection included a 'Pearly pink voile dress' with 'fabulous full pantaloons gathered in at the ankle...pink periwig in full bloom and matching flowers in ravishing ruffs round throat, arm and ankles', a 'Singular sweet flowering seventeenth-century dress' with 'light snow white organdie collar and cuffs in full bloom' and a 'Highly entertaining party pink culotte dress' with 'Neck and cuffs lightly gathered into frivolous feathery pink frills of organza.' In March

1969, the *Daily Express* reported that twelve British models had flown to New York to model a collection of clothes produced by British manufacturers under the title of 'The New Romantics'.

It was not only fashion journalists who used the new romantic label during this period. It was a time of protest against the Vietnam war and, reporting on riots in Paris in the spring of 1968, the Montana newspaper, *The Billings Gazette*, carried a news agency report which referred to the rebellious Paris youth as 'new romantics' who appeared to be 'a cross between an underprivileged army and clowns playing war games.' A story in the *San Antonio Light* of 21 November 1971 carried a quote from Otto Miller, the chairman of Standard Oil Co., who referred to ecologically minded critics of the petroleum industry as, 'at best, new romantics who idealize yesterday at the expense of today and tomorrow. At worst...new prophets of doom.' Somewhat less harshly, young Americans were described by Dr Nell Griffin, associate professor of English at Jacksonville State University, as the 'new romantics' because they had a number of idealistic traits 'in accord with the ideas of the 19th century romantics' and her essay appeared in *The Anniston Star* of 30 April 1972 under the headline, 'Today's young: The new romantics'.

At the same time, throughout the 1970s, fashion collections labelled 'new romantics' continued to appear with surprising regularity. In March 1971, the New York newspaper, the *Oneonta Star*, reported that sportswear was staging a big comeback and, under a headline, 'On Sport scene it's favored classics plus new romantics', said that this included, 'variations on every theme from the classics to new romantics'. The *California Oakland Tribune* of 25 February 1971 carried an advertisement for 'fanciful dresses' called 'THE NEW ROMANTICS' while the *Albuquerque Tribune* of 28 July 1972 included another advertisement offering literally 'hundreds of new romantics' as part of its 'exciting fall coat collection'.

If you wanted to gown yourself 'in great spills of ruffles and flounces and lacy trips' in 1973, you could acquire 'the sound of new romantics in petticoats and quills' from the ZCMI department store, according to an advertisement in the *Salt Lake Tribune* in February. Later in the year, the same newspaper carried an advert for a collection of dresses 'in a soft haze of polyester double knit...they're the new romantics and long on fashion.'

At the end of 1973, the December (U.S.) edition of *Vogue* carried yet another feature entitled 'The New Romantics' with celebrities Isabel De Rosnay and Jacqueline Bissett now amongst those said to be new romantics who were: 'Independent, vital bright – and unabashed to be beautiful.' Again it seems that, according to *Vogue*, the concept of new romanticism incorporated only beautiful, modern looking and intelligent women as it was stated that, 'The New Romantics...wear feathers as well as jeans, carry fans as well as books, and are not afraid that clear, good minds might be behind allure. Nothing could make a New Romantic swoon other than events, ideas, objects so beautiful or enlightening or so astonishing that an aware man could swoon beside her.' Meanwhile, Dillard's apartment store in Texas in 1974 was offering, 'The simple romanticism of the peasant look', with 'detailed flounced skirts, tucker or laced bodices' and 'sheer cuffed sleeves' in its 'scene stealers...the new romantics' collection.

If you were in the state of Montana in the spring of 1975 thinking about fashion and value, there was a good chance you were also thinking Discount Fabrics and their 'beautiful selection of pastels with floral patterns as pretty as a spring garden' which they called 'New Romantics'. In Colorado in 1976, the salon Lillie Rubin was selling some 'exciting new romantics', while, over in Missouri in 1978, what else could they call their 'soft dresses' with 'Flouncing hemlines, tiered skirts [and] billowy sleeves' but 'New Romantics'? Meanwhile, in the spring of 1978, Estée Lauder launched a range of three fragrances: 'White Linen', 'Celadon' and 'Pavilion' which it collectively labelled 'The New Romantics'.

In the literary world, the American academic Robert A. Hipkiss wrote a book in 1976 entitled *Jack Kerouac, Prophet of the New Romanticism* in which he identified writers J.D. Salinger,

James Purdy, John Knowles and Ken Kesey as four 'New Romantics', and Salinger's *Catcher in the Rye* would, as it happens, one day find its way into the lyrics of a Spandau Ballet song. Over in England in 1977, a professor of sociology at the University of Bath was warning, in a letter to the *Times,* of the similarity between the intellectual climate of Britain and that of the Weimar Republic, commenting that new ideas in education reflected the ideas of the 'new romantics' who, he said, challenged the idea of objective knowledge and celebrated relativism.

By the late 1970s, then, the term 'New Romantics' was one which had been used throughout the twentieth century albeit that its precise meaning was undefined and its membership uncertain. It was so familiar that in 1979 a rock group in London called Sneaks changed its name to The New Romantics and performed a gig at The Brecknock in Camden on 17 January, although it does not appear to have lasted long and had nothing to do with the New Romantic movement that was soon to burst onto the scene.

Even in early 1980, when the concept of new romanticism was not yet linked to the movement emerging from Blitz in London, fashion collections could still be described as 'new romantic' without any unwelcome or undesirable cultish connotations. Thus, Marylou Luther, the fashion editor of the *Los Angeles Times,* described new sportswear collections launched by Ralph Lauren and Perry Ellis in May 1980, featuring 'Lord Byron jackets' and 'Heathcliff capes', as 'The New Romantics'; Ms Luther also quoted Ralph Lauren as saying: 'Clothes are becoming romantic – a timeless, forever kind of romantic.' The same collection was described in the *Chicago Daily Herald* of 13 May 1980 as having, 'The vivid plaids, the lace-edged jabots, the ruffles, the blacks, the brights, the full skirts...warm coats...with double caplet collars...fitted styles that swirled out at the waist or were trimmed, rimmed and edged and collared and cuffed in fur.'

So, as the Eighties began, we can see that the 'new romantic' label was one which had been applied in various contexts, albeit usually fashion related, during the previous few years. It was not a new label but it was one which was soon to become massive in England and throughout the world. However, at the start of 1980, it was not yet a label applied to the movement which had begun at Billy's in Dean Street and had now taken over Blitz in Great Queen Street on Tuesday (and soon to be Thursday) nights. Although music journalist Tim Lott, in *Record Mirror* of 24 November 1979, had referred to various labels being bandied about, such as 'new musick' or 'the cold wave' or the 'robot age', to describe the new electronic music of artists (most of whom were being played at Blitz) such as Human League, Ultravox, Tubeway Army and Cabaret Voltaire, the first person to consider, and at the same time reject, a label specifically for the movement developing at Blitz was Ted Polhemus in the November 1979 issue of the *Tatler*: 'Some of this crowd are New Mods', he said, 'but to reduce this potpourri of extravagant styles to that of any other label is a mistake…They are a tribe without a name and even if I could think of one I'd hope I'd keep it to myself.'

It was not long, however, before a label *was* created for this tribe without a name. The gossip columnist, Francis Lynn, while telling a light-hearted story in the January 1980 issue of *Ritz* about how Steve Strange ignored all his 'punk' friends at the Blitz Christmas party in December 1979, while hob-nobbing with his more famous guests, wondered if it would be the regular 'Blitz kids' who would fly out to the opening of a planned New York version of Blitz or Steve Strange's more elevated celebrity friends. This was probably the first ever appearance in print of the term 'Blitz kids' in relation to the Tuesday night patrons of the venue in Great Queen Street. It was, nevertheless, a pre-existing phrase from the Second World War, being the title of a 1941 book by Elinor Mordaunt about children who lived during the Blitz, and also the name of a group of child actors from the cast of the 1962 Lionel Bart musical 'Blitz!' who recorded and released one of the songs from the musical as a single, but may have suggested itself to Lynn from the fact that Strange liked to refer to the young patrons of Blitz as 'my kids'.

By this time, the national newspapers were picking up on the new musical and fashion scene to emerge from Blitz. On 4 January 1980, the *Daily Express*, under the headline, 'HOT 10 FOR THE 1980s', carried a small piece on Visage who were described as 'not so much a new band – more a stylised group of trend-setting fashion fanatics set to music'. Rusty Egan was quoted as saying, 'We want to bring sophistication and glamour to music'. Sections of the music press were also quick to pick up on the new electronic/synthesizer music. We have already seen *Record Mirror*'s reference to the 'new musick', and Mark Williams in *Melody Maker* of 5 January 1980 said, 'you can trust me when I say that the sound of the Eighties is the sound of the synthesizer'. Discussing the music of Gary Numan, Human League, OMD and Visage, amongst others, in its edition of 12 January 1980, reference was made by the *NME* to 'The New Pop', which was described as 'that which channels the sensibility of old pop through new instruments…the New Pop uses synthesisers a lot and repeats itself a lot.' In setting out a history of electronic music, the music paper also referred to the Futurists of the early twentieth century, such as Luigi Russolo, who had believed in using noise (or sounds of any kind) to create art (hence 'the art of noise'). 'Futurism', having already been used to describe the fashion aspect of the scene, subsequently became a term used to describe the new synthesizer based music.

Peter York, the style guru, whose art school contacts from the punk world, of which he was an avid observer and commentator, had tipped him off to the club nights at Billy's in 1978, causing him to pay a visit to 69 Dean Street one Tuesday evening to check out the music, look and fashion habits of the clientele, which, as he told the author in July 2017, he found to be 'wonderful', albeit that the clubbers were not then quite as flamboyantly dressed as they would subsequently become at Blitz, was also alert to the new futuristic trend. In an article in the January 1980 issue of *Harpers & Queen* entitled 'Post-Modernism', he said:

...by 1978 the crucial style was uncompromisingly modern – and you could hardly talk to a young person of sensibility without hearing how they hated anything retro, that we must look to the future, the technology for our salvation, and how they liked modern materials like plastic, neon and aluminium. The ultimate expression of this funny mood was the Neon Night culture that developed round an odd little chap called Steve Strange - ex punk and Generation X roadie, who started 'Bowie Night', a portable event at various London clubs in 1978. This scene was very modern - futuristic indeed. Look close however and it was...moderne, a rehash of a period idea of the future – Bauhaus and Sci-fi trash, Star Trek and Thunderbirds, art and 'Low' all mixed up. Sweet, a bit feeble and silly, dated from the word go, post-punk and, intractably, hopelessly post-modern.

The 'scene' described by York was still very much alive at the time his article was published. On 24 January 1980, David Johnson, in his 'On The Line' column in the *Evening Standard*, while announcing that Steve Strange was to begin a new Thursday night at Blitz, made reference to 'the 80s set', an expression which Ted Polhemus had used in a recently published issue of *Tatler*, explaining that by day you can be anything ('broker's runner or Tesco till girl') but by night you must put on 'Your Look'.

In February 1980, the fashion aspect of the movement emerging from Blitz was noticed by Paula Yates in *Record Mirror*, on the occasion of the transfer of PX (where the members of Spandau now shopped) from James Street to Endell Street. She said, rather presciently as it turned out: 'For the next year we're obviously going to have to get used to Beau Brummel style velvet pantaloons and frilly Tom Jonesque shirts with floppy cuffs.' Also circa February 1980, issue 9 of the arts magazine, *Viz*, carried a piece by one Perry Haines who referred to 'A new movement, as yet unlabelled', thus echoing the point made in *Tatler* that there was no name for this movement ('Blitz kids' not yet having caught on). Haines added that the movement 'respects romance and adores the classics'. At about the same time, the weekly magazine, *New Society*, of 7 February 1980, featured an article on Steve Strange and Blitz in which the supposed 'Futuristic' nature of the movement was referred to and one of the clubbers was quoted as saying that they called themselves 'the Artificial Aristocracy' who 'leave the proles to do the imitating'.

Shortly after this, on 3 March 1980, the *Daily Mirror* carried an influential article by Christena Appleyard headlined 'BLITZ KIDS LET THEIR HAIR UP' (and a sub-heading 'The new wave that makes even the Punks look normal'), with photographs captioned 'Whacky', 'Weird' and 'Sparkling'. The 'Blitz Kids' were said to dress in clothes ranging from crinolines to clown costumes, to listen to loud repetitive electronic music by cult bands and to dance using a mesmeric mixture of mime and robotic movements. The *Mirror* story was syndicated around the world over the next few weeks via the Associated Press News Agency and thus appeared in various newspapers in the United States with similar headlines, most relating to the Blitz Kids. The *Indiana Evening Gazette* ran with 'London's Newest Cultists Call Themselves 'Blitz Kids'', the *Minnesota St. Cloud Times* opted for 'The 'Blitz Kids' Invade London', the *Chicago Daily Herald* said 'Post-Punk cult Blitzes London' while the *Los Angeles Times* chose 'London's Blitz Look: Outlandish Is In'.

The *Daily Mirror* article appears to have captured the interest of the BBC. Tony Wilkinson of *Nationwide* immediately filmed a report from Blitz, centred around the life of one of the more flamboyant regulars, Theresa Thurmer, emphasizing her Cinderella-like transformation from bored secretary during the day to 'a star' on Tuesday nights in 'a dream life of glamour and excitement.' This was the central theme of Wilkinson's report: the fact that 'hundreds' of people in mundane 9 to 5 jobs were casting aside their work clothes, their cares and, indeed, reality itself, to dress outrageously and live a secret fantasy life, just like the wealthy 'party going, jet-set' or 'beautiful people', for one night a week. Lacking a label to describe this 'group in London' – the report did not even mention 'Blitz Kids' – Wilkinson described Blitz as having 'five hundred of the most bizarre members in town', featuring 'men wearing silk pantaloons' who stand 'cheek by painted jowl with white faced French trollops.'

At this stage, it wasn't only Blitz that was playing electronic music and attracting an outlandishly dressed crowd. As we have seen, Jock McDonald, together with Jimmy Lydon, had started club nights at Studio 21 in September 1979, featuring electronic music on Saturdays and had then borrowed heavily from Egan and Strange by starting 'David Bowie nights' on Wednesdays at that venue in January 1980. In addition, the St Moritz had positioned itself as 'an alternative club for alternative people who forever look ahead' (according to Perry Haines in *Viz*) and now the Chelsea Drugstore, a pub in the King's Road, attempted to get in on the act, advertising in *Sounds* and *NME* of 15 March 1980 the occurrence of a 'SCI-FI DISCO' electronic music night on Mondays, DJ'd by Stephen Pearce better known as Stevo, with the instruction to 'DRESS WEIRD!!!'. The fact that the ad was not repeated suggests it might not have been a terribly successful event, although Stevo continued his electronic disco events and was DJ'ing in Billy's six months later on Monday evenings at what would be advertised, without much originality, as 'Bowie Disco' nights.

On 17 March 1980, a report by Liz Smith in the *Evening Standard* about Spandau Ballet's gig at the Scala cinema earlier in the month was headlined 'Dandies in hand-me-downs', and references were made to 'this dandified group' and 'the new movement in style'. A 'dandy', according to the *Oxford English Dictionary* is 'one who studies above everything to dress elegantly and fashionably, a beau, fop, exquisite'. The term 'New Romantics' was not mentioned in the *Evening Standard* but the article included a quote from Perry Haines who, paraphrasing his earlier article in *Viz*, said Spandau Ballet were: 'Herald angels to a new movement, they adore romanticism and cherish classicism.' A review of the same concert by Robert Elms in the *NME* of 29 March 1980 – the same one which Steve Dagger had forced him to write – said: 'An air of dandy dilettantism fills the air as wing collars and cloaks come to the fore', while the *Daily Star*, a few weeks later on 8 April 1980, contained an article headlined 'Just dandy!' and said of Spandau Ballet that they were 'the new dandies of the disco scene who love dressing up just to please themselves'. So 'New Dandies' seems to have been the name of choice at this time.

A clue to the arrival of the term 'New Romantics' can be found in an interview with Gary Kemp in *Record Mirror* of 12 April 1980. He said: 'Now we dress very, very romantically. We want to be dandies not clones', and the magazine referred to Spandau Ballet's 'romantic image'. The *Sunday Times* of 27 April 1980 also picked up the romantic theme, calling the lace ruffle wearing individuals 'the romantic rebel[s]'. In the May 1980 issue of *Tatler* (in the shops at the end of April), Ted Polhemus, who had previously referred to them as a tribe with no name, now referred to Steve Strange's Blitz crowd as simply 'the poseurs'.

In the *Evening Standard* of 8 May 1980, under the headline 'Dandies for Dancing', David Johnson said of Spandau that, 'Their clothes echo the romantic eras of Shelley and Wilde' and introduced the expression 'London's party-going Now Crowd' into the lexicon. Gary Kemp was also quoted as saying: 'We want to look like dandies'. But were they dandies or just plain weird? The *Daily Star* of 29 May 1980 seemed to think the latter. A feature on Blitz and the 'Cult of crazy fashions' by Cathy Couzens was headlined simply 'WEIRDIES!'. As we have already seen from the Chelsea Drug Store ad, it wasn't only at Blitz where one could find the 'weirdies', and John Blake, in the London *Evening News*, reported on 18 June 1980: 'Oxford Street's Studio 21 club has become the latest haven for the very weird. Men with multi-coloured bee-hive hair styles mix with ragged-leather urchins while girls in full ballet dancers' tutus twirl to electronic music. It's a poseur's paradise.' In the same week, the *Sunday People* of 15 June 1980 referred to this 'new cult' of 'the Blitz Kids' – obviously from Blitz rather than Studio 21 – but, reflecting the earlier *New Society* article, said they call themselves 'the artificial aristocracy'.

Bill Reed, fashion correspondent for *Ritz,* said in the July 1980 edition of that publication: 'Hot flash:- The Blitz Kids. STEVE STRANGE's new shop in Endell Street (ex PX) supplies the clothes for those Wagnerian Punks who frequent Blitz' observing that, 'Journalists from all over Europe are coming to London to get a first-hand look at this new clothing movement.'

A review by David Johnson in the *Evening Standard* of LWT's *Twentieth Century Box* documentary in July 1980 once again used the expression 'London's Now Crowd', and Spandau Ballet were described as 'youths given to dandyism'. It also referred to Blitz regular Chris Sullivan, 'reciting some Futurist manifesto'. The preview of the documentary in the *TV Times* simply referred to 'the new youth movement of the Eighties' and its narrator, Danny Baker, described the crowd who turned up at the Scala to watch the band as 'the exotic people'. Tony Hadley followed the earlier comment of Gary by saying that the line being followed was 'a question of elegance and romance' but still no-one was calling them New Romantics. Indeed, a chart compiled by the DJ Stevo for *Sounds* in August 1980, featuring much of the music played at Blitz, such as Human League, Ultravox, OMD, Yellow Magic Orchestra, Gina X, Cabaret Voltaire and David Bowie, was called a 'Futurist' chart, not a New Romantic one.

A short piece on Spandau's trip to St Tropez in the 2 August 1980 issue of the *NME* referred to the band as 'London's late-night dressers' playing 'white European dance music' and a feature in the *Evening News* on London nightclubs included a visit to Hell in Henrietta Street, Covent Garden, where, after his Thursday night cabaret spectaculars at Blitz had failed due to lack of interest, Steve Strange had initiated Bowie-type nights on Thursdays and Saturdays, but the best journalist Val Hennessy could do was to describe the crowd as 'posing punks' ('Blitz Kids' not being suitable considering she was in Hell, as it were).

As late as 8 September 1980, a long article about Steve Strange and Blitz in the European edition of *Time* magazine referred to 'Blitzers' but did not mention the expression 'New Romantics' at all. Nor did the first issue of Perry Haines' and Terry Jones' new fashion magazine, *i-D*, which was published in late August 1980. *Sounds* journalist, Betty Page, had come close in the 9 August 1980 edition of *Sounds*, in the context of a review of a new single called 'Bullet Proof Heart' by the Scottish band Fingerprintz, when, referring to a phrase that her friend Andy Partridge of XTC had used during a private conversation, she agreed that 'we're approaching a new age of romanticism'. This review was (rather unfairly to Fingerprintz, whose song was enjoyed by Ms Page) headlined 'HOPELESS ROMANTICS' but, if one combines the concept of a new age of romanticism with the 'Hopeless Romantics' headline, it is a short lexicographical step from there to 'New Romantics'. When Robert Elms wrote an article about Spandau Ballet in issue 6 of *The Face* (which hit the streets on 28 September 1980, and would thus have been written in late August), he stated, 'no slick label has so far been found for a look which relies so much on individualism and changes as quickly as it has been recognized.' It was not long, however, before such a slick label *was* found. Indeed, by the time the magazine was on sale, that label had already been used.

CHAPTER EIGHT

The New Romantics Who Never Were

ACCORDING TO ROBERT ELMS, writing in February 1981, once Spandau Ballet came to the attention of the press in 1980, 'Someone, somewhere, remembered a term that one of us may have used – New Romantics.' Elms is typical of those within the 'movement' who believed, and probably still believe, that the term simply must have been invented by one of the clever young things who attended Blitz because, surely, no ordinary journalist, editor or sub-editor who did not mingle with the strangely dressed, but highly intellectual, crowd in the trendy clubs could have come up with something quite so creative, appealing and, most of all, lasting. His use of the word 'may', however, betrays his uncertainty as to who actually first used it.

Some sources, such as *Record Collector* magazine, say it was Spandau's original producer, Richard James Burgess, who coined the term 'New Romantics' while others, including Elms himself when he came to write his autobiography more than twenty years later, attribute it to Perry Haines, the fashion journalist. However, it is somewhat misleading to speak of who 'coined' or 'invented' the term because, as we have seen, it was already in existence in 1980 and had been used throughout the 1960s and 1970s in other contexts. The more sensible question to ask is: who first *applied* the term to the movement to emerge from Blitz?

In respect of the widely repeated claim that Richard James Burgess was the first to do it, this might have its origins in a comment by Adam Ant, quoted by the *Independent on Sunday* in 1994, in which he said: 'I think that the term New Romantic was really something the media made up. It was first quoted by Richard James Burgess, I think, and he was referring to Spandau Ballet…'. Having said this, unless Adam Ant simply invented that explanation or was confused, the notion that Burgess was responsible must have been a pre-existing notion, although no published record of it has yet been found. Burgess himself certainly appears to believe he was personally responsible; he was quoted in *Record Collector's* June 2004 issue as saying, 'I knew that we needed a name for the movement, and I was playing around with a bunch of descriptors such as 'futurist', 'electronic dance music'…and then the 'New Romantic' tag, which was more to do with the look of the Blitz scene and Spandau Ballet than anything else.' However, Burgess does not say when he came up with this tag and there is no independent contemporary evidence that he was responsible for being the first to apply it to the movement. Moreover, although a member of Landscape, it is difficult to see why he would have been considering a descriptor for the movement in any context other than as Spandau Ballet's producer, a role which he did not adopt until shortly before the band was signed in October 1980 by which time, as we shall see, the tag was already in use.

As for the notion that 'New Romantics' was first applied to the movement by Perry Haines, this appears to be based on a claim by Haines himself (reported in both *Record Mirror* in February 1981 and *The Face* in November 1981) that he christened Spandau Ballet 'romantics' (i.e. *not* New Romantics) and is probably only referring to his earlier mentions of 'romance' and 'romanticism' in *Viz* and the *Standard* respectively. In fact, in an interview for *Sounds* of 25 October 1980, Haines said his name for 'the new movement spearheaded by Spandau Ballet' was 'The Herald Angels', a phrase which he had of course used in the *Standard* seven months earlier (and which he repeated in the November

1980 issue of *i-D* magazine) but which did not catch on. In any case, Haines himself unequivocally stated in an article published in *New Sounds, New Styles* in March 1981 that it was 'the press' who invented the label 'New Romantics', so that conclusively rules him out.

Martin Kemp, who appears to have no problem accepting that a mere Fleet Street journalist could have devised the term, claims in his autobiography that the name 'New Romantic' was first used by a journalist on the London *Evening Standard*. However, the first appearance of New Romanticism in the *Evening Standard* was in a short article by David Johnson in his 'On The Line' page dated 18 September 1980 which, while not quite using the term 'New Romantics', captioned a photograph of the band, 'NEW ROMANCE and new music from the band Spandau Ballet', which was close. In the following week's page, on 25 September 1980, Johnson *did* use the exact term when he said of the fact that the Scala Cinema was now regularly hosting entertainment evenings involving obscure films and live bands that, 'The rock world is slowly waking up to the New Romantics movement and the number of fans who are simply not prepared to brave the beer-and-lout venues any longer.' This was not quite the first appearance of the term in print though.

That occurred somewhat out of the blue in Issue 5 of *The Face* which was published on 24 August 1980 (and was certainly in the shops before 30 August 1980 because the *NME* of this date carried an advertisement stating that it was 'at your newsagents now'). When setting out what was to come in the next issue, it was stated by the magazine's editor and publisher, Nick Logan:

> Place a regular order for THE FACE at your newsagents today. Next issue is on sale Sept 28 with THE B-52s (about time), MADNESS, BURNING SPEAR[,] THE NEW ROMANTICS (more pictures of people dressed up funny)....

There are a number of curious factors associated with this preview. Anyone reading it (i.e. the average *Face* reader) could not have known what was being referred to by the term 'The New Romantics' other than 'people dressed up funny', which might not have been easily understood. From the context of being in a list of band names, the casual reader might have assumed it was a reference to a band. There would certainly have been no real reason for anyone to connect it with the movement from Blitz. A diligent reader might have appreciated that 'more pictures of people dressed up funny' was a reference to a photographic feature (with some text) at the back of the same issue entitled 'You're Not Going Out Dressed Like That (Again!)' containing black and white photographs which had been taken by Virginia Turbett of individuals, who could be said to have been dressed 'funny', at Jock McDonald's Studio 21 on the evening of Saturday, 19 July 1980. The 'Again!' in the title of that feature harked back to the first issue of *The Face*, which had carried a double page photographic spread entitled 'You're Not Going Out Dressed Like That', for which five photographs of young people, including one taken by Janette Beckman of an unremarkable couple at Blitz but also one taken by Anton Corbijn in Streatham of two mods and one taken in an urinal of two rockers, were selected. So it wasn't really possible for readers of Issue 5 of *The Face* to have divined Nick Logan's intentions here.

In the event, the next issue of *The Face*, while featuring the B-52s, Madness and Burning Spear, did not carry an article entitled 'THE NEW ROMANTICS' or anything similar. It *did* contain an article by Robert Elms about Spandau Ballet, with some photographs of the band, but this is very unlikely to be what Nick Logan had been intending to convey in Issue 5 because he would certainly have mentioned the band by name, not least to ensure more sales of the next issue of his magazine. Issue 6 also carried a 'day in the life' feature about Steve Strange, with plenty of photographs by Janette Beckman, but, as it was only about him, the plural description of 'New Romantics' would presumably have been inappropriate. On the face of it, therefore, it would seem that Logan intended to carry an article about people dressed up funny in *The Face*, Issue 6, but this concept was either spiked or modified.

Nick Logan, speaking to the author in August 2014, does not, unsurprisingly, have an actual recollection of writing the preview in Issue 5 of *The Face* (although he confirms that he would have done so) but thinks that the Steve Strange photographic feature was the most likely thing on his mind when he referred to 'more people dressed up funny'. He says: 'Probably what I meant, was, what I was alluding to – I was probably looking for something else to say, not knowing what content I had. But I was sitting on some pictures here. I was always bound to have something. And probably Janette brought that session in with Steve Strange and I thought okay that's the one I'll run this time.' As for the phrase 'The New Romantics', he doesn't think it was something he came up with himself. Firstly, it was not the kind of expression he would have used to describe the strangely dressed people of the time and he is not likely to have connected them to the Romantic poets: 'I don't remember making that connection' he says. Secondly, he did not at all like the phrase. 'I thought it was too weedy, drippy, not punchy...a bit prissy', he recalls, and this might explain why it was not used as a headline of any story published in *The Face*. As Logan elaborates, 'I probably thought that would do for now but it does need explaining', hence the inclusion of the explanation in parentheses that the New Romantics feature would involve pictures of people dressed funny. In any event, as we shall see, by the time Issue 6 was being put together, *Sounds* had already used a 'New Romantics' headline and no editor would have wanted to repeat someone else's concept.

Given that Nick Logan does not believe he thought up the 'New Romantics' tag, where did it come from? According to Logan, 'I don't think I made it up. It must have been in the air. Why would I have said that? Why would I have made that up? It's quite a fanciful jump to that. I don't think I made it up. It must have been floating around.' It may well be, as Logan also speculates, that someone at *The Face* suggested the tag to him and one candidate for this is Janette Beckman, whose photographs were included in the feature about Steve Strange which might originally have been entitled 'The New Romantics' but which was transformed into 'A Day In The Life of Steve Strange'. Ms Beckman was not only a regular clubber at Blitz but had studied for a year at St Martin's School of Art and would likely have been familiar with concepts in the fashion world such as new romanticism. She might have told Logan that she had some photographs of 'New Romantics' which is what influenced him to use this as his temporary title for the feature in Issue 5. However, in an email to the author in August 2014, Ms Beckman denied being responsible.

We may also note that as Issue 5 of *The Face* was being compiled, or shortly after it went on sale, Nick Logan received a visit from Robert Elms who convinced him that, in view of his connections with the up-and-coming Spandau Ballet and the Blitz scene, he should be commissioned to write about them for the magazine. Subsequently, Issue 6 featured a piece by Elms on Spandau Ballet (entitled 'Spandau Ballet: An Immaculate Conception') and Issue 7 featured an article by Elms on the whole Blitz phenomenon, which meant there was still an opportunity for Logan to have used the 'New Romantics' headline had he wanted to – but the piece was instead entitled 'The Cult With No Name'.

The ultimate decision on the headline for the story rested with Nick Logan and he certainly preferred 'Cult With No Name' to 'New Romantics'. 'That's a harder sounding phrase to use', he says, 'more journalistically enticing…It's a little bit dangerous, it's a little bit of a sexual thing, it's an otherness, you know what I'm saying…that's why I would have liked it, as opposed to "New Romantics" being a bit woolly.'

Elms says in his autobiography that he deliberately called his article 'The Cult With No Name' in an effort 'to avoid limiting the whole thing.' In other words, for his own purposes, he pretended that no catchy name had been devised for the movement, even though he was aware, and conceded in the article, that both 'Blitz Kids' and 'New Romantics' *had* been used (undoubtedly, in respect of the latter, a reference to its use as a headline in *Sounds* of 13 September 1980, as discussed below). Why would he do this? The answer may be that Elms was very good friends with Steve Dagger and if there was one thing Dagger did not want it was for a label, especially a 'New Romantics' label, to be applied to Spandau Ballet, thus limiting the band in a world where labels go out of date, and out of fashion, very quickly. Yet between Issues 4 and 7 of *The Face* (i.e. between August and October 1980) there had been a major development outside of Elms' and Dagger's control.

The aforementioned article in *Sounds* of 13 September 1980 (which would have been on sale in the shops on Wednesday, 10 September 1980) was written by Betty Page and was headlined 'THE NEW ROMANTICS'. The term 'New Romantics' was not actually used in the text of the article (only in the headline) and there is nothing obvious in the article to have triggered the headline, although it does refer to the band being part of a 'new wave' and 'some kind of new race'. Betty Page (whose real name is Beverley Glick) does not specifically recall how the headline of her article was devised but believes that it would have been the product of discussions between her and Alan Lewis, the editor of *Sounds*, with whom she had a very good working relationship. As she says:

> Knowing how we used to work, it was usually on a collaborative basis, us coming up with the headline. So it could well have been that I could have been talking to him [Alan Lewis] about the new age of romanticism that my friend Andy Partridge was talking about and he could have said "Ah, New Romantics!".

Betty had formerly been Alan Lewis' personal secretary but showed a talent for music journalism and was appointed a staff writer by her boss, who insisted that she be hired, in the teeth of opposition from the (male) owners of *Sounds* who did not like the idea of secretaries becoming journalists. In fact, this opposition had meant she started writing under the pseudonym of 'Betty Page' so that the owners did not know that she was also a secretary employed by the company.

It was Alan Lewis who was the driving force behind Betty doing the interview in the first place. According to Betty, i.e. Beverley:

> It was really Alan who gave me my first big project to get an interview with Spandau Ballet. No-one had got one. No mainstream publication had got one at that time. That was my job. There I was, a terrified twenty-two or twenty-three-year-old. I was even frightened of picking the phone up. But I had – he gave me – I had Steve Dagger's number. So I thought, "I've got to do this". I had to prove myself. It was my first big assignment. So I phoned up Steve. He was kind of, not suspicious, but he really made me jump through hoops. I'm not sure how many journalists would have put up with it actually...He said he wouldn't let me interview the band unless I'd seen the documentary that had been made about them, the one that Janet Street-Porter made. So I said fine, I went to their offices and watched the documentary. He sort of vetted me a bit, he was practically interviewing me. Once I'd met him and he'd sort of sussed me out a bit he said, "Okay you can interview me and Gary". So it wasn't really the band it was him and Gary. I said, "Yes, that's fine". That's how I got the interview. I think they decided to go with it...because I was impressionable. They knew they could say what they wanted to go in print and it would come out as they said it, which was true because it was basically all direct quotes. So they knew that I wasn't going to put a spin on it.

One thing that the band could not control was the headline of the article, and, according to Betty, this was probably decided upon before she even met the band, photographs of whom, posing at the Ritz Hotel in their most fashionable Blitz-like clothes, were taken prior to the interview by Virginia Turbett on 12 August 1980. These would have set the tone for the headline and, says Betty, 'It was clearly something that we cooked up...I remember the photographs were done before I did the interview, so it could have been partly us looking at the photographs, thinking it looks quite romantic...I'm pretty sure that he [Alan Lewis] told me that he wanted to call it "the New Romantics" but that could have been based on our conversations about the band.'

It is also possible, one imagines, that the small, almost invisible, mention of 'New Romantics' in the preview section of *The Face* a few weeks earlier might have influenced Betty and Lewis, perhaps subconsciously. Speaking to the author in July 2014, she felt, looking back, that the phrase 'new romantics' was 'in the ether' and she had, for many years, believed, like Martin Kemp, that she had seen it in the *Evening Standard* but perhaps it was the inclusion of it in *The Face*, a few weeks before the publication of her article, that had caught her eye.

Given that *The Face* had not made clear what was being referred to when it trailed its supposedly forthcoming feature on 'New Romantics' at the end of August, the *Sounds* headline of 13 September 1980 was the first time, at least in print, that the term 'New Romantics' was expressly linked to the Blitz movement via Spandau Ballet. In an article in *Record Collector* magazine of June 2004, Ms Page rightly referred to her act of 'giving a label to what had previously been called the Cult with No Name' (perhaps more correctly 'tribe without a name' because Elms' article had not yet been published when *Sounds* of 13 September 1980 hit the streets) and, at the press conference to re-launch Spandau Ballet on 25 March 2009, Gary Kemp stated his belief that Betty Page had coined the term 'New Romantics' in her *Sounds* article, a belief he repeated in his subsequent autobiography. In fairness, although Nick Logan appears to have intended to have used the term for an article or photo-spread in *The Face*, it is clear that it is a combination of Betty Page and Alan Lewis (the latter also having the distinction of coining the phrase 'New Wave of British Heavy Metal') who are jointly responsible for applying the term 'New Romantics' to Spandau Ballet and thereby to the entire Blitz movement.

Following the Betty Page article of 13 September 1980, the 'New Romantics' term slowly started to seep into popular usage. Surely not by coincidence, in the following week's *Melody Maker* of 20 September 1980, Ian Pye referred to the Irish rock band U2 as 'Dublin's new romantics' although, of course, the band had no connection with Spandau Ballet, synthesizer music or the Blitz scene. More pertinently, Issue 7 of *The Face*, which was in the shops from 22 October 1980, with its article by Robert Elms about the underground club scene headlined 'The Cult With No Name', said of the cultish clubbers: 'They've been referred to as Blitz Kids, The New Romantics and (yeeuk) the Now Crowd, but have so far resisted a definitive handle.' However, very much against the obvious wishes of Elms, 'New Romantics' was, in fact, soon to become the definitive handle. On the very same day, Christena Appleyard in the *Daily Mirror* of 22 October 1980, writing about Spandau Ballet in an article headlined 'COMING UP POSES', was more certain, saying: 'The group and their followers, who hate being labelled, were originally dubbed the Blitz Kids…Now they are called The New Romantics.'

The following day, 23 October 1980, saw the launch of Peter York's book, *Style Wars*, in which York outlined the beginnings of the movement which he traced to Louise, the lesbian and punk club in Poland Street which Vicki Bird had attended on the evening of the Silver Jubilee Street party in 1977, where Steve Strange and other 'Bowie freaks' had hung out with members of the Sex Pistols before the Bowie Nights had started at Billy's. The book had gone to the printers before the emergence of the 'New Romantics' descriptor and York chose to call the young people who went to Billy's 'the freaks', most of whom, he said, were into Bowie, and he referred to the subsequent 'Neon Night[s] at the Blitz, the ascent of Steve Strange [and] Studio 21' as 'the whole new old world'. The book's launch party, attended by some of these 'freaks', who had been brought along by Steve Strange, was featured in a double page spread in the *Daily Mail* of 24 October and photographs of them, accompanying the main article by Tim Satchell, were captioned 'High Punks' and 'Free Form Weird'.

Also in October 1980, Marylou Luther, the same fashion editor of the *Los Angeles Times* who had earlier in the year described the

Ralph Lauren/Perry Ellis collections as 'The New Romantics', applied the new romantic description to Spring collections designed by Zandra Rhodes (herself a Blitz regular) and Thea Porter, which took the costumes worn by the Blitz Kids as their inspiration. Rhodes was quoted as saying: 'People want to be individuals now at any cost. With the kids, Tuesday night at the Blitz Club is like a Berlin cabaret in the late 30s. You see a little 1950s bouffant, a little Marie Antoinette bouffant – a real mix of tough and romantic.' Under the heading 'Punks and Posers Create Another London Blitz-Krieg', Luther wrote in an article, published by the *Los Angeles Times* on 28 October 1980, that: 'The new romantics...are sometimes called posers and they are taking their clothes cues from the first Queen Elizabeth whose ruffs have joined the realms of street fashion along with velvet knickerbockers and ruffled shirts.'

However, 'New Romantics' was not a name universally adopted at this stage by any means. When reviewing a gig by the then unsigned Duran Duran at the Holy City Zoo in Birmingham, Tim Davies, writing in the 8 November 1980 issue of *Musicians Only*, connected Duran to 'the current obsession for veneer and fashion chic' aimed at those 'who feel they ought to be one step ahead of the vanguard' and he expressly linked the band with the 'vogue worlds' of Gary Numan and Spandau Ballet but did not use any kind of label to describe them. Two months after the *Sounds* article, *Record Mirror* of 29 November 1980 called the movement 'the new clan of the beautiful people'. An article in the same issue entitled 'BRAVE NEW FACE' referred to four 'Futurist' groups (Soft Cell, Naked Lunch, Shock and Spandau Ballet) from what it called 'the movement of the eighties' and did not mention the term 'New Romantics' at all. Instead, it referred to 'a certain circle of people, the Blitz kids' within which Gary Kemp was said to move. An interview with Steve Strange in the same issue also did not refer to New Romantics although it did mention Steve's 'romanticism' and called him a 'new dandy'. Picking up on Gary's 'we want to be dandies' theme, the *NME* of the same month called

Spandau Ballet 'the figureheads of the new dandyism'. A feature in the same issue on designers Melissa Caplan and Simon Withers and shops Modern Classix and PX made reference to 'the New People'. Robert Elms writing in Issue 8 of *The Face*, published in November 1980, about the closing of Blitz and Hell, referred to the 'Blitz Kids' and to 'London's extravagantly dressed people' but did not mention New Romantics, or the Cult with No Name for that matter.

In December 1980, David Johnson in the *Evening Standard* mentioned Stephane Raynor of PX and referred to 'the highly romantic clothes' he sold, calling him, no doubt to the disgust of Elms, 'the leader of the Now Crowd'. In the same month, an article in *Smash Hits* about Spandau Ballet began: 'Nobody's found a handle for this lot. "The New Romantics", "The Blitz Kids", "Post-Punk Blank Poseurs", "*Them*" – these are all names attempting to sum up the crowd of people Spandau Ballet refer to as "what's happening now".' Betty Page quoted Steve Strange in *Sounds* of 6 December 1980 as saying that, while he thought it was good that there was a Futurist chart, he did not like the label and that 'we had a lot of that before, like the New Romantics' (a label which, of course, Page, or at least her music paper, was directly responsible for getting into circulation). Paul Tickell in the *NME* of 13 December 1980, also writing about Steve Strange, spoke of 'the new glitterati', also known as 'The Metropolitan new romancers', and said, 'The New dandyism has arrived. More and more people are dressing up – outrageous elegant up – and fancily romancing'. Strange himself said, 'Kids are glad to be dressed up and escaping work and all the greyness and depression...it's all about style and being romantic.'

Across the Atlantic, the *Los Angeles Times* was also writing about the New Romantics. Under the headline '18th-century punk', on 12 December 1980, Jo-An Jenkins wrote: 'Watch them pour through the doors of Covent Garden's Blitz disco just before midnight. The romantic young men in their gleaming, jabot-collared shirts and elaborately brushed pompadours. The girls in their black lace ball gowns, hair piled high on their heads and trailing cascades of curls. Ruffles and knickerbockers, white gloves and patent-leather dancing skippers, fluttering fans and flowing evening capes are all part of London's new romantic look.' Steve Sutherland in London also picked up on the term in *Melody Maker's* 27 December 1980 issue, referring to Steve Strange as being 'the inspiration behind those outrageous looking youngsters labelled the new romantics.'

Nevertheless, despite the increasing use of the term to describe the movement, *Record Mirror's* review of 1980, in its end of the year edition dated 27 December 1980, put Spandau Ballet in the category of 'Futurists' not 'New Romantics' (a term it did not use). When Paul Colbert reviewed Visage's debut album in *Musicians Only* earlier in the same month, he spoke of 'high fashion leader Steve Strange' as opposed to the 'New Romantic leader' we would almost certainly think of today. A review in the *Times* of the gig at Heaven at the end of December described Spandau as 'the house band of the Blitz kids' but did not mention New Romantics, although a review of the same gig by Robin Denselow in the *Guardian* referred to Spandau as 'the unofficial house band for the newest youth fad of bright young things, described as the New Romantics.' The *Economist* of 27 December 1980, echoing Robert Elms' earlier *Face* article, referred to 'Britain's latest social cult, known variously as the Blitz Kids, the New Romantics, the Now Crowd, or – confusingly – 'the cult with no name'. However, an interview by Betty Page with the Birmingham band Duran Duran in *Sounds* during December 1980 made many comparisons between Duran and Spandau but, ignoring the headline from her earlier interview with Spandau, Page did not mention New Romantics at all. Furthermore, when, for the December 1980 issue of *Ritz*, Nick Monson interviewed Steve Strange (who was wearing an outfit consisting of a cape of highland tartan, Lincoln green knickerbockers, page boy shoes and 'a look of blasé indifference that would have done credit to a Regency fop'), he described him as 'a peacock punk' not a new romantic.

So 'New Romantic' was just one of a number of terms being used at the end of 1980. It was certainly not yet the 'official', or commonly accepted, name of the movement. Blitz Kids was still preferred by many. In January 1981, the front cover of *Melody Maker* proclaimed: 'Spandau Ballet and the Blitz Kids'. An inside article also referred to the band as 'the so-called Blitz Kids.' However, tucked away in a paragraph towards the end of the article, it did also state: 'you don't necessarily need a private income to belong to the New Romantics', so the name was slowly gaining currency. Robin Denselow in the *Guardian* of 5 January 1981 referred to 'the first stirrings of what are now tagged the New Romantics or Blitz Kids' and Denselow was also the reporter for a BBC *Newsnight* feature about 'a new youth cult, the New Romantics or the Blitz Kids' broadcast on 23 January 1981: his commentary concluding, 'Behind the posing and the dressing up, the New Romantics are at the very least optimistic and creative and at least someone is trying to dispel all the gloom.'

Despite this, the *NME* in January 1981 (in an article about Duran Duran headlined 'Just Fine and Dandy') spoke of the 'New Narcissists High Fashion scene for which Spandau Ballet have set themselves up as musical spokesmen' and thus missed the chance to put the seal on the 'New Romantic' movement. 'New Narcissists' was, not surprisingly, rarely heard of again.

That there was no consensus about the name at this stage, despite having been mentioned on the BBC, is evidenced by the following comment in the 30 January 1981 issue of *Time Out* which said: 'The New Movement has no name, although 'New Romantics', 'New Dandies' and 'Futurists' are contenders', and the accompanying article by Ian Birch referred repeatedly to 'The Movement' or 'The New Movement' but not to New Romantics. When a reader of *Sounds* wrote to defend Spandau Ballet, Classix Nouveaux and Ultravox from 'selling out' in its 24 January 1981 issue, he called them 'the Blitz groups' *not* 'the New Romantic groups' as we certainly would today. His letter was headed 'Blitzkid bop'.

Interestingly, another reader of *Sounds* in the same issue was angry that one of his favourite bands, the little known (and perhaps even mythical) Avenue Foche, had been described as 'a

Blitz group'. He did not, he said, want them to be associated with 'empty headed clothes horses', as he called Visage and Spandau. His point was that Avenue Foche was a proper 'Futurist' group and had no connection with the 'half-baked 'High Tech' wet dream of Steve Strange and company' who, he said, were 'as Futurist as the Angelic Upstarts'. His letter ended 'Long Live Futurism!', thus showing that Futurism and New Romanticism were not regarded as synonymous by everyone. A third letter in the same issue of *Sounds* came from 'an ageing Liverpool born punk' who had obviously been following the recent linguistic developments quite carefully. In response to a previous reader, Jane Buchanan, who had written in to defend Steve Strange, while claiming at the same time not to be 'a Blitz Kid', this Liverpudlian wrote: 'of course she isn't, after all the vogue/fad/movement has gone through two more changes since then. Maybe not Blitz Kid, probably cult without a name or New Romantics.'

The *Guardian* of 2 February 1981 referred to the existence of a 'new romantic cult signalled by the success of Spandau Ballet' while *Sounds* of 7 February 1981 introduced a cheeky new variation on a familiar theme in a feature on Spandau's instruments which was headlined: 'Make Way For The New Technologists'. Interestingly, Spandau Ballet were described as being far from a bunch of 'hopeless romantics', thus echoing the Fingerprintz related headline from *Sounds* of August 1980 which preceded the more famous one in September. At the same time, various attempts continued to be made to define the movement. John Blake in the *Evening Standard* of 26 January 1981 chose to call it 'the curious posers cult' while his colleague, Andrew Hogg, said of Steve Strange on 19 February that, 'he leads The Cult with No Name, variously known as the Futurists, New Romantics or Blitz Kids'. However, the previous day, 18 February 1981, Thames TV had broadcast a programme called *Afternoon Plus* which, according to the *Times*, featured an item on 'the latest youthful phenomenon, the New Romantics', showing that the label had now definitely and firmly entered the mainstream.

Even so, in both the national and music press, it was still not universally adopted and was by no means the first choice label. When the *Sun* published a two page centrespread special on 'the fantastic fashion revolution sweeping the nation', on 10 February 1981, there was no mention whatsoever of 'new romantics', perhaps because its readers could not be expected to understand such a difficult concept. Instead, the newspaper referred to the 'new movement...of young Londoners switched to sophisticated fancy clothes' as 'Peacock Punks' and asked: 'What do Peacock Punks like? Where do they go?' Spandau Ballet and Visage (as well as Adam & The Ants) were referred to as 'Peacock rock bands'.

Likewise, Issue number 5 of *Flexipop*, which was published around this time, referred to 'the so-called Peacock Punk revolution gathering momentum all the time'. While the 'Peacock Punk' tag was reasonably descriptive of the new movement, whose devotees were, by and large, either former punks like Steve Strange, disillusioned by the aggression and violence or bored by the sameness of punk fashion, or those like Gary Kemp, who had been inspired by punk – and it is certainly true that many of them were 'peacocking' in their choice of clubbing outfits – the label never really took hold in the media or in the public imagination, probably because the word 'punk' had so many negative connotations by this time and was hardly appropriate as a description for the rather more restrained and dandified members of this post-punk movement. Furthermore, to the extent that the original punks could also be said to be 'peacocking', it was tautologous and failed to encapsulate the newness of the movement. Thus, while it had the advantage over other labels of being nicely alliterative, it was not the one that would last. The *Sun*'s main article, which was headlined 'PUTTING ON THE BLITZ!' despite the fact that nights at Blitz were by then long over for the fashionable crowd, did not refer to 'Blitz Kids' either but this label was used in a historical context within a side feature about Steve Strange which stated that, soon after Strange opened at Blitz, 'everyone was dropping in to check out the wild new styles of The Blitz Kids and the even wilder new bands they were listening to.'

Three days after the *Sun's* attempt at describing the movement, the *Daily Mail* had a go on 13 February 1981. Reflecting the uncertainty about what to call them, the *Mail* did not mention 'Peacock Punks' although 'young night-time peacocks' were referred to in a sub-heading. The authors of the *Mail* piece, Simon Kinnersley and Kathy Phillips, stated, somewhat perversely in view of recent usage, that 'The new trend has no name yet', adding: 'They have been called New Romantics, Blitz Kids, Futurists and New Dandies, but none of these descriptions gives a true insight to what it is really all about.' However, a sign of which of these descriptions was to stick in the future could be found in a sub-article below the main piece which stated that 'devotees of the new romantic look, boys and girls alike, flock there [to Vivienne Westwood's King's Road boutique] for baggy trousers, huge billowy shirts, giant sashes to be worn as belts, shawls, turbans – anyhow.'

It was next the turn of the *Times* to explain the new scene to its readers as its fashion editor, Suzy Menkes, having no problem with what to call the movement, said in an article entitled 'Post punk' on 24 February 1981 that, 'The New Romantic look' was 'jolly, extravagant…a lighthearted relief for the jeans-and-sweatshirt generation'. She described new romantics as 'putting on the fancy dress – brocade waistcoats, slashed sleeves, fancy hose and hats – mostly in the clubs of Covent Garden (and their equivalent in other urban centres).' According to Menkes, 'Because romance has a far wider appeal than punk (even in its most watered-down version) could ever have, it is going to be Big.' In *Sounds*, however, the same Betty Page whose September 1980 article had been headlined 'THE NEW ROMANTICS' now hedged her bets, referring to 'the mysteries and 'curious habits' of the 'Blitz Kids/New Romantics/Cult With No Name', whatever you fancy labelling it.'

When Page wrote a piece about The People's Palace Valentine's Ball at the Rainbow Theatre in Finsbury Park, hosted by Strange and Egan, in the 28 February 1981 edition of *Sounds* – an event, incidentally, which caused a noticeable, if brief, cooling of the previously close friendship between the members of Visage and Spandau Ballet after the latter made a late decision to pull out of a planned appearance at the ball, having decided that the Rainbow was not the type of venue with which it should be associated – the article was headlined 'Futurist flashback', although it did also refer to 'a celebration of New Romance' (and 'New Romantic' was used for one of the photo captions). James Hamilton in *Record Mirror* had already noted that the Rainbow bash had been described as 'the biggest New Romanticism event ever', commenting that 'New Romanticism is still sufficiently ill defined for its followers to be unsure of what it is that they ought to like', while Mike Nicholls, in the same publication, called the evening a 'St Valentine's Day Ball for the New Romantics' but also referred to it as 'reaffirming the cult of lots of identically-dressed individuals'.

In its 28 February 1981 issue, Record Mirror started to publish its own Futurist chart, with Spandau's 'The Freeze' at number one, but not without reservations. Commenting that he had been 'greatly excited by the New Romanticism vibe for some time', James Hamilton, the Disco section editor, noted that, 'The danger in listing stuff as being 'Futurist' is that an immediate pigeon hole is created for a type of music that record companies, never known for originality of thought, will immediately adopt as another formula to flood the market.' However, he believed that this 'new music', which he described as being 'a fusion of Wally Eurodisco with white rock', had 'far wider pop appeal for a cross section of Britain's indigenous population (plus it's such fun dressing up!)'. Speaking of New Romantics and Futurists as if they were two sides of the same coin, which indeed they were, Hamilton pointed out that 'many of the New Romantics were Soul Boys before, and certainly in London's leading Futurist venues a wide variety of musical styles are mixed up, unexpected contrast being an important ingredient.' For Hamilton, the music New Romantics danced to was not 'new romantic' as such but 'futurist'. He wasn't quite sure how it was best described though because a few weeks later he was referring to 'The Futurist / New Romanticism / Electronic / Hi-Tech / Bright Young Thing scene'.

Yet, despite the variety of alternative names still being used in this period, it was clear that 'New Romantic' was fast emerging as the leading descriptor for the new movement, a fact which was not missed by Robert Elms, who complained at some length in his column in the London weekly music magazine *Trax* of 18 February 1981 about the 'crass' and 'shoddy' handle of 'New Romantics' being widely used by the media. It was in this context that he claimed that 'one of us' may have created the term 'New Romantics' but that it had been wrongly used by the media long after its time had passed so that 'now we are left with an appalling and pointless moniker that can only lead to a new tribalism.' His diatribe did not impress one reader of the magazine, rocker Dave Hardy from Thornton Heath, who wrote, in a letter to the editor, that Elms, 'whines about being labelled a New Romantic, but like all the rest, just wants to be noticed – by anyone and everyone.'

Elms' public hostility towards the 'New Romantics' label did not deter journalists from using it, at least not all of them. In the *Daily Express* of 19 February 1981, Anne Nightingale, writing about Steve Strange, said that, 'His gang are called New Romantics', while a feature on youth culture in the *Daily Mirror* of 24 March 1981 said, 'today we have the new Romantics, the new Eccentrics with their wild fancy dress' who 'just want to look amazing for when the bomb drops.'

Yet *The Face* magazine, writing about Spandau and others in its March 1981 issue, did not mention 'New Romantics' at all (no doubt because Nick Logan simply did not like the term) but referred to 'The Movement' and also to 'The New Electronics'. Indeed, the headline on the front cover read: 'SPANDAU BALLET AND THE NEW ELECTRONICS'. In its review of *Journeys To Glory*, *The Face* asked, 'how do you describe 'To Cut A Long Story Short' or 'The Freeze'? The New Dance Music perhaps....'. Equally, when *Sounds* of 21 March 1981 published an embarrassing set of photographs of Tony Hadley, extracted from the photo-love story in the April 1978 edition of *My Guy*, he was referred to by *Sounds* as having been 'a budding Cultist With No Name' at the time of the photo shoot, not 'a budding New Romantic', which they would surely have said if they were writing about it today.

A good example of how, as late as March 1981, 'new romantic' was by no means the only expression used to describe the new fashion and clubbing movement can be found in an article by Steve Taylor about Birmingham's Rum Rummer club which appeared in the *Observer* magazine of 15 March 1981. Taylor spoke in the club to a clothes designer called 'Melvin' and wrote:

> Like most of his fellow revellers, Melvin is reluctant to put a name to the movement; he simply says it's 'modern, different, weird'. Outsiders, usually taking a stance of stiff-upper lipped suspicion, have tried to foist titles on the clubgoers: the New Romantics, the Glitterati, Futurists, Poseurs, The Cult With No Name, the Blitz kids (after the best-known London venue for such goings-on).

Taylor followed this list of titles by saying confidently, if questionably, 'None has stuck.'

At the same time, the main section of the *Observer* of 15 March 1981 carried an article entitled 'Enter the Electronic Futurists' which stated (in parentheses) that Futurists were 'also characterized as 'New Romantics'', while *Smash Hits* of 19 March 1981 referred to 'bands currently wearing the Futurist/New Romantic tag.'

It may also be noted that the 7 March 1981 issue of *Look-In* (described as 'the junior TV Times'), not known for being at the cutting edge of music and fashion, referred to the nicknames, 'the Blitz Kids...or the New Romantics' in an article about Spandau Ballet, so there is no question that New Romanticism was a very well-known concept by this time. Indeed, it had come so far into the mainstream that the women's magazine *Weekend* of 17 March 1981 contained a two page photospread under the headline 'STEVE'S STRANGE ROMANTIC FOLLOWING' with the accompanying text referring to 'the New Romantics, who think that Punk has passed its prime and the New Wave is a washout', also noting that, 'the only way to be accepted as a New Romantic is to dress in clothes that most people wouldn't be seen dead in.'

Another sign of how the concept had fully entered the mainstream by March 1981 is that it was being discussed in the regional press. The *Bath Weekly Advertiser* of 19 March 1981, for example, carried an article by the Women's editor, Margaret Chesworth, entitled simply 'The New Romantics'. According to Ms Chesworth:

> Every so often fashion throws up a revolution...not just a few new styles but a whole new look. It looks as though we are on the brink of one right now. It's the romantic look and it will hit the shops in the autumn. It's almost theatrical – perhaps because we've had such an austerity winter, culminating in the Budget, and fancy dressing often seems to go hand in hand with hard times. Escapism no doubt. The new look is a kind of Annie Get Your Gun or Brigitte Bardot playing-a-Western scene – high-necked romantic shirts, frilly skirts and, maybe, a bandolier or neat boots to go with it. In London girls are already collecting this gear.

Such things were no doubt being said in local newspapers all around the country.

By the end of March 1981, the New Romantic label was sufficiently established for *Melody Maker* to use the term as a headline in a story relating to a non-new romantic band. Thus, a short piece about Public Image Limited's forthcoming album, 'The Flowers of Romance', was punningly headlined 'PiL – the new romantics', a rather ironic development considering that it is exceedingly rare to find the term 'new romantics' in a headline during 1980-81 but when we do find one it is in respect of a band which was not new romantic!

Even children were affected. Karen Ashton, a fourteen-year-old reader of the *Daily Mail,* living in Wigan, whose musical tastes had obviously developed very early in her life, had a letter published in the 'Junior Letters' section of the newspaper on 28 March 1981 complaining that she had formerly been labelled 'a mod' then 'a punk' due to the type of music she had liked and: 'Now when I buy records by Spandau Ballet, Ultravox, John Foxx and Gary Numan, I have acquired a new title. To my horror I am now considered a new romantic.' She rounded off her letter with a plea to the world: 'Can I not dress as I please, dance how I please and listen to what I please without having to join a tribe?'

The term was also sufficiently entrenched by this time for a reader of the *NME* of 28 March 1981 to write in to 'be the first to start a new romantic backlash!', explaining that: 'The music is not new! The gear and make-up is not such a wild romantic concept. Visage, Spandau and Duran Duran are all good but they're getting money for old rope'. The same issue of the *NME* carried a letter from the film director François Truffaut – goodness knows why *he* decided to get involved – in which he commented that it seemed to him that 'there is some sort of rift in the ranks of the so-called New Romantics', elaborating that, while 'the movement's primary spokesmen' (i.e. Spandau Ballet, Steve Strange, Rusty Egan) claimed not to want publicity, they were forever giving interviews and being photographed (a charge angrily denied by Rusty Egan in a later issue). Whether these claims were right or wrong, it is clear that the concept of new romanticism was now very familiar with the general public and was adopted by most journalists. Even Robert Elms, who affected to despise the label, described a Spandau fan who spoke to him at the Sundown Club in March 1981 as a 'new romantic looking chappy', in his weekly column in the 1 April 1981 issue of *Trax*.

Nevertheless, a joint feature on Duran Duran and Classix Nouveaux in *Melody Maker* of 4 April 1981, headlined 'Stepping out in the futurist disco', somehow managed to make absolutely no mention of 'New Romantics' at all and, in that feature, the members of Classix discussed not whether they were New Romantics or not but whether they were 'a Blitz group' or not. Furthermore, as late as May 1981, Andrew Hogg in the *Evening Standard* could write: 'The latest fad call it what you will Futurism, Blitz Kids or simply the cult with no name', showing that 'New Romantics' was not always even on the list.

By contrast, the *Daily Express* of 3 April 1981, when mentioning a new boutique opening in the King's Road called Minirock, said that, 'New Romantics devotees will find lots of lacey blouses', while an article about Landscape in the *NME* of 4 April 1981 said that Richard James Burgess had name-checks and production credits on 'all manner of New Romantic product' and spoke of 'the Futurist/New Romantic scene'. An article in the *Los Angeles Times* of 5 April 1981 by the English journalist Michael Watts spoke of 'a colorful new rock movement...dubbed the Pose, the New Dandies, the Futurists, the Modernes, the New Narcissists or even – by one of its archly named apostles, 21 year-old Steve Strange – the Cult With No Name' but added that 'the New Romantics is the most common description'. In *Record Mirror* of 11 April 1981, fashion designer Willie Brown of the Modern Classics label was quoted referring to 'the new romantics or whatever you want to call them', another article on Landscape in *Record Mirror* of 18 April 1981 referred to that band as being 'at the forefront of the electro-funk movement, the futurists, the new romantics, the cult with no name or whatever handle the market can accommodate', while Anne Nightingale in the *Daily Express* of 28 April 1981 spoke of the 'pretty packaging of the New Romantics'.

A visit of Spandau Ballet to New York, accompanied by a small army of fashion designers, helped to deliver the concept of New Romanticism to Americans in May 1981. The monthly music paper *NY Rocker* promised 'NEW ROMANTICS' on the front cover of its May 1981 edition although, in case its readership did not know what they were, also called them 'PEACOCK PUNKS' which was, perhaps, easier to understand. In the paper itself, neither the term 'New Romantics' nor 'Peacock Punks' was actually used and the journalist who wrote a feature on Visage and Spandau fell back on 'the cult with no name', describing the 'new generation of London boys' as 'dressy kids'. Back in the UK, the use of the New Romantic label was growing almost by the day. A feature in *Record Mirror* in May 1981 about Spandau's Stateside visit carried a fused headline of 'New York' and 'New Romantic', while a report on the same visit in *Melody Maker* of 16 May 1981 referred to 'the current new romanticism craze in England'. An article in *The Face* of the same month about how Rusty Egan was going to tour the provinces was entitled 'New Romantic goes to the country', showing that even Nick Logan had succumbed.

Expanding out from the music press, a feature by Sue Heal in *Woman's Own* of 9 May 1981 headlined 'After Punk – the New Romantics?' said that 'these Beau Brummels of the recession' were 'known variously as the Blitz Kids, New Romantics or just simply the Movement'. It used all three descriptors in the article, stating that 'The Movement is making ripples in the fashion world', that, 'Dressing up, to the Blitz Kids, means transformation' and that, 'The New Romantics choose a theme from Hollywood, fiction or history and then kit themselves up to the hilt for a midweek rave-up at one of their élitist clubs.'

From the spring of 1981 onwards, the term 'New Romantics' really started to take hold in the wider British media. This may be attributed to three factors. Firstly, the engagement of Prince Charles to Lady Diana Spencer, announced on 24 February 1981, not only put romance at the top of the agenda (an article in the *Evening Standard* on 21 March 1981 about the wedding, for example, was headlined 'A Return to Romance') but also focused international attention on British culture. Designer Annette Worsley-Taylor was quoted in the *Standard* on 30 March 1981 as saying, 'the royal wedding has generated enormous interest in our grand occasion clothes. Visitors to London want to see the New Romantics on the streets'. Thus, from being a virtual secret cult, the New Romantics were now an international tourist attraction! Worsley-Taylor described 'New Romance' as meaning 'certain fabrics, tweeds, cords, suede and leather, taffeta and brocade or it means softer skirts or trousers tucked inside cuffed boots, knickerbockers and coulottes.' The *Evening Standard* journalist, Liz Smith, concluded by saying, 'The New Romantic look is extremely British.'

Lesley Ebbetts, in the *Daily Mirror* of 4 March 1981, also linked the New Romantics and Lady Diana Spencer, asking, 'What have

Lady Diana, the new romantics and the Paris designers in common?' – the answer, apparently, being 'a little bit of lace'. As Ebbetts explained, 'The fancy dressed teenage followers of Adam Ant, Spandau Ballet and Visage wear lace as muffles, ruffles and jabots', while Lady Diana, she said, favoured ruffled lace blouses.

In a similar vein, *Vogue* magazine's May 1981 issue featured a photo shoot entitled 'Escape to the sun – The New Romantics...', with glossy images of beautiful English models in exotic locations wearing bloomers and breeches, lace smocks, skirts and blooms. The same edition of *Vogue* also carried a piece headlined 'THE MODERN ROMANTICS', describing the new fashion which had started at PX in Endell Street and which had blossomed into the mainstream, 'with full-blown bloomers, breeches, billowing shirts and lace...Embroidered blouses, chemises, camisoles...petticoats and scarves of pure lace knotted like whimsies round heads and necks.' The magazine made the point that, with the economy still in recession, 'in these doom and gloom times, when being sensible is the rule for survival, fantasy in dress provides escapism.'

Of course, this is a very fashion-based definition of New Romanticism but the term was also applied on a musical level. By the spring of 1981, not only had a second Blitz band (Visage) charted but Duran Duran, whose first single, 'Planet Earth', was released on 2 February 1981, had entered the spotlight with a bang. Coming from Birmingham, and not being part of the London scene, 'Blitz Kids' or 'Blitz group' was totally inappropriate for them and they were soon labelled 'New Romantics'.

In fact, Duran had been quick to latch onto the term themselves. They had read 'THE NEW ROMANTICS' headlined article in *Sounds* written by Betty Page in September 1980 and this had directly led them to amend the lyrics to 'Planet Earth' to include a line about New Romantics looking for the TV sound. As Simon Le Bon recalled in a 1993 online interview on www.poptrash.be (in which he confused *Sounds* with the *NME*): 'Spandau Ballet were really the band to first have the name 'New Romantics' applied to them. I can remember an article in I think it was the NME and they were standing there in these great clothes, really great clothes and the words "New Romantics" were there in the article and I pinched them and I put them in Planet Earth.' This move obviously helped to popularize the term and, according to none other than Betty Page: 'I think that's what really made it become something to be honest. If they hadn't done it, I don't know if it would ever have caught on so much. So I think them doing that kind of immortalized it really.'

In a review of 'Planet Earth' in February 1981, David Hepworth of *Smash Hits* called Duran 'New Age Romantics' (which is a novel twist but close enough) while an *NME* journalist, reviewing one of their gigs in March 1981, said that, 'Between sets the New Romantics writhe to a real futurist and new funk soundtrack', although he also spoke of 'the Futurist way forward' and said 'The Movement is a foppish uniform worn over an empty heart', thus showing that the old terms had still not died out completely and were being applied to Duran.

With both Spandau and Duran (and others) in the charts, it appeared that a new musical movement had indeed been born. The *Daily Mirror* of 16 May 1981 called Spandau, 'one of the leaders of the new romantics movement' while Alan Coulthard, reviewing 'Girls On Film' in *Record Mirror* of 18 July 1981, predicted that, 'along with the current Spandau classic ['Chant No. 1']' Duran's new single, 'should go a long way towards giving the 'New Romantic' scene a wider acceptance.' In an article in an American magazine called *Creem*, dated August 1981, Spandau Ballet were described as 'the spearhead for England's New Romantic movement' so the name was clearly very much in vogue by then, even across the Atlantic.

It was perfect in a way. It included the word 'new' – a common feature of many of the descriptions applied to the music and dress sense of the scene to show that it was something different to what had gone before, i.e. New Movement, New Electronics, New Dance Music, New Dandies, New Pop, New Mods, New Glitterati etc. – plus the word 'romantic', variations of which had been used by both Gary and Tony in April-May 1980 and which, mainly because of their 'romantic' image and outlandish fashion sense, was frequently used to describe people like Steve Strange and the Blitz Kids generally. As Sarah Gilmour, author of *20th Century Fashion of the 70s: Punks, Glamour Rockers and New Romantics*, puts it in her book: 'The 'romance' was in frilled shirts, bows, floppy haircuts and velvet knickerbockers. The 'new', futuristic element combined Bowie's Ziggy Stardust era with the military styling of Roxy Music's ultra-cool front man Brian Ferry.' So the name was descriptive and it was appropriate, even if it didn't seem on the face of it to make much sense. While some journalists did like to refer to the romantic nature of their music, early Spandau and Duran songs such as 'Muscle Bound' and 'Planet Earth' were not, in fact, particularly romantic. Indeed, Stephen Holden of the *New York Times*, when reviewing a Duran gig in September 1981, commented: 'It was hard to tell what was either New or Romantic about it.'

Certainly, Betty Page, the journalist responsible (with Alan Lewis) for the first ever 'New Romantics' headline – and thus the best person to ask – did not regard romantic music as a key feature of new romanticism. According to Betty, speaking to the author in 2014:

> To me it [New Romantics] always meant this kind of – there was obviously this allusion to the Romantic poets, Byron, Shelley and all that, but to me it was about this permission to express yourself in a way you looked, mostly; it was about a particular style of dressing quite flamboyantly; it was about creating your own style, your own image; it was about a blast of colour at a time when it was pretty grim in the late seventies, early eighties, there was a lot of unemployment, most of the clubs in London were just sort of relics from the 60s, you had all these kids coming along who were really creative. So I think the romantic element was more – was partly the style of it but also the creativity.

At the same time, it is interesting that Betty Page's mention of the approach of a new age of romanticism in her review of 'Bullet Proof Heart', in the 9 August 1980 issue of *Sounds*, was very much a musical reference in that her new age of romanticism (per Andy Partridge) involved songs with soft guitars and melancholic vocals, in contrast to the loud guitars and energetic vocals of punk and rock. While soft guitars and melancholic vocals were not a defining feature of New Romantic music, it is still true that the music of the New Romantics was very different to rock and punk music and certainly less guitar oriented, albeit that guitars still certainly featured.

The third factor which caused the 'New Romantics' label to take hold was simply the increased interest by television in the world of the Blitz, or more strictly the post-Blitz world, because there were no longer any Tuesday club nights hosted by Steve Strange and Rusty Egan at that venue after October 1980. Both *Newsnight* and *Nationwide* broadcast reports on the 'Blitz Kids' in the first few months of 1981 but, although they used that term to describe the participants, they actually filmed at two West End clubs, Le Kilt (*Newsnight*) and Le Beat Route (*Nationwide*), where Tuesday and Friday nights respectively had been taken over by Chris Sullivan (Le Kilt) and Ollie O'Donnell (Beat Route), both of whom were operating a Blitz type entrance policy, where only the 'outrageously dressed' were supposedly allowed in, although the music was now more uptempo dance and soul music as opposed to the rather stilted electronica which had been prominent in 1979. With so many of these new clubs now springing up, not just in London but throughout the country, the term 'Blitz Kids' was terribly dated, not to mention locationally inaccurate, and 'New Romantics' was much more appropriate.

Interestingly, although 'New Romantic' became the primary term to describe the new movement, the use of the description 'Futurists' never quite died and certainly, throughout the rest of 1981, 'Futurist' was used as an alternative description to 'New Romantic'. This prompted Gary Kemp to say in 1981: 'I don't think we're futurists – I mean, we don't sing about robots or anything do we?' By contrast, with so many available labels to use, the notion of a 'cult with no name' did die very quickly but its memory was kept alive during the summer of 1981 with the publication of *The Book With No Name*, advertised in *Smash Hits* of 23 July 1981 as 'The first book of The New Romantics'.

Ironically, the end of the New Romantic ride for Spandau Ballet could be said to have come at the very same time that the label started to become popular. The 'new romantic looking chappy' who spoke to Robert Elms at the Sundown Club in March 1981 said to him of Spandau's performance: 'They've changed, they've gone funky, it's supposed to be about the electronic music isn't it?' Elms' dismissive response in his *Trax* column of 1 April 1981 was: 'Poor boy, he obviously hasn't heard that straight electronics is about as trendy as a pair of platform boots, while funk is rapidly achieving the status of a new stylistic religion.' For Elms, Spandau Ballet had already moved on from being New Romantics, in both the music and fashion senses of the term, and, by describing the out-of-date fan as a 'new romantic looking chappy', Elms was putting distance between the band (and himself) and those who looked back to the fashion and music scene of Blitz.

Certainly, as Spandau ditched the synthesizer for 'Chant No 1', put on homely jumpers for 'Instinction', and then started to dress up in smart suits to promote 'True', it wasn't clear to anyone that they *were* New Romantics any more, considering that the whole point of New Romanticism was to play electronic music and dress outrageously (although, ironically, the songs could be said to have become more romantic in nature). In May 1983, at the height of the suited 'True' look, one reader of *Record Mirror* wrote in to complain that her mum liked Spandau Ballet and asked: 'what has happened to their shocking New Romantic image when mother used to scream in disgust whenever they came on TV...[?]' When, a couple of weeks later, another reader wrote to the same magazine to ask, 'how true are SB to their so-called New Romantic music?', the editorial response was: 'We all thought New Romantics went out with

Martin Kemp's last frilly shirt.' So the label didn't last long and it is much rarer to find descriptions of Spandau as New Romantics as the decade moves on.

Exactly the same is true of Duran Duran. Their early look was quintessentially New Romantic, with lots of frilly shirts and colourful outfits. Simon Le Bon was quoted in a 1984 book about the band by William Simmers as saying: 'We jumped on the bandwagon. We got our feet in the door as quickly as we were able'. However, he continued: 'But after a month or two we had to abandon that image because the frilly shirts looked stupid.' Ultimately no band likes to be pigeon-holed and Duran were no exception. They were, of course, aware that fashion changes very quickly and if you are a band closely associated with one sort of fashion you will be out of date in a heartbeat. As early as March 1981, Duran were already attempting to distance themselves from the New Romantic tag with Simon Le Bon quoted in *New Sounds, New Styles* as saying: 'I wouldn't necessarily include Duran Duran in the new romantics scene.' In the June 1981 issue of *Zigzag*, Andy Taylor stated that, 'The 'Futurist-New Romantic' thing doesn't really mean anything' and Nick Rhodes added: 'We don't like being labelled...we think it's unpleasant.' He also told Paul Morley of the *NME* for its 25 July 1981 issue, 'We were surprised to be tagged new romantic or futurist because we are not like that at all.' Similarly, in August 1981, Simon Le Bon was quoted in the *Daily Mirror* as saying: 'We don't intend to fade away when the fashion is finished. In fact, the new romantic thing is already dead as far as we're concerned.' To *Record Mirror* of 15 August 1981, Nick Rhodes complained about being portrayed as 'new romantic nancies' and said, 'I think we've shaken off that new romantic tag now'.

Furthermore, the New Romantic label was not very helpful to Duran's ambitions to break the United States. Thus, an Associated Press article from Los Angeles, headlined by Virginia's *Free Lance-Star* of 24 October 1981 as 'Duran Duran says it's not a New Romantic Band', stated: 'The first thing the guys in Duran Duran want to make perfectly clear is that, appearances to the contrary, they are not – repeat not – just another of the New Romantic bands currently making such a splash in London.' Back in London the following year, Betty Page, carefully avoiding the actual phrase, 'new romantic', noted astutely in *Sounds* of 29 May 1982 that Duran 'used the entire futuro-romantic kaboodle like any astute business mind would, skimming the surface but never diving in. Clever clever boys.' As John Taylor told *Smash Hits* from the States in its 19 August 1982 issue, 'The biggest thing we have to prove is that we're in a niche of our own and that we're not part of a pool of bands called 'New Romantics'', adding: 'There is a big reaction here against the English 'New Romantics' and that, unfortunately, is holding us up.' So Duran did not remain New Romantic for long either. Very soon they were simply another pop band of the era although, as with Spandau Ballet, the New Romantic tag was never entirely discarded or, rather, could never be fully shaken off.

We can actually identify the very end of the New Romantic period with some precision as being in August 1982. For in its 7 August 1982 edition, *Record Mirror*, with tongue firmly in cheek, referred to a 'sinister youth cult' involving 'the latest trend to grip the nation' and identified a number of artists, including Pale Fountains, Aztec Camera, Everything But The Girl and Carmel, as being 'The new New Romantics' who used the 'language of swing and showbiz romanticism'. With the appearance of the new New Romantics, then clearly, by this date, the original New Romantics were already history!

At this point, it might be worth considering who the original New Romantic bands actually were because identifying them is a far from easy task. It was, of course, Spandau Ballet the band, and the band alone, who were originally called 'The New Romantics' by Alan Lewis and Betty Page in *Sounds* in September 1980 but, as we have seen, the definition soon widened to incorporate not only the whole movement of 'Blitz Kids' but a number of other bands, not necessarily those with any connection to the Blitz club or even to London.

If we were to list the archetypal New Romantic bands there would probably be only three: Spandau, Visage and Duran. The essence of these bands is that they had both the look (i.e. the flamboyant clothes) and the sound (i.e. synthesizer based, futurist style, electronic dance music). Just having the look did not necessarily make a band a new romantic band.

Adam & The Ants, for example, in their swashbuckling and eye-grabbing piratical, or 'dandy highwaymen', costumes could be said to have had the look (they were certainly described as a new romantic band by the tabloids in the early 1980s) and, indeed, they were wearing kilts long before Spandau Ballet (hence Adam's inclusion in the *NME's* Tartan Chic feature of April 1979). Robert Elms also recalls in his autobiography that Stuart Goddard (a.k.a. Adam Ant) was a visitor to, and was influenced by, Blitz, although Goddard does not mention this himself in his own autobiography; on the contrary, in his book, *Stand and Deliver,* he says that (circa April 1980) he was convinced that his then girlfriend, Amanda Donahoe, wanted to be part of the new Blitz/New Romantic scene but he, himself, did not want anything to do with it. However, despite clearly having the look, Adam & The Ants did not have the sound; none of their records from the early 1980s featured any reliance on synthesizers and were instead based around heavy tribal drumming. Largely for that reason, they are not generally regarded today as a New Romantic band. Goddard certainly does not regard himself as such. 'I'm a punk rocker, I always was,' he told Steve Price for thequietus.com in April 2010, 'I'm not a New Romantic.'

Like Adam & The Ants, Culture Club too might have had the look – and there is no doubt that Boy George was one of the founders of the New Romantic movement and a Billy's original to boot – but their sound was rather more like pure pop, or perhaps reggae pop, not electronic dance. Conversely, any of the bands, like Kraftwerk, whose music was played at Blitz had the sound but they could not properly be described as New Romantic bands because they did not have the look.

A large number of bands that followed Spandau into the charts in the Eighties have been labelled as New Romantic. Thus, *Record*

Collector's 'New Romantic' special edition from June 2004 listed the following: A Flock of Seagulls, Blancmange, Classix Nouveaux, Culture Club, Depeche Mode, Duran Duran, Human League, Spandau Ballet, Ultravox and Visage as the ten key New Romantic bands, although some of those are questionable and, in respect of Culture Club, the magazine itself admitted that their 'membership of the NR circle is debatable'. However, *Record Collector* expressly excluded Adam & The Ants ('too punk to be New Romantic'), Talk Talk ('too interested in jazz'), Soft Cell ('too outlandish even for the fops'), Tears for Fears ('too mundane') and Japan ('too glam rock'). Another band often described as New Romantic, Kajagoogoo, were also excluded on their own admission: 'The New Romantic label didn't appeal to us, we wanted to have our own label.'

Of the bands other than Spandau, Visage and Duran, the best claim for membership of the New Romantic circle is by Classix Nouveaux who, as we have seen, were formed before Spandau in August 1979 and who had a futurist type single entitled 'The Robots Dance' released in August 1980 when *Sounds* described them as looking like 'right Blitz silly buggers' on the record sleeve. *Smash Hits* of 27 November 1980 referred to their 'glam Blitz-type image' and 'ropey futurist/Space Age lyrics' and the same publication noted in April 1981 that the band felt that 'Futurist/New Romantic' groups such as Spandau Ballet were 'only just catching up' with what they had been doing since August 1979, saying that 'there are certainly links' between Classix and the New Romantic bands such as, 'looks, white disco rhythms, a strong awareness of Europe and an interest in sci-fi.' According to Simon Tebbutt in *Record Mirror* of 29 August 1981 they were 'the oldest New Romantics' and were 'firmly labelled part of the New Romantic/Futurist movement. Their style and their sound place them alongside the likes of Visage, Spandau Ballet, Duran Duran, Ultravox and sometimes Landscape in the eyes and ears of the public.' So they had both the sound and the look and it is only their failure to make any real impression on the charts which probably counts against them when we consider who the key New Romantic bands were.

Lack of chart success, other than 'Einstein A Go Go', also counts against Landscape when we consider the key New Romantic groups of the era. Band member Richard James Burgess, who was, of course, the producer of Spandau Ballet's first album, was a Blitz regular and, as previously mentioned, *Record Mirror* of 18 April 1981 claimed that 'Landscape did in fact make the first electro-disco 12 incher specifically for Blitz kids called 'European man' and appeared to be a clear year ahead of the market.' Originally a jazz-funk band in 1979, Landscape quickly embraced the possibilities of electronics and computers, producing more experimental records than other groups. However, they did not have a particularly strong visual image and would not normally be categorized as one of the pioneering New Romantic bands.

The far more successful Ultravox (sometimes 'Ultravox!' – with exclamation mark) also have a claim to being classed as a key New Romantic group especially as (1) Blitz regular Midge Ure was part of Visage along with Billy Currie, (2) their early tracks were played at Blitz and (3) the band, described by *Record Mirror* in June 1981 as being 'the founding fathers of futurism', made heavy use of 'futuristic' synthesizer sound. At the same time, John Foxx, who was replaced as lead singer by Midge Ure in 1979, has denied that they were, in fact, a New Romantic band. 'We were never part of any particular movement' he told *Record Collector* in 2004 and, in truth, although some of its individual members had certainly dressed in true PX style in the past, they never quite had the New Romantic look as a group. Midge Ure points out in his autobiography that Ultravox never wore frilly shirts and headbands and he expressly denies that the band were New Romantics. This reflects what he believed in October 1981 when he told *NME* journalist Chris Bohn, 'We're no more new romantic than you are', explaining that he and his fellow band members only went to Blitz because 'we liked the music [and] there were always nice birds down there'. Furthermore, in May 1982, he was quoted in a publication called *Peacock Rock* as saying, 'We hate being lumped in with all this 'New Romantic' crap.' So, on their own statements, we can safely rule Ultravox out as being one of the key New Romantic bands.

One final group we should consider is Modern Romance, whose name is, of course, synonymous with 'New Romance', and 'New Romance' is but a syllable away from 'New Romantics'. Indeed, when we consider that Modern Romance was formed by two Blitz attendees, Geoff Deane and David James, in the summer of 1980, well before 'The New Romantics' headline in *Sounds* of 13 September 1980, we might wonder if the origins of New Romanticism are to be found here. In fact, the apparent similarity between 'Modern Romance' and 'New Romantics' is a coincidence; the name 'Modern Romance' came from the band's first single, appropriately titled, 'Modern Romance' which was released on 12 September 1980. From an examination of the lyrics of that song, it is evident that 'modern romance' is used in its literal sense to mean 'a contemporary love affair' and has nothing to do with the then so-called cult with no name. Modern Romance's early music, incidentally, was not futuristic, although they did use synthesizers. In *Smash Hits* of 26 November 1981, Geoff Deane revealed that the original plan was for the band to move towards a more futurist, 'white European dance', sound but: 'When Spandau broke, I was choked. On paper it was virtually exactly the sort of thing we had been talking about. Dance music made by, if you like, white boys in nicer venues. I thought, we've been beaten to it. And we were quite rightly because they were a lot better than the Modern Romance of the time.'

But were *Spandau Ballet* themselves ever actually New Romantics? Not according to Tony Hadley. In an interview published in the April 1981 issue of *International Musician and Recording World*, he said:

> As far as we are concerned, too many people have tried to label us 'Futurist', 'New Romantics', 'Cult with No Name' and electronic music etc. As far as we are concerned we've got nothing to do

with that...But this 'New Romantics' and 'Futurist' garbage, as far as I'm concerned, I can't see how we can be labelled...I don't want to be like a movement, I just want to be Spandau Ballet.

He repeated this viewpoint when speaking to *Radio Times*' John Craven in 1982. 'I wouldn't say we were new romantics,' he said, adding, 'Who needs a label anyway?' Tony was certainly reflecting the views of the rest of the band at the time, none of whom promoted the New Romantic label, regarding it correctly and suspiciously as a media invention, and they were worried it would put the band into a bracket or category from which they would never be able to escape. In *Sounds* of 28 February 1981, Betty Page noted that, 'Spandau have recently condemned the tag 'New Romantics' as a label that misses the point'. On a Spanish television programme in July 1981, Tony said, 'It's become very easy for the press, basically, to kind of use this to kind of like, to put us in a cubby hole', and Gary stated firmly during the same interview, 'We never call ourselves new romantics.' Indeed, it is certainly the case that none of the band members referred to themselves as new romantics in any interviews they gave during the key 1980-81 period. When asked if they had thought of themselves as new romantics, during an interview on British Forces Broadcasting Services in July 1984, Steve Norman said, 'At the time, not at all, we hated it.' Robert Elms has revealed that Gary Kemp once said to him, 'I for one am certainly not new romantic', and Gary was quoted by Elms in February 1981 as saying of the name, 'it simply serves to place limitations on a very creative group of people. Who the hell are they talking about anyway? I don't know anybody who would consider themselves a new romantic.'

More than this, the band actively took steps to prevent the media using the new romantic label. Robert Elms, in his weekly column in *Trax*, commenting on a proposed BBC *Nationwide* feature to be called 'New Romantics' Blitz Kids', said in February 1981 that 'Gary Kemp, Steve Dagger and yours truly tried to put them straight – drop the label and see the light – odds on they still won't get it right.' When interviewed for the programme, Gary said, 'It's best not to have a label really, I mean the danger of having a label obviously is that you're trapping yourself immediately, you know, immediately putting up barriers', and he expressly repudiated the 'New Romantics' tag claiming that it was 'insipid' and 'conjures up Clark Gable and *The Sound of Music* and things like that.' During the same interview, Tony called it a 'cheap label'.

The feature was broadcast on 16 March 1981 and, against Elms' odds, *Nationwide* was strictly on-message, expressly making the point in the report's introduction, clearly at the behest of the Dagger/Elms/Kemp triumvirate, that Spandau Ballet played 'a new type of electronic rock music which hopes to defy being labelled by constantly reinventing its style and usual appearance.' Contrary to Elms' gloomy prediction, the New Romantics label did not feature prominently in the BBC's report. Indeed, it was only mentioned once by reporter Pattie Caldwell and that was in the context of it *not* being the right label, as she said, 'They've been called decadent and elitist, the New Romantics, the Blitz kids, the Futurists – every time they get a new label they simply change their clothes, always keeping one step ahead of the media.'

It was the kind of positive angle to have the Spandau boys purring and, indeed, the inability of the media to label the movement was the central theme of the report, rounded off by Steve Strange saying: 'Change is our style, change and progression, and all the bands like Visage and Ballet are going to move on, that's why the paper can call it what they like, they can call it Blitz Kids, New Romantics, I'd rather call it Cult With No Name because they can never put one finger on it, because every time they come back the whole thing has changed.' This, in a nutshell, was what Dagger wanted the world to believe.

As the band did not like the name and never promoted it at the time, and as the period of New Romanticism was so brief, being over almost as soon as it began, it could be said that, in many respects, Spandau Ballet were the New Romantics Who Never Were.

CHAPTER NINE

Golden Years

ALTHOUGH THE RIVALRY BETWEEN and Duran Duran was very much of the friendly variety they *were* nevertheless rivals who appealed to a similar market. It began as early as November 1980 when the now signed and charting Spandau performed at the Botanical Gardens in Birmingham but declined to allow a then little known local band, Duran Duran, to support them. During an interview with Steve Sutherland in *Melody Maker* of 4 April 1981, John Taylor was quoted as saying that Duran liked Spandau and that: 'They're better than 99 per cent of bands around at the moment but they're nothing to do with us really. I mean, we've never even met. Well you've met one haven't you.' At this point, Steve Sutherland noted, 'Simon grunts in the affirmative'. This would appear to be corroboration of the following remarkable story told by Gary Kemp during a Radio 2 interview in 2001 which one would otherwise naturally assume to be apocryphal:

> We went to Birmingham. Of course we don't play a normal rock gig, we play the Botanical Gardens. We get a band asking us if they can support us and we say "no we never have support". We all got to sleep on this guy's floor that night. A whole load of us. And I remember sitting next to this other guy who said, "We wanted to support you tonight but you didn't want us to but the show was great, we really enjoyed it". And he was the lead singer with a band called Duran Duran!

Simon Le Bon's grunted acknowledgement that he had met one of the members of Spandau does seem to tally very nicely with Gary's story. Having said this, there is a counter version put forward by Andy Taylor who says in his autobiography that Duran invited Spandau to the Rum Runner after the Botanical Gardens gig where they were delighted to discover that Simon Le Bon was taller than Tony Hadley. Well now, considering that Tony Hadley is a giant of a man at six foot four inches whereas Simon Le Bon's height is normally recorded as six foot two inches, there is some reason to doubt the accuracy of this story.

In terms of establishing whether a band was successful or not in the 1980s, one really does need to focus on chart positions, however geeky or nerdy this might appear. Chart position was how artists judged themselves and were judged by others. A number one single in the Eighties (as in previous decades) was the ultimate indication of success and was much harder to obtain than it is in today's, internet streaming, file sharing, times which have seen greatly reduced sales of singles. A top number one single in the Eighties could sell a million units which would entitle it to a platinum disc, although a gold disc, awarded for half a million sales, was also desirable. For albums in the 1980s, 300,000 units would earn a platinum disc, which was rather easier to obtain.

The top ten single, 'To Cut A Long Story Short', was followed in early 1981 by 'The Freeze' and 'Muscle Bound/Glow', both of which did well enough in the chart. The album *Journeys To Glory* reached number five, going gold in May 1981 (thus selling 100,000 units), despite the Nazi related controversy stirred up by some parts of the music press. A new track, 'Chant No. 1 (I Don't Need This Pressure On)', was quickly recorded with Beggar & Co which gave the band their highest chart position so far at number three in the summer of 1981, although an otherwise favourable review of the song by *Smash Hits* referred to 'Tony Hadley's pompous foghorn vocals', which created the nickname 'Foghorn Hadley'.

The second album, *Diamond*, was coolly received by the music press and, indeed, by the record buying public in general. Tony had found it a very difficult album to record the vocals for; he revealed in his autobiography that, severely lacking confidence, he was seriously thinking of walking out on the band at the time. It wasn't really his fault. The songs, a number of which were experimental in style, were not Gary Kemp's best compositions and Richard James Burgess was not on top form as producer while recording the album. 'Paint Me Down' could not get into the top twenty despite a controversial video banned from *Top of the Pops* featuring the band members near naked on Primrose Hill; and Paul Tickell commented in *NME*'s review of 1981 that the band were 'ending the year in some desperation'. Then, at the start of 1982, 'She Loved Like Diamond', a much better song, despite some impenetrable lyrics, but poorly arranged and produced, could only make number 49 in the singles chart. Steve Dagger felt that urgent action was needed and Trevor Horn, producer of ABC and Dollar, was hurriedly drafted in to remix 'Instinction'.

It was a sensitive subject. When *Record Mirror* of 27 February 1982 printed a rumour that Burgess was for the chop and about to be replaced by Horn following 'the last two smashes (snicker)', the next issue, of 6 March 1982, reported that Steve Dagger had personally rung *Record Mirror*'s office during the week to deny the story. However, much to *Record Mirror*'s amusement, a Trevor Horn remix of 'Instinction' *did* indeed appear in April; and that magazine's reviewer charitably described it as Spandau's best single so far. It contained a rarity in 'Gently' – a brand new song on the B-side which was not on the album – something which had only happened once before with 'Glow' (which was, in fact, a double A-side with 'Muscle Bound') and, was, surprisingly never to happen again: the band recording their standard eight Gary Kemp compositions for all their albums (with the exception of *Heart Like A Sky* which has an additional Steve Norman composed track) and no additional material, something which may have hindered sales of singles taken from the albums. Whatever Gary Kemp's qualities as a songwriter, and there are many, he was certainly not what one would call prolific.

The remix of 'Instinction' appears to have done the trick and came out in the nick of time just before the band's UK tour, or rather 'series of special appearances' (because Spandau Ballet did not yet officially do tours, per Steve Dagger). The original concept was that these 'special appearances' would be advertised by word of mouth only but, in response to inaccurate speculation and reports of fake tickets being sold for phantom gigs, the (eight) venue locations were, in the end, announced by the band in the music press. The live performances were very successful and it was reported that there were 'a few thousand screaming nymphettes' at the Brighton Centre on 8 April and, exactly one month later, 'swarms of young girls...screaming and fainting' at the Liverpool Empire.

And how had Spandau Ballet transformed itself from a cool, fashionable, musically credible, electronic rock/dance band into pin-up boys being idolised and screamed at by teenage girls? Well, the new video for 'Instinction' might have helped (and the stills from the banned 'Paint Me Down' video had probably done no harm) but, perhaps more influentially, in the weeks leading up to the 'series of special appearances' there had been a concerted effort to repackage the band as heartthrobs in teenage girl magazines. Thus, Steve Norman stared out at the readers of *Heartbeat's* 6 March 1982 issue in full glossy colour on the front cover with another full page colour picture of Gary Kemp on the back. In the following week's issue, it was Tony Hadley's turn to grace the cover, with John Keeble on the back and a centrefold spread of the whole band in the middle. Then, on the cover of the 20 March issue, the *coup de grace*: the blue-eyed boy, Martin Kemp, oozing sex appeal and no doubt making thousands of girls go weak at the knees. It was a noticeable change of marketing strategy by the band, whose front cover appearances had until then been confined to the music press, but it was very much a sign of things to come.

Amidst all the screaming and hysteria, an old friend from The Same Band, Jess Bailey, joined the group on stage playing keyboards. As a bonus, the live performances were well reviewed across the spectrum of the music press, with all reviewers agreeing that the band members could certainly play their instruments and sounded tight as a unit. There was an audible shift in the band's sound as well as its image during this time as the boys moved towards the smoothness and slickness for which they would soon become world famous. Nothing demonstrates this more than their version of 'She Loved Like Diamond', captured for posterity on the *Old Grey Whistle Test* of 6 May 1982, which, with its rough edges smoothed out, Tony's maturing voice on top form, Steve knocking out an attractive rhythm on bongo drums and the inventive Jess Bailey adding relaxed piano fills, sounds today like it could easily have been a track from the *True* album.

By the end of the tour that was not a tour, Spandau Ballet were back in the top ten, just, and they quickly followed this up with the single 'Lifeline', also top ten. This track had been produced at Red Bus studios in central London during August 1982 by Tony Swain and Steve Jolley who had impressed the band as producers of Imagination. Swain and Jolley were recruited by Dagger for one song initially and worked very well with the band – Tony Hadley in particular recalls it as 'a very enjoyable' recording – and were thus retained for the next album.

During this period, while the girls and young women of England screamed for Spandau Ballet, many boys and young men around the country were still smitten by the girl in the film from the spring of 1981, that girl being Gregory's girl (at least she was in the last reel) otherwise known as Clare Grogan. She had captured many teenage hearts with her cute on-screen performance as Susan in the film *Gregory's Girl* and then all over again in the following year as the bubbly lead singer of Altered Images. Despite already being in some form of relationship (with hairdresser Lee Andrews), Gary Kemp was lovestruck in real life, taking a number of trips to her home town of Glasgow to see her. She gave him a book by Nabokov in which he read of seaside arms and pills on tongues and, we can speculate, he gave her J.D. Salinger's *Catcher in the Rye* in return (in January 2000 he confessed on his website that the book 'meant something to me and a certain person') but, despite putting so much into her life, his love for her was, it seems, frustratingly unrequited. As a member of a band, she might have written him a song telling him that she approved but, if she did, well, he must have misunderstood and he remained, as it were, far from her arms on any night. This long-distance platonic relationship, which Gary only felt comfortable enough to reveal publicly for the first time at the age of nearly fifty, led to a creative explosion and inspired arguably some of the best pop songs of the 1980s, recorded appropriately enough at Love Beach in Nassau's Compass Point Studios in October and November 1982.

The songs recorded in Nassau for the *True* album were, as a whole, certainly the best in the band's entire repertoire and the five band members were undoubtedly at their happiest in the Caribbean sun. On a musical level, every track seems to work. According to Gary, speaking in February 1983, 'I think they're the best things I've ever written, easy'. His lyrics had previously been described as 'epic nonsense' – not quite the insult it may seem because it is a neat trick to write commercial songs with attractive sounding but nevertheless meaningless lyrics – but now he seemed to have something to say, even if it was only about 'being young and having a good time, or being in love', as William White of the *NME* succinctly put it. 'Code Of Love', 'Pleasure' and 'Heaven Is A Secret' are probably the band's finest album tracks (at least of those which were never released as singles) and all the songs were beautifully crafted by Gary, with lush production from Swain and Jolley, inspired sax solos from Steve Norman, some outstanding percussion and dreamy backing vocals from Gary, with Tony's memorable lead vocals, swirling with pre-delayed reverb, sounding particularly smooth and strong without any of the earlier foghorn element of which *Smash Hits* had complained. 'It was all relaxed, it just felt good' recalled Tony in a 2007 Radio 2 documentary, adding that: 'Tony [Swain] would always put this really nice warm delay on the vocal and it would always sound just warm and lush'. Even the artwork for the album by David Band, whom Gary Kemp had met through their mutual but competitive 'friendship' with Clare Grogan, was well chosen.

Steve Dagger was certainly feeling pleased with the new recordings. On his return from Nassau in late November, he mentioned to an *NME* journalist at the Wag club that the album was finished, 'but the tracks all sound so good that we can't decide on a single. It's all pretty commercial, but there are a few slow tracks that will surprise a few people. Some of it's not quite what you'd expect.'

In the event, the first single from the Bahamas recording, 'Communication', was not perhaps the best of the bunch but they knew they had 'True' up their sleeve and this effortlessly sailed to the magical number one position on 26 April 1983. 'I love that track so much' Gary had said in February 1983: 'I've always wanted to write a track that made me go all silly. I wrote it a while before the rest and I was scared to show it to the group 'cos I didn't want it to be messed up and 'cos I was a bit embarrassed about how personal the words were and how soft sounding it was.' As he later explained: 'I was 22, suffering from unrequited love and the song just came.'

The collective memory of the morning the band found out they were number one in the singles chart while together in a hotel in Sheffield (about to play at Nottingham that evening during something resembling a conventional UK tour) is probably the happiest one ever for the band. Martin summed up the occasion in an interview in *Number One* in 1990: 'I remember when it happened we were on tour and we just went crazy, jumping up and down on the beds, pushing John Keeble up and down the corridor on a laundry basket with a bottle of champagne in his hand. Just sitting at breakfast drinking champagne and crying…a brilliant feeling.' As if to increase the pleasure, the *True* album also soared to number one in May and went platinum, selling 300,000 units, a couple of weeks later. This album spent an astonishing sixty-four consecutive weeks in the Top 100 album chart. It also enjoyed a certain amount of critical success from a music press which had disliked *Diamond*. In *Record Mirror*, for example, Betty Page called it 'a chunk of creamy, dreamy funk with satisfyingly rounded edges.'

Unfortunately, Spandau never managed to achieve another number one single (or album for that matter) and, to some extent, the shadow of this failure hung over them like the sword of Damocles throughout the Eighties. The need for a second number one – another classic like 'True' – put pressure on the band, and on Gary Kemp in particular, that slowly drained the energy when it did not appear. To some extent, they only had themselves to blame. Following the success of 'True' there was a long delay while the band, which had contractual control of such matters, dithered over which song to release next – 'Foundation' was mentioned as a possible follow-up – but when the obvious choice, 'Gold', finally came out in August, the band were engaged in promotional work abroad and reportedly declined to return for a *Top of the Pops* performance which might well have seen them overtake KC & The Sunshine Band to the top spot. In the end, they had to settle for number two and not even a gold disc for 'Gold'.

Nevertheless, it was unquestionably a very good year for the band. 'True' was the sixth best-selling single in the UK during 1983 and the album was the fifth best-selling of the year. The song 'True' was nominated for an Ivor Novello award and Gary Kemp personally was nominated for writing the theme tune to Noel Edmonds' *Late Late Breakfast Show*, with a tune not dissimilar to the intro from 'Foundation', although neither actually won. However, the band did collect the Sony Award for Technical Excellence at the Brit Awards in February 1984 although, as Culture Club won the award for Best British Group, they might have regarded this as a kick in the teeth. The success of 'True' was slightly double-edged for one band member. Martin Kemp had been replaced on bass by an electronic keyboard and would always feel that he was not really a part of the success of the record, a factor which no doubt led him to start thinking about a possible acting career after the band.

There was another long wait of nearly a year for the next Spandau Ballet single. 'Only When You Leave' – a song written by Gary before the release of the *True* album – was finally released in June 1984. It is one of the band's best but, ironically, the fact that they had so many fans dashing to the record shops to buy the single in its first week of release possibly hindered its chart success. 'Only When You Leave' debuted in its first week at number five. Today that would not be considered anything special, and indeed probably a disappointment for most big acts, but it was Spandau's highest new entry chart position and was quite a rare achievement for any artist of the period. Indeed, by the time of the release of 'Only When You Leave' in June there had only been two singles that had debuted higher than number five during the first half of 1984 – Queen's 'Radio Ga Ga' and Wham!'s 'Wake Me Up Before You Go Go' – which both entered the chart at number four. 'Wake Me Up Before You Go Go' made it to number one in its second week, as one would have expected from a song entering the chart so strongly, but 'Radio Ga Ga' had been blocked from making the top spot by a song called 'Relax' which was the sensation of 1984 and it was the surprise success of Frankie Goes To Hollywood that was to destabilise Spandau Ballet's assault on the charts in that year.

Following a *Top of the Pops* appearance, 'Only When You Leave' rose a couple of places to number three but in many respects it had peaked too soon and was falling down the chart before most non-Spandau fans had become familiar with it through radio plays. A fairly ordinary promotional video to accompany the song did not help. However, it never had any real hope of making it to number one because, after its first week of release, Frankie Goes To Hollywood released 'Two Tribes' and this made a spectacular new entry straight to the top of the chart, easily leapfrogging Spandau's effort and dislodging Wham! from the top spot.

At the time, Spandau appeared nonchalant about the new competition. 'It doesn't bother me,' said Gary during a Capital Radio interview, 'they're not a big band....They couldn't compete with us live on stage. I don't think they can compete with us as a band.' Nevertheless, Spandau Ballet's follow-up single wasn't released until after 'Two Tribes' had held the number one spot for nine weeks and it was clear from its volume of sales that no-one was going to be able to dislodge it during that period. Matters were made worse by Frankie's choice of slogan in one of their advertisements which said, 'It makes Spandau look soft' and, if the *Daily Mirror* of the time is to be believed, this insult nearly caused a fight between Gary Kemp and Paul Rutherford (of Frankie) at a party in a country house in Hertfordshire hosted by the Thompson Twins, only being kept apart by Duran's John Taylor who supposedly acted as peacemaker.

As if this was not bad enough, the new album *Parade* was held off the number one spot in the album chart by Bob Marley's posthumously released *Legend* album in July although it did go gold (selling 100,000 units) in its first week. Typically, Spandau Ballet, having found a winning formula in the Caribbean sunshine with an appealing and original fusion of laid back funk, soul, reggae and pop, had decided to change it by recording the album in the urban industrial surroundings of Munich's Musikland Studios (albeit still with Swain and Jolley) and the new tracks sounded less laid back, less soulful and less funky as a result. Whether this was an improvement is open to question and most of the music press thought not. Betty Page, until then a staunch ally, rather turned against the band in her review of *Parade* in *Record Mirror*, calling it 'bland, tedious, swiftly accessible pop rock for housewives with no depth, no feel, no soul' and only *Smash Hits* of the major music papers gave it a really good review, with Ian Birch awarding it a mark of nine out of ten.

Tony tried to put a brave face on it all during a *Record Mirror* interview published in August 1984. Of the failure of 'Only When You Leave' to reach number one, he said, 'Well, number three's not bad...number three on reflection was great, I can't say I'm disappointed' but his ambitious state of mind was revealed when he added: 'you tend to think that everything you release is going to be number one…sometimes other people take the number one spot, but you can't start moaning about it, you just have to release something else and do bigger and better things.' Of the failure of *Parade* to get past Bob Marley in the album chart, he said, 'It doesn't really bother me that much because this was only the first single off the album and I think the album's going to go in the number one slot later on.' These were confident words but could the band achieve the kind of success that Tony was taking for granted? And what would happen if they did not?

When the follow-up single, 'I'll Fly For You', was eventually released in August it was a good one, and probably should have done better than to peak at number nine, but it takes nearly two minutes from the start of the track to reach the chorus, which is quite long for a hit single. It was not unknown for music television programmes of the time to terminate the video, expensively filmed in New Orleans, before it reached the first chorus, although, as its narrative appears to make no sense, based around some sort of incomprehensible courtroom scene, this might not have been such a bad thing. The song was not well reviewed in the music press, with Adrian Thrills, who had previously been supportive, calling it a 'lifeless tome' and matters were not helped when John Peel commented on the track on *Top of the Pops*, after the video had been played, by saying, 'That song gets me right here', while pointing to his stomach. One might wonder why he accepted the job of presenter if he did not like the songs being broadcast. Whether his words had any effect on sales can never be ascertained but it might have put doubt into the mind of any potential purchaser of the single.

In any event, as an indication of the type of competition Spandau were up against, when Frankie was eventually toppled from the top spot in August it was by George Michael's peerless pop ballad, the classic, 'Careless Whisper'. Although Spandau no doubt desperately hoped 'I'll Fly For You' would give them their second number one, in truth it didn't stand a chance bearing in mind the emergence of so many major new artists with huge numbers of fans in 1984, and the band were made to pay for their long delay of almost a year before having released some new material.

Their next single, 'Highly Strung', released in October, was not one of their best and Gary's use of the diplomat/laundromat rhyme is frequently cited as one of pop music's worst rhymes ever, although he has defended it by saying, 'That was purposely crass. It was a twee lyric like a nursery rhyme. I thought that was really funny.' Even another ludicrously expensive and pretty baffling video, filmed for no apparent reason in Hong Kong, could not push the song into the top ten. The fact that Wham!'s 'Freedom' was now at number one shows the type of competition the band were up against. As if to rub salt into the wounds, Duran Duran, the band which had been forced to stand in the audience when Spandau victoriously played the Botanical Gardens in November 1980, had by now had two number one singles in the UK, the most recent being 'The Reflex' in May 1984, and were in the middle of a run of ten consecutive top ten hits, most of them in the top three, usually accompanied by much cleverer videos than those produced by Spandau. If that wasn't bad enough, 'The Reflex' had also made number one in the United States, being their sixth consecutive top ten hit single in that country. The boys from Islington were a little off the pace.

There was some consolation in that *Parade*, although never reaching number one as Tony had hoped it would, went platinum in October, having sold 300,000 units and, indeed, was the twentieth best-selling album in the UK during 1984, beating both of Duran's long playing offerings: *Arena* (at number 31) and *Seven and the Ragged Tiger* (at number 53). It was in the singles department, though, where sales were not as they ought to have been. 'Only When You Leave' was the 88th best-selling single of the year and 'I'll Fly For You' only the 100th best, which compares unfavourably with 'The Reflex' at number 17 – although it has to be said that both Spandau and Duran were comprehensively trounced by Black Lace, whose 'Agadoo' was the eighth biggest seller of the year.

Things may be a bit different today but there were a number of ways to consider the success or otherwise of a musical act in the 1980s. The obvious one, as already mentioned, was chart position which was clear, mathematical and easily understood by everyone. The higher you were in the chart, assuming it was not rigged, the better you were doing. This was certainly how most people, including the acts themselves, judged whether they were successful or not. It was not a perfect method, though, because a single reaching number one could sell fewer records than another song which failed to hit the top spot in another week because of different overall sales. So total record sales, rather than chart position, was another reasonable indicator of success. However, while, in theory, if you sold a lot of records or achieved a high chart position, you should have produced an objectively good song which people wanted to buy, this was not necessarily the case if you had a loyal fan base, because you might have made a poor record which nevertheless shifted lots of units. So another measure of success was whether a song had received critical acclaim, usually by considering the reviews received in the music press. This method was often favoured by acts which did not attain high chart positions or sell many records but were still widely admired. For those artists with poor chart positions and sales, whose songs were panned by the music press, there was yet one more fallback position. If you were selling a lot of tickets for your concerts you could be said to be doing better than someone merely shifting units or getting good reviews. By October 1984, Gary Kemp was preferring to focus on the fact that Spandau Ballet had sold out a number of large venues, including the Birmingham NEC and Wembley Arena, for their forthcoming tour and, perhaps putting his blind eye to the telescope, claimed: 'I don't see us as a band that's sold on seven-inch singles any more.'

For the final single from the album, four being the usual number of tracks one could respectably release in the 1980s if one was not Michael Jackson, the band were persuaded by Peter Powell of Radio 1 to select his own personal favourite song, 'Round and

Round', although with hindsight, and perhaps even with foresight, if they were going to sign off the year with a slower number, 'With the Pride' would probably have been a better choice. 'Round and Round' did not do too badly for a fourth single off an album, just sneaking into the top twenty, but it was certainly not the kind of chart busting success the band was looking for before their long disappearance on their so-called 'World Parade' tour and then to Ireland on a tax break.

Before jetting off to start their world tour in 1985, the band did perform on a number one single in 1984: Band Aid's 'Do They Know It's Christmas?', the best-selling single of that year despite being on sale for just three weeks of it. The standard version of the story of how this came about, as told by Bob Geldof, goes that the morning after the famous television news report from Ethiopia by Michael Buerk, Bob woke up to find his partner, Paula Yates, had left for Newcastle for that week's recording of *The Tube*, having placed a note on the refrigerator saying that everyone who visited the house that day must contribute £5 for famine relief. Bob then visited the Phonogram press office and mentioned to a few people that he was thinking of doing a record for Ethiopia, after which he telephoned Paula at the TV studio in Newcastle and asked her who was filming for *The Tube* that week. Paula called over Midge Ure, who was there with Ultravox, and handed him the receiver. Having listened to the persuasive Irishman's idea, Midge immediately agreed to help Bob write a song for a charity single. Having put the phone down to Midge, Bob then called Sting who agreed to be part of it without hesitation. He then telephoned Simon Le Bon whose reaction was also positive.

On a roll, Geldof happened to spot Gary Kemp in an antiques shop in the King's Road and Gary said that Spandau would take part as long as the recording could be held back until after the band returned from Japan, where they were flying out for a tour lasting from 10 to 18 November. In some versions of the story told by Bob, he *then* sees Simon Le Bon in the street and ropes him into the project (rather than earlier on the telephone). In Bob's autobiography he also says that, later that night, he spoke to Martin Kemp at a party (presumably the party at Xenon to launch the Wham! album, *Make It Big*, which both Geldof and the members of Spandau were reported as having attended) and it was only then that the notion began to form in his mind that his project could be massive. In his own autobiography, however, Martin gives the impression that the first he and the rest of the band heard of Geldof's project was on 24 November, the night before the recording, when they were in Germany filming for a TV programme and Dagger broke the slightly unwelcome news that they needed to wake up early the next morning to fly back to London in a Lear jet.

However, quite aside from this difference of recollection between Bob and Martin, the facts do not quite match the rest of the story. Before dealing with this, we need to bear in mind that, although the first of Michael Buerk's reports was broadcast on a BBC news bulletin on Tuesday, 23 October 1984, there were two different broadcasts by Buerk on consecutive evenings (one from Korem, one from Makele) and the one seen by Geldof was first broadcast on Wednesday, 24 October 1984. We know this because it was the broadcast featuring a young British nurse whom Bob has spoken of many times as a major part of his inspiration behind the project. So the chronology should be fairly straightforward. Bob saw the TV report on Wednesday, 24 October 1984, and the next morning, which would have been Thursday, 25 October, Paula took the train to Newcastle (as she did every Thursday at that time) from where she spoke to Bob on the telephone before handing over to Midge who was getting ready to appear on *The Tube* on Friday, 26 October.

The problem with this account is that Ultravox were not on *The Tube* on Friday, 26 October 1984. In fact, they did not appear until the 50th edition of that show on Friday, 2 November 1984. Bearing in mind that Ultravox's performance was a live one, presumably it was Thursday, 1 November 1984, over a week after the first broadcast by Michael Buerk, when Bob and Midge first spoke about doing something for the starving in Ethopia. This would certainly fit with the fact that the Xenon party to launch the *Make It Big* album was on the evening of 1 November.

Midge's recollection, however, is that he and Bob did not mention a charity single during their telephone conversation but they agreed to meet and discuss what to do over lunch on the following Monday and it was only during this lunch that they decided that writing and recording a Christmas song was the best way forward. So, it would appear – assuming Geldof had not secretly started making arrangements for a charity single before discussing the idea with his eventual co-writer – that Bob could not have spoken to Sting and Gary Kemp about the Band Aid project until Monday, 5 November, at the earliest, after his lunch with Midge. Nothing really turns on this, and there is no doubt that the footage affected him greatly as soon as he saw it, but it is a curiosity of history and one wonders what Bob was actually doing during the week after the broadcast. It is possible that he watched a repeat the following week, because Buerk's broadcasts were frequently repeated at the time, but it would be somewhat surprising if he was not aware of them until a whole week after the first broadcast because people were talking about them from day one. In any event, regardless of the precise chronology of events, participating in the Band Aid single was certainly one of Spandau Ballet's better moments from 1984, despite their notoriety achieved by turning up to the recording session in limousines.

Quite aside from Band Aid, and despite the failure of Spandau to secure either a number one single or album in the year – *Parade* peaking at number two in the album chart – 1984 was by no means a complete write-off for the band. The annual *Smash Hits* poll was not necessarily the best indicator of popularity, being open to forgery and manipulation by fans able to send in multiple entries, but we may note that, whereas Spandau Ballet finished fifth in the Best Group category for 1984, and Tony Hadley was eleventh in the Best Male Singer category, the album *Parade* was nevertheless voted the second best album of 1984 (finishing runner up to Duran's *Seven and the Ragged Tiger* which had actually been released in November 1983, as Gary complained to Smash Hits at the time). Considering that the *True* album had only managed to come sixth in the equivalent 1983 poll, it was, perhaps, some consolation and surely reflects the quality of the album or at least the appreciation of it by the readers of *Smash Hits*. The UK tour was also successful, with six successive nights played at Wembley Arena.

More misery for the band, however, came in April 1985 when Steve Norman tore a knee ligament while sliding on stage at the Universal Amphitheatre in Los Angeles, which resulted in the final gig of their tour of the United States, in San Francisco, as well as their proposed tour of Italy and Spain, being cancelled. In his autobiography, Tony expresses the view that the tour should have continued, with Steve playing his sax while sitting down, and Steve himself has said that, on reflection, this would have been the best approach, but they have no doubt both forgotten that the medical advice for Steve would have been to take a complete rest. Indeed, Gary Kemp told a reporter for *No.1* magazine of 4 May 1985 that Steve's doctor had said that he was 'not allowed to do anything energetic for six to eight weeks.' While it might sound easy to play a sax in a wheelchair on stage, a tour involves a lot of travel and physical exertion so that the only sensible option, in the absence of deploying a replacement, was to return to London where Steve could recuperate.

The cancellation of the United States' tour is often cited as a reason why Spandau made no further impact in America, but only one gig in the States was actually cancelled on that tour and it is unlikely to have made much difference. True, the band were subsequently forced to cancel a second planned (six week) tour of the United States supporting The Power Station in the summer of 1985 because Steve had still not fully recovered, it being reported at the time that, 'the doctors say he should not undertake a gruelling month-and-a-half on the road until he is 100 per cent fit.' *This* cancellation certainly might have had an effect on the band's success in the States.

The year in Dublin was tough for the band members, being apart from their families, and the long absence did not help them build on the successes of *True* and *Parade*. A dispute with Chrysalis, following legal proceedings in the High Court instituted by Steve Dagger, also delayed their next studio album. The main complaint was that the record company had failed to promote the band properly in the United States where, despite the fact that, following a Top Five success with 'True', 'Gold' made it to a respectable number 29 in the singles chart and 'Only When You Leave' got to number 34, the band were nevertheless regarded as a one hit wonder. There was one silver lining of their time in Ireland which was that Gary was inspired to write 'Through the Barricades', regarded by many as one of his best songs.

Before recording this track, the band returned to London for Live Aid in July 1985, when, with Steve Norman's knee sufficiently recovered to allow him on stage for fifteen minutes, they played three songs at Wembley: 'Only When You Leave', 'True' and a brand new track called 'Virgin'. They were criticised for including a new song in their short set when most other bands were playing standards, and Dylan Jones, author of *An Event That Rocked The World,* has teased out from Steve Dagger the fact that Dagger now believes it was a mistake to have used the occasion for promotional purposes. But at least it gave their fans an opportunity to hear some new material and, if those fans were prepared to pay for it by making a telephone donation to the Live Aid charity, it might have made a contribution to the 'global jukebox' concept. 'Virgin' was the only new song they were ready to perform which is why that particular one was chosen. However, according to an uncharitable Paul Gambaccini, speaking on a TV documentary about Queen, 'Nobody remembers Spandau Ballet were at Live Aid', so perhaps it doesn't make any difference.

Despite being hidden away in Dublin, Spandau Ballet remained in the public eye in England during November 1985 when Chrysalis released a greatest hits compilation, *The Spandau Ballet Collection*, against the band's wishes and without their permission. Steve Dagger managed to obtain a temporary injunction against a television advertisement for the album but this injunction was overturned by the Court of Appeal and the album reached a very respectable number three in the charts. By this stage, there had been 'a complete breakdown in the working relationship' with their record company, according to the band. The whole matter was settled in early 1986 when Spandau were released by Chrysalis from their recording contract and then, after a short period of negotiation, signed to CBS in June of that year, with a famous clause in the contract preventing release of any records in South Africa, a country then under apartheid.

The band was back in July 1986 with their first CBS single, 'Fight For Ourselves', which only made number 15 in the UK and, ironically, considering the stated reason for the change of label, it was not even released in the United States. Although full of bravado and pomp, the song lacks a genuine hook and this was reflected in the fact that Gary appears to have had difficulty naming it. The *Daily Mirror* of 11 January 1986 reported that the new single was going to be titled 'We're Fighting for Ourselves' while, a couple of weeks later, the *Evening Standard* reported that the group had recorded their new single: 'Everybody (We Have Got to Fight For Ourselves)', information which can have only come from official channels, perhaps exposing rare uncertainty in the mind of the normally confident and decisive songwriter.

Matters were not helped by the fact that Spandau signed to CBS just as it commenced a bitter dispute with record retailers, including the national chain Our Price, over new trading terms it imposed from 1 July 1986 which reduced the ability of retailers to return unsold albums. During the dispute, which lasted for three months until the end of September, some record stores refused to stock any CBS product at all and this issue delayed the release of Spandau's next single. Furthermore, there was evident tension in the fledgling relationship between the band and its new record company. It was initially announced in the music press that 'Swept' was to be released as the next single by CBS, then it was said that the band wanted to release 'Cross the Line'; it wasn't until

October that it was confirmed that the band's sixteenth single would, in fact, be 'Through the Barricades', also the title track of the band's forthcoming album.

Following the relative failure of their comeback single, the band must have been highly confident that the impressive 'Through the Barricades' track would repeat the success of 'True' but, disappointingly, it refused to climb higher than number six in the UK singles chart and did nothing in the States.

The band appeared to have lost many fans during their long absence. Sales of the *Through the Barricades* album, produced by Trevor Horn's engineer, Gary Langan, were disappointing and Spandau hadn't helped themselves by ditching the lush production of their previous two albums in an attempt to capture their harder edged, guitar orientated, live sound on vinyl. The sniping from the critics in the music press appears to have affected the band before they recorded the album. John Keeble acknowledged at the time that, 'There was a lot of criticism levelled at us after the Parade album that it hadn't moved too far from True and it sounded a bit soft. I think some of that criticism is fair', while Gary said: '…people always thought that we were better – well certainly more aggressive and powerful – on stage than on record. People who weren't very keen on our records used to go to gigs and come out quite keen, simply because we were more raw and livelier live.'

It is certainly the case that critics of their singles and albums in the music press were usually forced to concede that Spandau Ballet was an excellent live band. The problem here, though, was that their commercial success had come from some extremely well produced studio albums. If they had wanted to capture their live sound, a live album might have been a better choice. Clearly, Spandau wanted to improve their credibility and aspired to become more of a rock band than a pop group but the type of person buying serious rock music was not likely to add Spandau Ballet to their record collection.

At the same time, the music scene from 1987 onwards changed drastically, with Stock, Aitken & Waterman and dance music, both using new studio technology, starting to dominate the charts –

even Duran were not competitive any more at the highest level – and Spandau's live drums and guitar-based sound, regardless of how good the songs were, did not really fit into the period so that the band were in danger of becoming irrelevant. Gary blames it on the emergence of Acid House in his autobiography but this new phase of youth culture wasn't dominating the charts in the same way that the New Romantic culture had done during the earlier years of the decade. It did not, for example, affect the Pet Shop Boys who had three number one hit singles within a twelve-month period during 1987 and 1988. They were just two men without a guitar or drum kit between them but they emphasised the new reality; songs could be programmed and created in a studio by anyone, incorporating sounds previously unheard of, and for a few years at least, until the novelty died down, there was very little room at the top of the British charts for traditional guitar bands. PM Dawn's effort a few years later, when they incorporated the riff from 'True' into the beautifully relaxed 'Set Adrift on Memory Bliss', provides an example of the musical direction Spandau *could* have taken had they been so minded. The failure of 'How Many Lies' to break into the Top 30 in February 1987 was a disaster and put enormous pressure on Gary Kemp to deliver more hit singles for the next album.

CHAPTER TEN

When the Monolith Cracks

'I think the most disastrous thing that I ever see with bands is that people who have been together since school end up splitting up over money which is an incredible thing to happen but that does happen.'

—Martin Kemp, Radio 1 – July 1986

UNKNOWN TO THEIR FANS AND most of the media at the time, the members of Spandau Ballet started to fall out in 1987. The first sign of trouble appears to have been an argument between Gary and Tony, while they were in Germany, about whether the artists who had participated in Live Aid a couple of years earlier had done so out of a genuine wish to help the starving of Ethiopia or a selfish desire for publicity and increased record sales. It was a rather trivial dispute but seems to have ruined the previously good relationship between the band's lead singer and songwriter although, surprisingly, despite pondering the origins of his fallout with Tony, Gary does not even mention the incident in his autobiography.

Perhaps a dispute between the two men was inevitable. Although Tony was happy to do what he was told by Dagger and Gary in the early years, as he grew older he inevitably and understandably began to have his own ideas about what the band should be doing and wanted more control over his career. Gary on the other hand was a self-confessed 'control freak' and liked to be the dominant member within the band. His close and longstanding relationship with Steve Dagger undoubtedly helped him to achieve this, which must have frustrated Tony. In his 2004 autobiography, Tony speculated that Gary wanted to be the lead singer of the band, a remark which seemed paranoid at the time the book was published but, as Gary subsequently admitted in his 2009 autobiography that he had harboured thoughts of singing the lead vocal on 'Through The Barricades,' it was not quite such an outlandish notion. Gary and Tony also had different political outlooks. Gary had always been an idealist, as reflected by his socialist political leanings and had, for example, played on the anti-Thatcherite Red Wedge tour in 1986. Tony (contrary to the suggestion made in 1981 that all the band members were left wing) was more of a pragmatist and inclined towards conservative political views. An early public indication of their differing outlooks can be seen in an issue of *Smash Hits* in July 1986 when they were both asked if the royal family should be scrapped. Gary gave a long answer, complaining that the royal family was a 'very dated and patronising part of British society' and that 'the whole thing is ridiculous…it stinks', to which Tony, who had been quoted two years earlier in the *Sun* as saying, 'I love the Royal Family and all that tradition..', responded bluntly, 'Gal, that's bollocks. You *know* it's a lot more involved than that'. While there is no necessary reason that this kind of thing should have interfered with their ability to co-exist within the band, the fact that the two men had to spend so much time together on tour and in rehearsal and recording studios meant that the conflicting political opinions began to grate.

But there was more to it than just a difference of political opinion or desire for control. Gary had become irritated that he was doing all the important work of the band on his own and, according to judge Andrew Park, 'felt that other members of the band were being carried by him to an unacceptable extent, that in between albums they were doing nothing in particular while he was working hard writing songs for the next album.' This was an important issue. Between recording, touring and promotional activity, the other four band members were free to relax and spend time with their friends and families while Gary was labouring away on new material. Although the song 'Through the Barricades' was written in only a few hours, that was an exception and it took considerable time to compose an entire album. Gary was also seriously affected by the pressure arising from the need to deliver more hit singles and was no longer enjoying his songwriting. These annoyances and pressures all led to Gary making a decision to stop the payments of songwriting royalties which went to the band members (and Steve Dagger) via Marbelow. However, as they were not speaking to each other at the time due to some form of disagreement or falling out, Gary asked Steve Dagger to convey the news to Tony, John and Steve rather than informing them directly.

Another problem related to the production credits of the *Heart Like a Sky* album, with Gary insistent that he was to be individually credited as a producer much to the annoyance of Tony, John and Steve. Indeed, Steve made a highly critical comment about Gary on a BBC *Young Guns* documentary, broadcast in September 2000, when he said, 'He grew into a control freak at that point. It just seemed to me that was the point where he really overstepped the mark and his decisions he was making were purely selfish ones.' There also appear to have been some personal issues between some of the band members in 1988 but one major cause of the problems seems to have been that Gary and Martin agreed to star as the lead actors in a film, *The Krays*, initially without telling the rest of the band. Curiously, Tony does not mention this in his own book although his major gripe on the *Young Guns* documentary was that Gary and Martin agreed to star in the film without consulting him (his exact words being, 'I would have liked to have been asked'). The very fact of their involvement in the film, however, clearly did not go down well with the rest of the band. According to Gary, interviewed for a 2005 BBC documentary,

Brothers in Arms, 'Some of the members were really unhappy. They saw it as being a bit disloyal. I guess they were scared really it may be the end of the group'. In Martin's view, 'what split us up was the movie'. He was evidently more enthusiastic about the film than about Spandau's next album and this affected his friendships with the rest of the band. There was enormous tension and unhappiness in the recording studio during the making of the final album although this was well hidden from the public, with Gary being quoted in an August 1988 interview (published in *Record Mirror* of 3 September 1988) as saying that the key to Spandau's survival was: 'Respect for each other. We just happen to like working together.' As the band members were barely speaking to each other at this time that was a bit rich.

Following the failure of any of the singles released from the album to trouble the compilers of the Top 40 chart, the band eventually fell apart in 1990 – their final appearance together, at least for a while, being in Edinburgh on 6 March 1990.

Things remained reasonably civil in the early 1990s during which time Tony gave a televised interview to Tim Grundy on a 1992 programme in which he answered the question: 'Are Spandau Ballet over?' by saying:

> No. Definitely not. We're still very much together and, I mean, remembering we were, sort of, at school together and stuff like that, there's a good camaraderie between the band anyway and we were only out two or three weeks ago having dinner, cracking a few bottles of champagne and remembering our old times and stuff and we were talking about doing a new album sometime in 1993.

But Tony's positive mood was soon to change. His solo 1992 *State of Play* album flopped, being withdrawn from sale almost instantaneously with its release, and it wasn't long before he was released from his record company, EMI. At this time, he was in debt and struggling financially. He had bought a new house which needed renovation and had turned into a money pit. While he would have received some limited income from an equal share of performance royalties for plays of Spandau Ballet songs on radio and television, as well as some royalties from compilation albums featuring Spandau songs, there was no longer any money flowing in from payments for songwriting royalties which now all went to Gary Kemp. In 1993 or 1994, Tony tried to speak to Gary to reinstate those royalty payments, which had, as we have seen, been stopped five or six years earlier, but it appears that Gary, who was busy working on his own solo album, did not want to talk to him on the subject. This was hardly surprising because Gary must have thought the entire issue had been resolved in 1988 when he had asked Steve Dagger to deal with it by speaking to Tony and the rest of the band to inform them of his decision.

In 1994, Tony took legal advice and then, after an unexplained delay, together with John and Steve, issued a writ of summons in the Chancery Division of the High Court in London against Gary Kemp and Reformation Publishing Company Limited on 21 May 1996. The writ claimed that Tony, John and Steve were entitled to damages for breach of contract and/or a share of all past and future publishing income received, and to be received, by Gary Kemp and Reformation in respect of all fifty-seven songs said to have been written by Gary Kemp and recorded by Spandau Ballet. This figure included remixes and oddities: 'Man with guitar', 'Re-paint', 'Feel the chant', 'Highly re-strung,' 'Live and let live', 'Barricades...intro' and 'Fight...the heartache', none of which can properly be said to be separate compositions. The correct total of Spandau songs written by Gary during the band's lifetime was fifty, comprising eight tracks on each of the band's six albums (*Journeys To Glory, Diamond, True, Parade, Through the Barricades, Heart Like A Sky*), making forty-eight, plus 'Glow' and 'Gently' which were not included on those albums. Martin officially remained neutral in the legal proceedings although, from comments he later made in his autobiography, it is clear that he strongly supported his brother.

A few days after the writ was issued, Tony was quoted in the *Sun* as saying: 'I'm sad it's come to this but I'm afraid no-one puts one over on me and that's what Gary as Spandau's main songwriter has tried to do. When I found out how much we were owed I could not believe it. I rang Gary to try and sort things out privately, but he has not returned my calls. In the end myself, John and Steve had no option but to take legal action.' To the surprise of no-one, he also said, 'the chances of us reforming now I think are zero'. It was all out war.

In April 1998, Tony's legal team made an interesting tactical decision. Having originally claimed in 1996 that Gary had reneged on a contractual agreement for the payment of royalties, they now chose to make a new and totally different claim that Tony, Steve and John were actually co-authors of all of Spandau's songs (although they later excluded the eight Gary Kemp compositions on the *Heart Like A Sky* album which had been developed in a different way). This claim was made despite the fact that Gary Kemp had always been credited on all the band's records as the sole composer. The problem with making such a claim in respect of copyright, almost two years after issuing proceedings, was that they risked giving the appearance to the trial judge that they did not have sufficient belief in the strength of the original, contractual, claim. Furthermore, this was the first time ever that Tony, John and Steve had claimed to have co-written Spandau's songs. They were all subsequently to confirm in court that they put forward the copyright claim because of legal advice they received in 1998 and that it had not crossed their minds before this that they might be the joint owners of the copyright. By making two different claims against Gary, the obvious danger was that both of them were weakened in the eyes of the trial judge.

Tony was nevertheless confident of success and, together with his co-plaintiffs, Steve Norman and John Keeble, would have anticipated making something in the region of one million pounds in damages from Gary Kemp plus a share of future royalties from all Spandau Ballet's songs. According to Tony's version of events as set out in his autobiography, there was never any question of settling the litigation out of court. However, Gary has given a somewhat different account. In a statement posted on his official website following the court case, he said:

> We were offered a lot of money to take Spandau out on a tour just before the court case started and I felt that this would be a way to get us back together and make everyone happy creatively and financially. We contacted John Keeble, who agreed to meet us the following day, but on that day we received a call from Tony's new manager saying that no discussions to do with Spandau could take place until after the trial.

Although this statement was made by Gary in September 1999, Tony had nothing to say about it in his 2004 book, which made no reference to any settlement offer or possibility of a Spandau Ballet tour as a way of settling the case.

On 4 January 1999, three weeks before the trial was due to begin in the High Court, Tony's new manager, John Glover, applied on Tony's behalf to register the Spandau Ballet trademark. Although not the manager of Spandau Ballet, he nevertheless paid a £350 registration fee and made an application to the Patent Office to register the trademark name 'Spandau Ballet' on behalf of Tony Hadley, Steve Norman and John Keeble in classes 9 (recording), 16 (artwork), 25 (clothing) and 41 (performance). Registration of a trademark effectively gives the trademark owner a commercial monopoly of use on that name in the classes for which the registration is made. The application was thus designed to give Tony, John and Steve control over the band's name in respect of recording, live performance and merchandise (although it was eventually dropped in respect of merchandise).

Yet Spandau Ballet did not exist in any form in 1999 and had not existed as a functioning band for almost a decade. Why did the Spandau Ballet name need any protection? Especially in classes for live performance or merchandise when there were no live performances or merchandise to protect? A possible answer to this question soon suggested itself. Almost immediately after the court case finished in late February 1999, but before the judgment had been handed down – so no-one yet knew who had won – Tony, John and Steve announced plans to reform Spandau Ballet, record a single and perform live concerts. However, any such plans were instantly blocked by the Kemps' lawyers who, on 18 March 1999, forced Tony, John and Steve to undertake that they would not use the name 'Spandau Ballet' for any professional or promotional purposes whatsoever.

At this stage, Tony was still confident of victory and his legal advisors appear to have believed things had gone well in court. Had he won, this would have meant that he would have had a share in Spandau Ballet's royalties and might well have been credited as a co-author of all of Spandau's songs. He, Steve and John would still have owned half of Marbelow and, in addition, would have owned the Spandau Ballet trademark. His legal costs would probably have been paid by Gary Kemp. He would, therefore, have been in an extremely good position. However, there were some fundamental problems with Tony's case.

Firstly, almost twenty years after the events in question, memories had faded and there was no solid evidence that Gary Kemp had ever entered into a contractual arrangement to provide the other band members with his publishing income, certainly not in perpetuity. As the judge commented, if Gary had said something to the other band members to the effect that he was entering into an agreement with them, 'No one can tell me what it was, when and where he said it, or put in the context of an entire conversation.' There was overwhelming evidence that Steve Dagger believed during the early 1980s that the payments, being voluntary, could be stopped at any time and had told employees of Marbelow that this was the case. The band's solicitor, Brian Carr, had no knowledge of any agreement having been made by Gary to pay royalties to the others and he, too, had believed it to have been a voluntary arrangement. With the evidence of the existence of a verbal contract between Gary and the other band members being so thin, this part of Tony's case was quickly dismissed by the judge.

In respect of the copyright claim, the problem here for Tony was that the evidence was clear that Gary had substantially written all of Spandau's hit songs on his guitar or piano before he presented them to the band and there were very few changes made to them in the recording process. Furthermore, although there was some legal precedent for musicians to be considered co-writers of songs, and so John Keeble and Steve Norman had a chance of succeeding in their claim, it was going to be virtually impossible for Tony, as a singer, to be able to persuade a judge that he had been part of the process of composing any songs unless by singing them he had significantly changed Gary's melodies (which he hadn't) or added additional lyrics (which he hadn't). While Steve Norman had a reasonable case that his memorable saxophone solo should make him the joint author of 'True', Gary instructed a musicologist who gave evidence that the solo was basically derived from Gary's melody (which, without an expert of his own, Steve was unable to effectively challenge) and, in any case, the judge ultimately decided that it was too short for Steve to be considered a joint author of the track. Gary had also been credited as the sole author of all Spandau's singles since 1980 and the judge declared that even if he had found that Tony, John and Steve were joint composers of Spandau's songs (which he didn't) it would have been unconscionable to award any damages after all that time.

It may be noted that the exclusion of the *Heart Like A Sky* songs from the litigation can be explained by the fact that technological advances had allowed Gary to record the songs for that album as complete demos before the rest of the band got anywhere near them. In those circumstances, where the songs already existed in recorded form before being recorded by Spandau Ballet, it was far more difficult, if not impossible (hence the dropping of this part of the claim), to argue that the other band members were joint composers. This inevitably raised the question that if Gary could single-handedly produce fully arranged and recorded versions of the tracks on the *Heart Like A Sky* album, could he not have done the same thing for all of Spandau's earlier songs, had the technology existed? And would this have proved that he, not the other band members, was the real composer of those songs?

There was also a bitterly fought evidential battle during the hearing over an issue which was very minor in the context of the claim (and of no significance at all once the judge decided there had never been a contract between Gary and the other band members) but very important in understanding why the legal proceedings had been instituted in the first place. In England, one cannot usually issue a contractual claim more than six years after knowledge of the facts of the claim. Steve Dagger said in evidence that he had told Tony, John and Steve during separate telephone conversations in 1988 that Gary was stopping the publishing income payments to Marbelow, yet the three of them had not launched the legal action, claiming a breach of contract, until eight years later, after the limitation period had expired. Tony, John and Steve denied all knowledge of any such conversations with Dagger: probably because, with the passing of time, they had forgotten all about them. All they remembered was that Martin had told them (in a hotel jacuzzi in California) that Gary was stopping the payments in respect of the *Heart Like A Sky* album only.

Whatever the truth of the matter (and the judge preferred Dagger's version of events) there was no doubt that Gary had instructed Dagger to inform the others of his decision and believed that Dagger had done so. From the point of view of Tony, John and Steve, who the judge quite rightly found to be honest witnesses, Gary had suddenly stopped the publishing payments, without telling them, years after the band had split up. From Gary's point of view he had stopped the payments in 1988, while the band was still functioning, having done everything properly and openly, with no objection having been raised against his decision. Thus, it seems that the entire legal proceedings, and the years of bitterness and enmity that followed, arose as a result of a simple misunderstanding.

The judge announced his decision to the parties on 30 April 1999 and Tony, John and Steve were shocked to discover that Gary had won on every point. Despite this, Tony still appears to have been intent on reforming the band. On the very day he lost, and was refused leave to appeal, he was talking about getting Spandau Ballet back together, being quoted in the following day's *Daily Mail* as saying outside the High Court, 'We are going to be asking Martin and, even under the difficult circumstances, Gary as well and hopefully the planned tour will be next Spring.' In the *Sun* he was reported as saying, 'It would be great if we re-formed.' So soon after the end of such a punishing and divisive trial this wasn't a realistic option but there was no reason why Tony, John and Steve couldn't perform as a trio, although the question would be under what name. At this stage, neither the Kemps nor Steve Dagger had any idea that Tony, John and Steve had made an application to register the Spandau Ballet trademark and, consequently, on 20 May 1999, the Kemps allowed Tony, John and Steve to refer to themselves as 'ex Spandau Ballet', as long as the name 'Spandau Ballet' was not given undue prominence in any promotional materials.

In his book, Tony says that, following a serious offer from a promoter for a Spandau Ballet tour, he went to great lengths to try and persuade Martin Kemp to give his permission, as director of Marbelow, for him, John and Steve to tour as Spandau Ballet even if this would mean the exclusion of both Kemps from the band. Tony apparently dates this to after 30 April 1999 (the date of the judgment) because he supposedly told Martin that in return for his agreement he was prepared 'to drop the appeal', by which he must have meant the application to the Court of Appeal for permission for leave to appeal the judgment of Mr Justice Park which was eventually dropped on 15 October 1999. A story certainly appeared in the press at this time that Tony, John and Steve were planning 'a comeback tour' as Spandau Ballet. It is strange, though, that Tony was expecting Martin to vote against his brother considering that Martin had already blocked the attempt to reform the band in March 1999 but, putting that issue aside, if Tony, John and Steve (or John Glover on their behalf) had been planning to reform Spandau since January 1999 this would certainly provide an explanation of the trademark registration in that month. It would also explain how John Glover was able to sign a declaration to the Patent Office that there was a bona fide intention for Tony, John and Steve to use the trademark 'Spandau Ballet'.

Once Tony, John and Steve dropped the appeal in October 1999 and admitted defeat, Gary pursued Tony for his legal costs and Tony had to give up his share in the company which owned the rights to the Spandau Ballet name. On 3 May 2000, Tony, John and Steve sold their combined total of fifty per cent of the shares in Marbelow to Gary Kemp for a total value of £200,000 after the whole company had been valued by accountants as being worth £400,000. Gary Kemp, therefore, now owned 64 out of the 96 shares of Marbelow, making him the majority shareholder in the company and thus, in effect, the owner of Spandau Ballet. This seemed to spark off a rather entertaining battle of wills in which Tony continued to insist on his right to perform and record Spandau Ballet songs while Gary tried to block him from doing so.

First, in February 2000, Tony attempted to release a live album called *Obsession* featuring some covers of Spandau (Gary Kemp) songs. This was prevented by Gary and the original album had to be scrapped, being released later in the year with all Spandau songs removed. In an interview with the *Birmingham Evening Mail* at that time, a rather paranoid sounding Tony was reported as saying, 'It seems a bit petty to me, but I was forced to take off Through the Barricades and Gold from the live album...I guess they are just getting at me, but that suits me fine.'

In April 2000, Tony, Steve and John announced they were to go on tour performing Spandau Ballet songs. Some reports actually announced that Spandau Ballet were to reform. In fact, the band performed as 'Hadley, Norman & Keeble' also described as 'ex Spandau Ballet'. This did not initially cause a problem but in late 2001 it was announced on some radio stations that *Spandau Ballet* would be performing in 2002 on a Here & Now tour. Advertisements in the national press referred to the appearance of ex

SPANDAU BALLET in large letters, with the names of Hadley, Keeble and Norman in a smaller font. Gary was unhappy with this because he felt that Spandau Ballet would never have appeared on the same bill as the other artists lined up for the Here & Now tour and he believed that it devalued the Spandau Ballet name, or brand, which he wanted to protect, especially because he hoped that one day the band would reform: 'I still think the credibility of the name Spandau Ballet is worth preserving,' he said at the time, 'We still trade on the good name we created and I don't want it devalued with pathetic Eighties revival tours.' Any appearances, or apparent appearances, of members of the band under the Spandau Ballet name would, he thought, reduce the commercial potential of a future full reunion.

Gary came under a certain amount of criticism for this approach. His critics shouted that there would never be a Spandau Ballet reunion, that there were too many bridges burnt between the members and that Tony, focused on his solo career, would never contemplate sharing the stage again with the Kemps. Many thought that Gary was seriously deluded for even *thinking* that Spandau Ballet might reform, never mind expressing this view publicly. The Chosen One, however, knew better than any of them.

In normal circumstances, it might have been difficult for Gary to have prevented his former colleagues trading on the band name because Tony, John and Steve were legally entitled to earn an income as performers and to refer to the name of the band of which they were formerly members, but it just so happened that he discovered in late 2001 that Tony, John and Steve had registered the Spandau Ballet trademark (the application having been formally approved in June 2000) and Marbelow's solicitors wrote to Tony's management company, Blueprint, on 20 November 2001 requesting that the trademark be transferred to Marbelow. Blueprint replied on 13 December 2001, saying that they were prepared to transfer the trademark but only if Marbelow would permit Tony, John and Steve to use the words 'ex Spandau Ballet' in the promotional material for their tour. Marbelow's solicitors believed that Blueprint had no right to introduce such a condition and, on 20 December 2001, they issued proceedings in the London High Court (Chancery Division) on behalf of their client to demand both the transfer of the trademark and a restraining order on the use of the Spandau Ballet name.

Shortly after this, on 11 January 2002, Marbelow made an application for summary judgment (a legal procedure to obtain judgment in its favour without a full hearing on the basis that Tony, John and Steve had no real prospect of successfully defending the claim) and a few days later, on 14 January 2002, the *Sun* newspaper reported, inaccurately, that 'Eastenders star Martin Kemp is suing his ex-Spandau Ballet band mate Tony Hadley for using the group's name on a nostalgia tour' (inaccurate because Martin, albeit a minority shareholder and director of Marbelow, was not a party to the proceedings) and quoted Tony as saying: 'I've been told we must not refer to ourselves as ex-Spandau Ballet. I think it's my individual right.' Tony did not, however, mention that he had also been told that he must return the trademark to its rightful owner. Instead, the *Sun* reported him as saying, 'We are going to defend the case.' No quotes from anyone connected with Marbelow or Gary Kemp were provided by the *Sun* and there was no mention of the trademark registration.

The following day, the official Tony Hadley website announced the following:

> Tony and John received an early Christmas present from Martin + Gary Kemp's Company 'Marbelow Limited' in the form of court writs trying to prevent them performing as 'Hadley, Keeble and Norman', Ex Spandau Ballet on the upcoming 'Here and Now tour' which will start in April. In the meantime The Kemps have applied for a summary judgment which means the case will go before a judge on Monday the 21st of January. Since this got known, loads of emails from fans worldwide came in showing their support. On behalf of the guys and management I would therefore like to thank everyone for their wonderful support. It's all highly appreciated.

But did the fans who were giving their 'wonderful support' know what the court case was about? Apparently not. There was no mention on Tony's website or in the press of the trademark issue. Nor was there any mention of the trademark on Tony's website which, following a brief court hearing before Mr Justice Jacob on 22 January 2002, reported:

> In this morning's day in court (22-01-2002), Tony, John and Steve agreed to bill themselves as HADLEY, NORMAN AND KEEBLE - Ex Spandau Ballet – with Ex Spandau Ballet being 75% of the size of HADLEY, NORMAN AND KEEBLE. Marbelow have accepted this temporarily pending the full hearing which will be sometime later on this year in which they still want to prevent Hadley, Norman and Keeble the right to use 'Ex Spandau Ballet'.

Yet, in addition to agreeing to bill themselves in this way (and with the words 'Ex Spandau Ballet' in a different font), Hadley, Norman and Keeble had also agreed, through their lawyers, to return the trademark to Marbelow (and indeed the court had ordered them to do so, albeit by consent). This was not considered newsworthy enough for Tony's website. However, the *Times* newspaper reported on 23 January 2002 that:

> Three members of the former Spandau Ballet group lost a legal battle over the name yesterday. Tony Hadley, John Keeble and Steve Norman applied to register it as a trade mark excluding two other former members. The High Court ruled that the trade mark belonged to the band's trading company, Marbelow Ltd, controlled by one of the two excluded former members.

The *Times* report was slightly misleading because the trademark had already been registered but the cat was now out of the bag. The registration was a surprise to everyone not directly involved with the case, especially because Tony had appeared not to want to have anything to do with Spandau Ballet since the conclusion of the 1999 court proceedings and the failed attempt to reform the band, albeit that the application to the Patent Office had been made prior to this. Tony's fans learnt that, as a director of Marbelow, as he had been at the time, he had no legal right to apply to register the trademark 'Spandau Ballet' (a name owned by Marbelow) without the consent of the full board of directors of the company. Thus, despite Tony's claim that he was going to defend the case, there was never any realistic prospect of him defending that part of the case relating to the return of the trademark.

John Glover, the manager of Hadley, Norman and Keeble, provided an explanation for the trademark registration in response to questions raised on the forum of the official Tony Hadley website after the report in the *Times*. In a statement posted on Tony Hadley's website on 28 January 2002, Glover said:

> Here is the full story on this current Spandau Ballet litigation....In 1999 during the first court action, Tony, John and Steve discovered that the name Spandau Ballet had not been trade marked for the band or for Mar[below] Limited. All bands are advised by their record companies to trade mark their names to assist in the prevention of piracy and bootlegging. This is normally arranged by the artist's lawyer and or manager, but in this case it had been overlooked. In order to protect the whole band Tony, Steve and John at their own expense arranged to register this trade mark. It was never their intention to keep this for themselves. It was always intended to be for the benefit of all five members. Martin and Gary's solicitors have sent us numerous letters complaining about the way in which we advertise HNK.

Although billed as 'the full story', Glover did not explain why a band which did not exist and which was not even signed to a record company or planning to perform would be advised to trademark its name nor did he reveal who, if anyone, had given such advice. He did not explain what possible problem there could have been in 1999 with piracy and bootlegging of Spandau Ballet material considering that there was no market for Spandau merchandise or recordings at the time. Glover also did not explain why, if he believed that Spandau Ballet's manager had overlooked a crucial trademark registration, he did not simply inform Steve Dagger about this fact and let him pay the £350 registration fee and register it if he felt it necessary. No doubt Mr Glover had perfectly valid and legitimate reasons for making the registration, and was acting in the best interests of his clients at the time, but when questions were raised on Tony Hadley's forum about his statement, the entire forum was closed down. In a long explanation posted by the webmaster of Tony's site on 30 January 2002 entitled 'Forum closed indefinitely' it was stated:

> Why is it that everyone all of a sudden has a law degree, knows everything about promoting and the entire music industry and did (sic) management for artists etc? What is it that everyone thinks they are right? Why is it so hard to accept that the information given is all that will be told.

When the forum was eventually restored, all the previous posts on the subject of the trademark registration had been deleted.

Tony Hadley has never explained why he agreed to the trademark registration and he did not take the opportunity afforded by his autobiography to do so. As we have seen, according to Mr Glover, the registration was made in order 'to protect the whole band' but, in a subsequent statement posted on his official website, Gary Kemp confirmed that he, Martin Kemp and Steve Dagger were 'never informed' of this trademark registration and only found out about it by chance in late 2001.

As if the legal action was not enough, more trouble arose in January 2002 when Gary Kemp's publishing company, Reformation, prevented the broadcast on the *Richard & Judy* show of a Spandau Ballet video to promote Hadley, Norman & Keeble's appearance on the Here & Now tour and this news was revealed in rather sour terms on Tony Hadley's official website:

Minutes before Tony's appearance to talk about the upcoming Here and Now tour, the show's producers were informed that they were not allowed to show the Spandau Ballet video they planned alongside the introduction. This was stopped by the publishers of Gary Kemp's songs which coincidently happens to be Gary Kemp.

Tony now took every opportunity to be insulting about the Kemps in the press. Here, for example, is what he is reported to have said about them in the *Daily Star's* magazine published on 11 May 2002:

> I get on really well with Steve and John from Spandau…But as for the others… I don't get on with them at all. I would have to cross the road to avoid them. People say: "Come on if they put enough money in front of you, Spandau would get back together." But they just don't know me. You could offer me £10 million in cash in a suitcase and I still would not get on stage with those w***ers.

Presumably Tony was referring to 'those wankers' rather than 'those winners'!

On 16 May 2002, the *Sun* published a story which said that Gary had tried to make peace with Tony in the foyer of the Dominion Theatre before the premiere of the Queen musical *We Will Rock You* but Tony was reported as replying to Gary: 'I'm telling you, f**k off or else' (the asterisks being inserted by the press). While unconfirmed, and quite possibly untrue, this story has never been denied by either party.

In February 2003, a cheeky Gary Kemp appeared in a BBC episode of *Murder in Mind* in which a character called 'Hadley' ended up being stabbed to death by Gary's character! In the same month, there was an attempt to release a DVD called *Evening of Gold* which was packed with Spandau Ballet songs performed live by Hadley, Norman & Keeble. The DVD was advertised for sale on Tony's official website and in the March 2003 issue of his fan club magazine but Gary Kemp refused to grant a synchronisation licence and the DVD was withdrawn from sale before being released, although it did, eventually, somehow trickle out through a few internet outlets.

At the same time, Tony gave an interview to London's free *Metro* newspaper, published on 7 March 2003, in which he stated of the 1999 court case that, 'we had a judge who made a pretty appalling decision'. Offering a rather obvious hostage to fortune, he also said: 'I want nothing to do with Spandau ever again….A reunion tour for any amount of money? I wouldn't do it. There's too much bad blood.'

Shortly after this, Tony appeared on the so-called 'reality' show *Reborn in the USA*, a karaoke type singing competition, staged in front of bemused audiences in small venues in the United States, between supposedly washed up British artists from the Eighties, hence the chance to be 'reborn' (although, amusingly, and perhaps in response to complaints by the participants, after a couple of episodes the emphasis changed and the artists were suddenly referred to by the show's presenter, Davina McCall, as highly successful acts in Britain, thus making a mockery of the entire concept). Marbelow's solicitors apparently wrote to the makers of the programme in advance to ensure that Tony did not use it as a platform to air his grievances about the still ongoing legal action relating to the use of the Spandau Ballet name and this fact was somehow leaked to the *Sun* on 11 March 2003, with a standard quote from Tony ('The Kemps seem to be getting their knickers in a twist'). During his publicity interviews for Reborn, Tony also got in a dig at Martin, telling the *Daily Mirror*'s *The Look* magazine: 'I didn't follow my former Spandau Ballet colleague Martin Kemp when he was in Eastenders. I'm currently facing another court case with Martin and Gary. I'm not going to comment on Martin's acting skills. The less said the better, in my opinion.'

Reborn in the USA was a very strange programme with a somewhat loosely defined set of rules. In an Elvis themed week, the contestants were tasked to perform unsuitable and newly learnt covers of Elvis Presley songs to diehard Elvis fans in Memphis whereas Tony, who appeared last in the running order, was allowed to sing a cover version of the 1991 Mark Cohn track, 'Walking In Memphis', which he regularly performed live at his own gigs and which had even appeared on his live album, *Obsession*, released three years earlier. Not surprisingly, in contrast to the previous round when he ended in the bottom two and was saved by the UK audience vote, Tony stormed it and won that week's competition with ease.

Having reached the final, singing cover versions of various songs not written by Gary Kemp, Tony then, surprisingly, performed a Gary Kemp composition, 'Through the Barricades', in the final on Saturday, 26 April 2003, which was broadcast live on ITV. If this was in any way supposed to be a way of sticking two fingers up to Gary in order to show him he could still sing Spandau songs on prime time national television, it backfired. His victory could now be put down as a victory not for Tony but for Spandau Ballet. Indeed, the official Spandau Ballet site, run by Steve Dagger and Gary Kemp, was quick to congratulate Tony on his victory while pointing out that it was a Spandau Ballet song that had won it for him. At the same time, in response to suggestions that there might one day be a reunion, Tony made the point that, 'The Spandau thing went too far and it's wrong of any former member to intimate to fans that we'll get back together. It's absolutely dead', adding, when asked about his feelings towards the Kemp brothers, 'I don't want anything to do with them ever again.' By contrast, when Gary was asked during an interview for *New* magazine's 5 May 2003 issue about how he felt watching Tony's success in *Reborn* he said, 'I just hoped he would win.'

On 23 May 2003, the Marbelow legal proceedings were finally settled with Tony, John and Steve accepting the restrictions on the use of the 'ex Spandau Ballet' name although, ironically, after all the fighting over this appellation, it was hardly ever used again by Tony, who now promoted himself as 'winner of Reborn in the USA' rather than ex Spandau Ballet.

Matters came to a head in July 2003 when Tony was invited to perform for a charity event at *Party In The Park*. Once again he chose to sing Spandau songs but this time Gary was able to block their broadcast on Channel 5. This appears to have set Tony off into an apoplexy of rage, at least according to the *Sun* of 7 July 2003, which quoted Tony as calling Gary Kemp 'petty and childish' and saying: 'I hate Gary. He's shown he's absolutely pathetic. This is a children's charity.' On stage he also said sarcastically to the crowd, 'I'd like to dedicate this to a very good friend of mine Gary Kemp – I'd like to wish him all the best.'

A few weeks later, in an interview by an *Evening Standard* journalist published on 4 August 2003, Tony called Gary 'a bloody hypocrite' and was reported as saying, 'If I saw him or his brother, they'd bleeding well know about it, if you know what I mean.' During this interview, Tony also claimed that Gary 'used to give the rest of us a small cut for our creative input' which Gary had then withdrawn. Subsequently, however, the *Evening Standard* was forced to publish an apology to Gary in which it was stated that, 'Mr Kemp has asked us to emphasise that the payments he made to the other members of the group were not for 'creative input'' and, the newspaper said, 'We apologise to Mr Kemp for any contrary impression which may have been created.'

Against this background, it came as somewhat of a surprise when a story announcing 'Spandau Ballet are reforming' appeared in the *Sun* on 19 March 2004 but it was later rubbished by Tony, who explained that his friend Shane Richie, had, apparently without his knowledge, approached Martin and Gary at an awards ceremony to suggest it was time Spandau got back together, leading them to believe Tony himself was interested. In Tony's autobiography, published in the first week of May 2004, he claimed there was 'no chance' of a reunion. Despite this, Gary told fans who came to see him perform in a play called *Pignight* at precisely the same time that he was extremely hopeful that Spandau Ballet *could* get back together with Tony as lead singer. Gary had been encouraged by the recent re-establishment of friendly relations with Steve Norman, and a detailed offer was put to Tony by promoters to which, instead of 'no chance', he was now saying 'never say never' and actually thinking about it. In the end, it was not to be and talk of a possible reunion fizzled out. One of the sticking points appeared to be that Tony did not want Steve Dagger to manage the band, which is presumably why, at the start of 2005, Gary suddenly announced out of the blue that he would not agree to reform Spandau Ballet unless all six of them were involved, including Dagger.

Tony's book was itself a weapon in the dispute as he took the opportunity to criticize the detailed 1999 judgment of Mr Justice Park by saying, 'I think he was wrong' – although his analysis pretty much stopped there. Relying on his memory, he also muddled up the legal matters, apparently believing that the judge had given him leave to appeal when, in fact, this had been refused. His two main gripes against Gary in respect of this litigation were that he had apparently been too busy to meet him to discuss the royalty payments before the writ had been issued and that, following judgment, he had pursued him for his full legal costs, although, as Gary's victory had fully entitled him to do this, it sounded rather like sour grapes.

Tony was also critical in his book of Gary for not allowing him to use the 'ex Spandau Ballet' name but he omitted to make any mention at all of the 1999 trademark registration which had been the central issue in the 2001 litigation, referring only to 'a trademark issue' which he did not explain. His biggest complaint, however, seemed to be that he had received notification of the legal claim on Christmas Eve, thus ruining his Christmas, and this made such an impact on him that it was actually how he chose to begin the story of his life. But the timing of events would have been out of Gary's hands and can be explained by the fact that Tony's management did not reply to the 20 November letter from Marbelow's solicitors, Charles Russell, demanding the return of the trademark, until 13 December, with the claim form consequently issued at court just over a week later on 22 December, which meant that, by the time it was served on Tony through the postal system by Charles Russell, who were no doubt attempting to effect service as quickly as possible, it was Christmas Eve when he received it. The timing was just one of those things but Tony gave the impression that it was part of Gary's persecution of him. The possible reunion being discussed at the time of publication caused the book, with its focus on the dispute with Gary, to be out of date almost as soon as it was in the shops and, when the paperback edition came out in March 2005, the new extra chapter it included was all about Tony's agonizing over whether to accept the offer of a Spandau tour or not.

Shortly before Live8 (Bob Geldof's follow-up to Live Aid) in the summer of 2005, a story somehow reached the press that Spandau Ballet had been offered a slot on stage but a certain unnamed former member of the band had refused to appear. There were no prizes for guessing who it was. This story was even repeated on the official Spandau Ballet site. Furthermore, after Live8, Gary Kemp was quoted in the Glasgow *Sunday Mail* of 31 July 2005 as saying:

> Tony doesn't want to perform with Spandau any more, that's the simple truth. Bob Geldof wanted us to do Live8 but I think our problems are harder to solve than the problems in Africa. I want to move on from the court case of 1999 but I don't think Tony is ready....It didn't occur to me Tony might not want to bury the hatchet. Steve was able to do that and we're friends again. Tony sings my songs on his solo tours and good luck to him. But he'd be able to sing them to more people if we all got back together.

That was a double whammy from Gary, publicizing both that Tony refused to do Live8 and that he (Gary) was friends with Steve Norman again, something which was not widely known at the time. Indeed, that particular rapprochement had happened quite suddenly and out of the blue, apparently in the early part of 2004. Until that point, Tony, Steve and John had appeared to be solidly united against an isolated Gary (the support of his brother could be said not to count) and this unity gave some moral force to Tony's position that Gary was the villain of the piece. Steve's switching of sides tended to undermine this simplistic view. It had only been a few weeks earlier that Steve had written in his and Tony's official fanclub magazine (December 2003 issue) of an unnamed 'ex-band member's selfish behaviour' which had caused him to seek to distance himself from Spandau Ballet as much as he could. With hindsight, it is unclear exactly which band member Steve was referring to.

In September 2006, Gary asked to be added as one of Tony's friends on MySpace but Tony, or whoever was running his MySpace page, declined to add him. Subsequently, Gary amended his MySpace page which had said that 'Tony Hadley' was the person he would most like to meet and replaced him with his late grandfather. In January 2007, Tony gave an interview to the *Weekend* magazine of the *Daily Mail* in which he was quoted as saying that he was 'too trusting of people and too gullible'. It wasn't hard to work out what he meant. The magazine also claimed, presumably because Tony told them, that there had been a gentleman's agreement between the band members made as school friends 'always to share the band's royalties between them', something which the judge in the 1999 court case ruled had not happened. In a February 2007 interview to the website Remembertheeighties.com, Tony was quoted as saying that 'there were a lot of things that went on personally behind the scenes that I couldn't write about and could never appear in a book or in interviews' and, although he didn't mention Gary, the implication was clear enough that he had somehow been injured even more than he had let on in his book.

However, in April 2007, Tony stirred up media speculation when he appeared as a guest on the Shane Richie show on Virgin Radio and mumbled vaguely about the possibility of Spandau reforming for the band's thirtieth anniversary in 2009, a date which he described as providing a 'window of opportunity' although he also said that a lot of things needed to be remedied first. Tony's words at this time were subject to closer scrutiny than announcements from the Politburo in the days of the Soviet

Union and this subtle change of emphasis (albeit no different in substance to what he had said in his revised paperback) seems to have excited the other band members. Gary reveals in his book that, towards the end of the year, John Keeble contacted Steve Norman to commence the process of reconciliation, following which Gary met up with Tony and John in a Soho pub.

Rumours started to surface in 2008 that there was actually, and incredibly, going to be a Spandau Ballet reunion. Indeed, the *Daily Star Sunday,* on 3 August 2008, announced that the band was set for a comeback. When the press was informed in early March 2009 that there was going to be an announcement on HMS Belfast on 25 March it could only mean one thing. Against all the odds, Tony had managed to put aside his differences with Gary and rejoin the band for a new tour. Not only that, but the two men hugged each other aboard the Belfast. It was probably the greatest public reconciliation of two former enemies since Mohamed Fayed and Tiny Rowland had settled their bitter eight-year dispute over the acquisition of House of Fraser, shaking hands in the food hall of Harrods in 1993 underneath a stuffed shark that Fayed had named 'Tiny'.

In many ways, the Spandau Ballet reconciliation was as inevitable as the break-up had been. All the pressures on Tony, who was the key to the whole thing, were pushing him in one direction. Both Steve and John, who had continued as musicians without great financial reward, wanted a lucrative comeback tour and Tony must surely have felt that he owed them something, having led them down the path to defeat in the High Court. John had loyally stuck by Tony for ten years and for Tony to have continued to have refused would not only have left him isolated as the only member against a reunion but it would have been unfair to John.

Of course, the financial attractions were so great for everyone, not least for Tony. Although, by the time the reunion was announced, he had long since repaid all the debts incurred from the court case, he had also separated from his wife of twenty years and the ensuing divorce must have been costly. It is also easy to imagine that such a life-changing event had an effect on the way he thought about a Spandau Ballet reunion, especially as he became open to new influences from the people around him. He certainly appears to have become more humble following the separation from his wife as uncharacteristic comments by him, such as 'I was stupid and selfish' which appeared in *Closer* magazine in January 2004, suggest. As we know, some of Tony's friends, such as Shane Richie, thought a reunion was sensible, and Tony was having to deal with the question of a reunion in virtually every interview he gave. He was probably hearing the same question from every taxi cab driver he ever hired. Moreover, Tony's own son, Tom, appears to have played a part behind the scenes in about 2007, secretly meeting with Gary's son, Finlay, to plot a reconciliation, paving the way for their respective parents to shake hands, although it was John Keeble whose quiet diplomacy ultimately appears to have been the decisive factor in getting all sides back together.

Had it just been the lure of money alone, Tony might well have resisted but once he agreed to walk into the same room as Gary and share a few drinks he obviously realized it was pointless to continue with the grudge. As Tony said on the Belfast, 'Time is a great healer'. His autobiography had allowed him to get his grievances out in the open and publishing it must have been cathartic, enabling him to move on. It is hard work to maintain a grudge against a former friend and colleague, especially such a public one, and it must have had a punishing emotional impact on Tony over the years. In a philosophical moment during the summer of 2009, Tony said, 'As you get older you think you don't want to pop your clogs before you've put a few things to rest'. Making up with Gary made too much sense not to do it.

Tony was able to deal with the inevitable press questions as to his apparent u-turn with ease, pointing out that he had previously said 'never say never'. This was a touch disingenuous because his 'never say never' comment only originated in 2004, following receipt of an offer of a lucrative reunion tour, and he had, in fact, spent the previous few years literally saying he would never do it. But it would be churlish to criticize him for this and, generously, no journalist ever pressed the point. Tony has also pointed out that 'loads of people' said to him: 'Good on yer son, make yourself a few quid' and one can hardly argue with that.

Funnily enough, no-one ever asked Martin about his change of mind. He had previously said a number of times that there was no way he would ever go back into the band, claiming to David Vincent in an interview for Amazon.com in 2000, for example, that the idea was his 'worst nightmare'. In The *Westminster & Pimlico News* of 2 January 2003, he was quoted as saying quite categorically, 'I would never be in Spandau Ballet again…I think you can only move forward and that would be going backwards. I think it would kill me.' However, his own acting career had come to a bit of a pause – the low point being the change of broadcast time by ITV for his gangster series, *The Family*, which suddenly, and ludicrously, switched from 9:30pm on Tuesdays to 11:30pm on Wednesdays mid-series after poor ratings – and a reunion made as much sense for him as it did for everyone else.

For Gary, too, a reunion was an obvious way forward. Following *The Krays* and smaller parts in *The Bodyguard* and *Killing Zoe*, he seems to have become disillusioned with acting, unhappy with the lack of control and creative input enjoyed by actors, although he still took occasional roles in stage plays and appeared in the odd film or television drama. His solo songwriting career had, somewhat surprisingly, never really taken off. His 1995 album, *Little Bruises,* had not been a commercial success and, although his live solo performances of 'Through the Barricades' prior to that song's release had been generally well received by the audiences, if not by the critics, at a number of charity and political concerts during late 1985 and early 1986 (i.e. The Snowball Revue in aid of battered women, Red Wedge and Artists Against Apartheid), his singing voice, in all honesty, wasn't strong enough to carry him as a lead vocalist. His musical about the life of Yeats entitled *A Terrible Beauty* never saw the light of day and, although he wrote tracks for other artists, none of them enjoyed commercial or even artistic success. By 2008, he appears to have been doing voiceovers for Peugeot car adverts (at least, the chap doing it certainly sounded like him) which is probably not how he had hoped he would end up earning a living.

The tour, culminating in two sell-out nights at the O2 Arena in London's Docklands, on 20 and 21 October 2009, was supposed to be a thirtieth anniversary tour but the dates did not quite work. Spandau Ballet had not come into existence until after the Halligan's gig on 17 November 1979 so, with the anniversary tour commencing on 13 October 2009, the band had not yet quite reached the thirty year anniversary mark. It is interesting that Gary Kemp mistakenly claimed in his 2009 autobiography that the Halligan's gig was in October 1979 which possibly suggests that there was a complete mix-up in the organization and the tour started a month earlier than it ought to have done in the belief that the Halligan's gig had been in October. Or perhaps Gary simply convinced himself into thinking Halligan's must have been in October 1979 when he wrote his book because he knew October 2009 was when the tour was to start. But, well, even Chosen Ones cannot change history.

EPILOGUE

And Then There Were Four

IT DIDN'T LAST. It couldn't last. Of course it couldn't. For six years, following the triumphant, well-received 2009 reunion, the band performed live, off and on, every now and then, in various countries around the world, churning out all the old hits. In a sign of the times, the modern Spandau Ballet was now 'powered by' Ecotricity, an energy company, with the band's new official website proclaiming that, 'Spandau Ballet are happy to recommend that fans switch to Ecotricity for their power supplies'. An album called *Once More* was released in October 2009, featuring stripped down, acoustic versions of classic Spandau Ballet songs, plus two brand new tracks, 'Once More' and 'Love Is All', the former being jointly written by Gary and Steve, the latter being, for the first time for the band, a Tony Hadley sole composition. It wasn't exactly what one would call a proper album though.

Things seemed to be going reasonably well for a year or two – Gary and Tony appeared to be comfortable together both on and off stage – but, in 2011, Tony was already making noises in public about preferring to resume his solo career. Appearing on ITV's *Loose Women* in May 2012, he told Janet Street-Porter that it was 'very doubtful' that he would tour again with Spandau Ballet. There was, nevertheless, another single recorded and released in 2014, the band's best new song for many years, 'This is the Love', written by Gary Kemp and produced by back-in-favour Trevor Horn; and perhaps, one might have thought, the love had returned to the group. The less memorable 'Soul Boy', another Hadley composition, recorded to accompany the 2014 release of *Soul Boys of the Western World*, followed a few months later and there were to be some more live performances in early 2015 – during which the band got on 'splendidly' according to Steve Norman – but this seemed to mark the end of the new journey as there were to be no more public appearances of the five band members together.

In September 2016, according to a statement posted (much later) on the official Spandau Ballet website, Tony 'made it clear' to his colleagues that he did not want to work with the band any more. Things went silent for a few months but, on 31 January 2017, the Spandau Ballet website teased fans that there was 'some rather splendid Spandau news on the horizon'. No such news was ever announced but the fact that something big was being planned which never went ahead may provide a clue as to what was causing tension within the group; according to Ashleigh Rainbird in the *Daily Mirror*, quoting an unnamed source, 'The band were offered a string of lucrative opportunities...But Tony opted to focus on his solo career, meaning everyone missed out'.

The next Spandau news was, as a result, not 'rather splendid'. Instead, on 3 July 2017, Tony issued a terse, carefully worded, statement in which he said that, with deep regret and due to circumstances beyond his control, 'I am required to state that I am no longer a member of the band Spandau Ballet'. He did not explain why he was 'required' to state this nor what the circumstances were that were beyond his control but, according to the *Sun* newspaper, 'a source' provided information that Tony preferred to do 'small solo gigs making money for himself than performing with Spandau' and the newspaper claimed that the rest of the band were 'totally bewildered' by his decision. So bewildered were they, in fact, that Steve Norman issued his own personal counter-statement four days later in which he said that he found Tony's claim that his decision to leave the band was out of his control to be 'utterly confusing' – he insisted that the decision was Tony's alone and that he wasn't pushed out by the rest of the band. Nevertheless, for the first time ever, including the years of the hard fought legal proceedings, the band actually, formally, split up. One wonders if the wounds created many years earlier had ever really healed.

In truth, Spandau Redux 2009 hadn't quite been the same; but then again how could it? That amazing, almost spiritual, camaraderie between five young, innocent and optimistic friends in the early eighties with their whole lives ahead of them, fuelled by all sorts of creative possibilities, could never be replicated by five middle-aged men, their best years apparently behind them, fuelled by all sorts of commercial possibilities, with a history of mistrust and arguments. But at least they tried.

The remaining four members have suggested that they will keep the band going in some form or another so, perhaps, the journey to glory will continue?

AFTERWORD

The Two Spandau Ballets and the Three Bass Guitarists

IT IS, I THINK, an indication of how strongly they feel about their creative achievement of devising a brilliant band name having been erased from history that, not far short of forty years after the event, all the members of the *original* Spandau Ballet were not only happy to give up their time to speak to me, in order to allow me to understand how their band was formed and disbanded during 1978 and 1979, but also to search through dusty drawers and cupboards to locate old documents, articles and photographs to supplement their story. Of the three founding and constant members of the band, Mick Austin went on to become an award winning artist, Mark Robinson went on to run his own design company and become a highly successful golf artist, and David Wardill went on to become a proper pop star but all of them, to a greater or lesser extent, have carried a sense of indignation throughout their lives that they have not received recognition for their moment, or possibly moments, of inspiration. The same is true for Michael Harvey, now a solicitor. Gordon Bowman, who went on to study Business Studies at college and then worked in retail before transferring to the area of health and social care, had no part to play in the actual creation of the band's name but he did play a huge role in disseminating that name around London with his green spray can and he, too, was very happy to give up his time to tell me his story.

Being someone who, as you know, liked Spandau Ballet's music during the 1980s, I was always intrigued by the band's name and have a distinct memory of the band members being asked on a Saturday morning children's television show where it had come from. Although I can't now remember exactly what they said, and haven't been able to track down that particular piece of footage, I seem to recall they were not terribly pleased to be asked, in similar fashion to other interviews I have located. At the same time, I was aware, either from their answer, or from the music press, that the name had supposedly been seen by someone written on a toilet wall. This did not seem very satisfactory to me because it did not explain what the name meant. What connection did a ballet have with Spandau? In my mind, it always brought up the image, as it clearly did for the writer Roy Bainton, already quoted in this book, of the constant rotation of the armies guarding Rudolf Hess in Spandau gaol but I wondered if this was what it was originally intended to mean.

My discovery of the existence of an earlier band called Spandau Ballet occurred back in 2004 when I was carrying out research at the British Newspaper Library, which was then in Colindale, for some articles I was writing for Deformation, a website that you might recall me saying I was running at the time. Looking through early issues of the *NME*, I was intrigued to discover an explanation provided by Robert Elms for the band name which had nothing to do with seeing any graffiti on any wall. I already knew that he had said something similar in the sleeve notes to the Gold compilation CD, which had somewhat baffled me because it was so different from the long-established story. Then I really became interested when I found the letter from 'Michael Austin', evidently written in late 1980 but published in the *NME* in early 1981, in which a clearly furious Austin claimed to have devised the name with his friend 'Dave'.

I naturally wanted to find out more about this early Spandau Ballet band. The only clue I had was that Austin had been living in

Ampthill, Bedfordshire, during 1980, because this was the address he gave to the *NME*, and so I began a search for him. He was rather hard to track down and, at one point, I sent a message to another Michael Austin whose email address I discovered somewhere on the internet. He wrote back from Australia to tell me that, while he was a musician (bass guitarist) from Bedford and had worked extensively in the UK, he was not *the* 'Michael Austin' I was seeking. To my surprise, he added that before he migrated to Australia he remembered there being a Michael Austin who was connected with Spandau Ballet who, he believed, lived in Ampthill. A follow-up email elicited the fact that his knowledge of the other Michael Austin came from Mick's letter in the *NME*, a letter which had caused some people to quiz this Michael Austin as to whether *he* had any connection with Spandau Ballet. He had even asked around at the time to find his namesake, but unsuccessfully.

At the same time, I was reviewing every edition of the *Ampthill News and Flitwick Record* from the 1970s in order to try and locate a mention of this band in their local newspaper but without any success. I also trawled through the listings sections of the back issues of the *NME*, *Melody Maker*, *Sounds* and *Record Mirror* but there was no mention in any of them of a band called Spandau Ballet before November 1979, or in any other published source that I was aware of, and I virtually gave up any hope of finding anything further.

The breakthrough came in late 2008 when I realized that, in May of that year, someone had added to Spandau Ballet's Wikipedia entry a sentence or two relating the story of the original Spandau Ballet, in the context of an explanation of the more famous band's name, which revealed that the full name of 'Dave' was David Agar Wardill, the bass guitarist of The Passions. A subsequent browse of a Passions website then revealed a posting, dated 30 August 2008, addressed to Wardill on the guestbook of that site from a Mark Robinson, referring to the old band they both used to be in. It said, 'Just a quick note to Dave. Do you remember the real Spandau Ballet? The Venue rehearsals etc.

Come on, speak up!! Hope you are well, Mark. Say hi to Mickey' and contained Mark's email address. I wrote to him and he quickly replied. His reply copied in Mick Austin, who turned out to have been the author of the Wikipedia addition, and David Wardill with whom he had regained contact following the posting. I had finally found the members of the band we would refer to as SBv.1.

Perhaps the most extraordinary aspect of the existence of the original Spandau Ballet was that 32 Sibley Grove, where David Wardill lived for about a year (and Mick Austin for a much shorter time) was a real New Romantic hot spot, in which seminal Blitz kids such as Kim Bowen, Lee Sheldrick, George O'Dowd (Boy George), David Holah and 'Electric' Barry, either lived or visited; and Kim, especially, was closely connected with Graham Smith, Robert Elms, Steve Dagger and the members of Gentry as they were then known. Leaving aside whether this connection had anything to do with the transmission of the name from one band to the other, it is amusing to think that if David and his fellow band members in early 1979 had considered writing the type of music their housemates liked, and dressed in the same way as them, they already had a name that would have fitted perfectly. They were Spandau Ballet and had a clear head start over all other bands if they had wanted to become the 'house band' of the New Romantic movement. But the thought never occurred to them and, frankly, I have no doubt they would have rejected the idea if it had, preferring to concentrate on the type of music they liked to play.

Another surprise for me was that David Agar (as he then was) was actually asked about his membership of Spandau Ballet by a music journalist shortly after he joined The Passions. His reply that he had been in such a band before the formation of Steve Dagger's band had been sitting there in black and white in the *NME* all along, ignored or misunderstood by everyone.

Talking of bass players, another key and invaluable source for me in writing this book was Michael Ellison, the original bass player in Roots. I contacted him through the now defunct Friends Reunited website and was delighted to receive a reply which enabled us to meet for an interview. He is a charming man who has continued to play the bass guitar in various bands, which he absolutely loves doing, and one can see how happy he is when he is performing on stage. He doesn't seem to have any regrets about leaving the band in 1977 and probably feels he would have been replaced by Martin Kemp in any event had he remained in it but I know that he would love to play with the other members of Roots one more time and it would be rather nice if the members of Spandau Ballet made that happen.

My biggest regret was that I was unable to make contact with Richard Miller, the bass player of The Makers. I tried to send messages to him in various ways but, if I was successful (which is not certain), I guess he does not want to discuss the past. Having said that, he doesn't seem to hold any kind of grudge against the band for replacing him, despite the rather underhand way it was done, and I understand (and I hope he won't mind me saying) that he was present at the Royal Albert Hall premiere of the Spandau Ballet film in 2014, suggesting that he is still in contact with his old bandmates.

In the end it was Martin who played the bass in Spandau Ballet (second version), and in some respects he literally *was* the chosen one; but chosen by Dagger, not the Bishop!

APPENDIX 1

The Boy and the Bishop

GARY PROVIDES FIVE 'CLUES' in his autobiography which could assist us with the dating of Bishop Huddleston's visit to his home:

1. It was during a *Top of the Pops* performance of 'Maggie May' by Rod Stewart.
2. The performance featured Rod Stewart and The Faces kicking a football around.
3. Jimmy Savile was the host of that particular night's *Top of the Pops*.
4. It was before a concert at the Oval to raise money for Bangladesh.
5. It was shortly before a Kemp family outing 'at the weekend' to a holiday camp in Westward Ho!

Unfortunately it is impossible for all five to be correct and Gary's memory has, quite understandably, let him down somewhere.

Anyway, let us take each of these 'clues' individually.

The track 'Maggie May' was initially released by Rod Stewart in the United States in July 1971 as a B-Side to the song 'Reason To Believe'. It wasn't long before a DJ in Cleveland, Ohio, decided to ignore the A-side and play 'Maggie May' instead. This evidently proved popular with his listeners and, with other radio shows following suit, the Billboard chart for the week ending 14 August 1971 listed the track, then slowly creeping up the chart to number 62, as 'Reason To Believe/Maggie May' whereas previously it had been 'Reason To Believe' alone. The following week, as the song's popularity grew across the United States, it was 'Maggie May/Reason To Believe'. By this time, the song had been released in the UK, again as 'Reason To Believe', but when Rod Stewart appeared with The Faces (with whom he was touring) on *Top of the Pops*, hosted by Tony Blackburn, on 19 August 1971, it was 'Maggie May' they performed (for the first time on British television) and no footballs were kicked around.

At this time, *Top of the Pops* allowed artists on the show even though they were not in the charts and this was the case with Rod Stewart who did not enter the chart until the last day of August (at number thirty-one) and, while 'Maggie May' was being played on the radio as if it was the 'A' side, the single was listed in the official chart as 'Reason To Believe' (although the *NME*'s chart recorded it as 'Maggie May'). It was not until 13 September that 'Reason To Believe' was finally replaced by 'Maggie May' as the official A-side and listed as such in the official UK chart – now at number eleven. Two days later, on 16 September, *Top of the Pops*, again hosted by Tony Blackburn, repeated the footage of 'Maggie May' that had been recorded and broadcast in August and this lifted the track to a chart position of number three. Then, with 'Maggie May' sitting nicely at number two in the chart of 28 September, Rod and The Faces were back at the BBC and recorded a new performance but still without a football. This was broadcast on *Top of the Pops* of 30 September 1971, hosted by Ed Stewart. The record buying public seemed to like it and sent the song to number one the following week, leading to a repeat of the recording on *Top of the Pops* of 7 October, hosted by Jimmy Savile. The same recording was repeated again on *Top of the Pops* of 14 October, hosted by Tony Blackburn but then Rod and the band were brought back to the BBC for a new recording, involving John Peel and a football, which was broadcast on a *Top of the Pops* hosted by Jimmy Savile on 21 October. This recording was probably repeated on both 28 October (with Ed Stewart as host) and 4 November (Jimmy Savile) before the track lost its number one position.

If the first three of Gary's clues were all correct then we would have little problem in identifying the date of the Bishop's visit as Thursday, 21 October 1971. On this date we have a *Top of the Pops* episode meeting all of Gary's criteria: it was hosted by Jimmy Savile and featured a performance of Maggie May by Rod Stewart during which, for the first time, a football was kicked around. However, 21 October was definitely not the date of the visit. For, that evening, Bishop Huddleston was at the Court Lodge County Secondary School in Horley where he was guest speaker – talking about world responsibility and his six years as Bishop in Tanzania – at the school's annual Speech Day. This is confirmed by the Bishop's diary (about which see overleaf) and a local newspaper report. The event commenced at 7:45pm, only a few minutes before Rod 'kicked off' on *Top of the Pops*, a programme which started at 7:25pm and concluded after playing that week's number one (i.e. 'Maggie May') shortly before 8:00pm, which makes it impossible for the Bishop to have interrupted Gary's enjoyment of the music show on that particular evening.

It is true that Jimmy Savile also hosted *Top of the Pops* on 4 November and this episode possibly included a repeat of the performance in which the football was kicked around but we can effectively rule this evening out as being the night of the visit. In the first place, Gary's account implies that the performance has stuck in his mind because it was the first time he had seen Rod Stewart. It may be a literary device, and Gary's telling of the story of the Bishop's visit reads rather more like an Alan Bennett drama than actual recollection, but Gary refers to Rod as 'the singer' when telling the story in his book, suggesting that, having missed Jimmy Savile's introduction, he did not even know who he was. The appearance of the football certainly seems to have taken him by surprise, being 'too fascinating to ignore'. Yet this account does not make any sense in the context of a visit on 4

November. As a devoted viewer of *Top of the Pops*, which he says he had been since March 1971, Gary would not only have been very familiar with Rod Stewart and Maggie May by the first week of November – the song having been number one for four weeks – but he would already have seen the performance of it with the football on Top of the Pops on 21 October (and probably again on 28 October).

Even if Gary had, for whatever reason, missed all previous episodes of *Top of the Pops* featuring 'Maggie May' there are other problems. Gary says that the Bishop told him he had been helping to put on a charity concert which was 'going to be' at the Oval cricket ground. This concert took place on Saturday, 18 September 1971, which means that any broadcast after this date does not fit the story. Of course, Gary could simply be confused and the Bishop actually told him that the concert had already taken place. After all these years such a memory lapse would not be surprising. Yet there is one more crucial fact which tends to demolish the 4 November date. The Bishop of Stepney's personal diary for 1971 is kept at Oxford's Rhodes House Library. Access to it is restricted for some reason but it was examined for me by the librarian with Gary's visit in mind. It shows that Huddleston had an appointment at St James the Less Church in Westminster at 7:00pm on 4 November 1971, making it highly unlikely that he would have been in Gary's home before 8:00pm that evening.

In fact, on the basis of Trevor Huddleston's diary we can probably also rule out all of October because his Thursday evenings during this month seem to be full and accounted for.

At this point, we need to ask ourselves about the reliability of Gary's memory in respect of both Jimmy Savile and the appearance of the football during the 'Maggie May' performance. Under normal circumstances, the chances of Gary recalling the presenter of a particular episode of *Top of the Pops* more than thirty-five years after the broadcast are effectively zero. However, Gary says that Savile looked like a younger version of the Bishop, which was a reasonable comparison.* So it is just about possible that it could have stuck in his mind for this reason. However, we need to consider another possibility. While attempting to refresh his memory during the writing of his book, it would only have been natural for Gary to search on the internet, specifically on You Tube, for a recording of 'Maggie May' on *Top of the Pops*. Had he done so, he would have found a clip of Jimmy Savile introducing Rod Stewart and The Faces with a performance interrupted by a short game of football. Certainly the performance with the football is the only TOTP recording of the performance of 'Maggie May' that still exists (the BBC having wiped all the other tapes) and is, therefore, the only TOTP performance of 'Maggie May' available on the internet. Seeing this footage, it would only have been natural for Gary to have assumed that *this* must have been what he saw, or rather tried to see, on *Top of the Pops* while Huddleston was distracting him as an eleven-year-old all those years ago.

So we have to consider the possibility of a performance of 'Maggie May' without Jimmy Savile and/or without the football. Returning to the Bishop's diary with this in mind, it is blank for Thursday, 19 August 1971, as it is for most of August, apparently because this month was set aside (like it was every year) as a holiday month. In August of the previous year, the Bishop had spent the first half of the month in Tunisia and the second half on the Isle of Arran but in August of 1971 he only went abroad in the last week of the month, when it is a matter of record that he flew to India on 25 August, returning to London on 1 September. We know that he did not visit any other countries during August 1971 because a newsletter to his flock in January 1972 stated that he only went abroad three times during the previous year: to Jamaica (in Easter), to Tanzania (in December) and India (at the end of

---

* In view of the now known activities of both Savile and Huddleston (the latter being visited by police in 1974 regarding allegations of gross indecency with young boys) it is also a rather unsettling comparison.

August). He was certainly out of London, on holiday, as at 6 August 1971 because his personal secretary recorded this in a letter to the Overseas Christian Communication Centre, but this leaves open the possibility of him spending the first two weeks on holiday somewhere (perhaps the Isle of Arran) and returning to London during the week commencing 16 August, thus allowing him to visit Gary Kemp on the Thursday of that week. We shall return to the possibility of the visit being on this night in August.

For Thursday 16 September, there is an 8:00pm appointment recorded in respect of an attendance at a meeting of the management committee of the St George's Adventure Playground Association, which would have been held at the St George's Methodist Hall in Cable Street, Tower Hamlets, and this allows us to rule it out as the day of the visit. The evening of Thursday, 30 September 1971, also looks unlikely because there is an entry: '8pm; Christ Church, Highbury, Youth Fellowship' in the diary. Having said this, the Kemp household in Islington was not too far away from Highbury and it is possible that Huddleston could have left Gary at about 7:45pm, allowing him to honour his appointment at Christ Church. With 'Maggie May' not yet being in the number one position it would probably have been broadcast before a quarter to eight. However, by 30 September, the Oval concert had already taken place which does not fit Gary's story.

If we can rule out 16 September on the basis of the entry in the Bishop's diary, the only evening of a 'Maggie May' performance that fits Gary's account of the visit being before the Oval concert is the evening of 19 August 1971. This date has the clear advantage of being the first time Gary would have seen Rod Stewart, as a solo artist, on television and quite possibly the first time he had heard 'Maggie May' which had only been released (as a B-side) a couple of weeks earlier. At this time, Rod was a reasonably well known recording artist and his album, *Every Picture Tells A Story*, from which 'Maggie May' was taken, had entered the Top Ten of the album charts, but he was not quite a household name, and had not previously charted in the UK, so the likelihood is that Gary would not have known who he was when he saw him on *Top of the Pops* on 19 August. Yet he was not so unknown that it would have been impossible for the Bishop to have been able to identify him when he saw him on Gary's television. It is true that the existence of the charity concert at the Oval, and the fact that The Faces would be appearing, had not been publicly announced as at 19 August – the announcement of the concert was not made until the end of the month and even then it was only stated that The Faces had been 'approached' to appear – so if the Bishop did mention the concert to Gary on this date it was an exclusive reveal. Yet the concert was presumably in the late planning stages at this time, so this is not impossible, although it is unlikely that the Bishop would have met The Who or The Faces, as Gary seems to suggest, at any time before the concert.

We ought, however, to consider if Gary's recollection about this part of the conversation is correct. Did the Bishop even mention a concert for Bangladesh? The conclusion has to be that he must have said something about it, otherwise how else could Gary even have known about his connection with it? Nothing about it appears on the internet nor is it mentioned by either of Huddleston's two biographers. None of the reviews of the concert in the music press indicated that the Bishop attended or was connected with it.

It is certainly well known that Huddleston was deeply involved in the issues relating to Bangladesh, or East Pakistan, where there was a famine and refugee crisis, following both a cyclone and an attack on the civilian population by the army of West Pakistan, and, on 25 August 1971, as mentioned above, he flew out to the country to see the situation for himself but there appears to have been only one contemporary mention of his involvement with the concert at the Oval. The *Evening Standard* announced on 17 September 1971 that Bishop Huddleston, amongst others, had been appointed to the Board of Trustees, with responsibility to oversee and administer the distribution of the funds raised by the concert, which was, in the event, £17,000. While possibly reported elsewhere, this appears to be the only publicly available corroboration that the Bishop was associated in any way with the concert so, clearly, Gary did not imagine or invent the connection and he is hardly likely to have trawled through back issues of newspapers from 1971 when writing his autobiography. Flowing from this, the fact that the Bishop mentioned the concert does seem to corroborate Gary's memory that he was watching Rod Stewart and The Faces perform 'Maggie May' on *Top of the Pops* at the time (or else why would the Bishop have brought the subject up?).

The fact that the announcement of the Bishop's appointment was the very day before the concert might suggest that Huddleston could not have visited Gary any earlier than this but Ray Foulk, the promoter of the concert, has kindly confirmed in email correspondence with me that Huddleston's appointment would have been agreed some weeks in advance of the concert, possibly in August (or earlier), and would have formed part of the promoter's pitch to the Surrey County Cricket Club in order to obtain clearance to use the Oval.

There is one clue which has not yet been considered, namely Gary's recollection that, at the time of the visit, his parents were packing to go to a holiday camp at Devon's Westward Ho! at the weekend. This may be the key to the whole mystery. Such a holiday would have lasted at least a week, possibly two, which means that Gary simply must have been on his school holidays at the time. School Term would have ended on Friday, 23 July 1971, and Gary would have been off school until early September (probably the week commencing 6 September) when he joined Owen's. There would, of course, have been a half-term at Owen's, almost certainly from Monday, 25 October, to Friday, 29 October, but holiday camp season was from May to the end of September. Although a small number of camps would remain open during the first week of October, it did not make economic sense to retain staff and stay open later than this, and the Kemp family would not have taken their summer holiday in the first week of October when their children were at school, so, it seems that, on the basis of the Westward Ho! recollection, we can rule out any date after

September. Considering the problems with the September dates, when Gary was at school anyway, it does rather look like 19 August must have been the day of the Bishop's visit assuming Gary's basic recollection that 'Maggie May' was on television at the time is correct. In this respect, we may note that, when Gary appeared on Radio 1's *My Top 12* show in August 1983, he told the story of the Bishop's visit, probably for the first time in public, saying: 'I remember vividly when he [Huddleston] was sitting there, Rod Stewart was on *Top of the Pops* doing Maggie May' and, indeed, he selected 'Maggie May' as one of his Top 12 records because it had made such an impression on him: 'Maggie May has always meant a lot to me since then' he said. While memory of even important events in one's life can be faulty, it is hard to believe that Gary could have got this one fact wrong.

There is one final piece of information available: Trevor Huddleston's diary – which one might assume would answer this whole question – does mention Gary Kemp, twice, but in a rather baffling way each time. Here is what it says:

Friday 30 July 1971: '*Gary Kemp. Westward Ho!*'
Monday 25 October 1971: '*Gary Kemp*'

In addition, both entries are crossed out. According to Marion Lowman, the librarian at Rhodes House Library, this would normally indicate an appointment that was cancelled.

Neither entry really makes any sense although the reference to Westward Ho!, which is expressly mentioned by Gary in his autobiography in the context of the Bishop's visit, is intriguing. Does 'Westward Ho!' indicate that Gary was in Devon on 30 July? If so, why did the Bishop note it in his diary? We know that the Bishop spoke to Gary at the prize-giving and it is possible that Gary told him when and where he was going on his summer holiday. Perhaps the Bishop, planning to make a visit to the Kemp home, made a note of it in order to avoid visiting while Gary was away, although if that were the case one would expect a return date to be included. Or perhaps the Bishop intended to visit him on 30 July, thus noting Gary's name in his diary, but later discovered he was on holiday, thus adding 'Westward Ho!' to the diary and, additionally, adding 25 October as an alternative date to visit. If we assume that the Kemps were off to Westward Ho! during the last weekend in July for a two-week holiday, commencing on Saturday, 31 July, this would bring them back to London on Saturday, 14 August, providing the opportunity for the Bishop during the week when a new performance of 'Maggie May' would be broadcast on *Top of the Pops*. It fits but, of course, does not sit at all well with Gary's recollection that his parents were packing on the day of the visit in preparation for leaving for a holiday in Westward Ho! at the weekend. If 19 August were the correct date, Gary's holiday in Westward Ho! needs to have commenced on Saturday, 21 August (Saturday always being the first day of a holiday in a holiday camp in the 1970s because it was the day the previous week's guests would leave en masse), in which case the Bishop's diary entry makes no sense.

And what about the entry for Monday, 25 October? It would probably have been the start of half term for Gary, which may be why the Bishop noted it, perhaps because the Kemps were planning to go away somewhere that week too, but this is pure speculation. There is no conceivable explanation as to why the entries have been crossed out which, as stated above, would normally indicate a cancelled appointment but, in this instance, there was no appointment in the first place, the Bishop's appearance at the Kemp home being unheralded and unexpected, at least according to Gary's understanding of events. One could, perhaps, draw the conclusion that the Bishop visited Gary on one or both of the dates noted in his diary and, while this is not impossible, neither of those dates fit with Gary's firm recollection of 'Maggie May' being on television at the time. There were no performances of this song on television on either 30 July or 25 October.

A 19 August visit may not fit perfectly, and the mention of Westward Ho! in the Bishop's diary in July is problematic, but it seems to be the most likely occurrence. Considering the school term dates, it is certainly the only possible day of a Rod Stewart *Top of the Pops* appearance on which Gary's parents could have been packing for a week's family holiday, as a holiday camp holiday must have been, at a minimum. Certainly a July or August date seems to be much more likely than September or October.

In one telling of the story by Gary, on a Radio 2 documentary broadcast on 17 November 2009, he said:

> Trevor Huddleston who was Bishop of Stepney then, later head of anti apartheid movement, was there handing out prizes and a few days later he arrived at my house….

Similarly, in the narration for the 2014 documentary, *Soul Boys of the Western World*, Gary said that the Bishop came to his house 'about a week' after the prize-giving. We should not read too much into this, it may just be careless talk, but with the prize-giving having been on Thursday, 8 July (which we know from the Bishop's diary), the next Top of the Pops (15 July 1971) was hosted by Tony Blackburn and featured a performance of 'Won't Get Fooled Again' by The Who (a band which would play at the Oval concert so that their appearance on the television could have caused Bishop Huddleston to comment on his connection with that concert). The episode after that (22 July 1971) was hosted by Jimmy Savile with T-Rex's 'Get It On' at number one and Jimmy Savile was back hosting again on 29 July, an episode which featured both The Who and T-Rex but, as with the previous two episodes, no Rod Stewart or The Faces. There is nothing in the Bishop's diary to have prevented him from turning up at Gary's house on any of those dates, although he has an entry in his diary for 15 July 1971 at 6:45pm to indicate he was meeting with an unnamed friend or colleague at that time, with "Evening London Hospital?" pencilled in underneath. For 29 July, his diary also refers to meetings with friends and colleagues "throughout the day", with "Chichester Theatre" added.

A visit on 29 July, or any date after this, cannot conceivably be described as 'a few days later' or 'a week later'. At the same time, it would seem most likely that the visit would have been sooner rather than later after the prize-giving. For the Bishop to have waited until the end of September or October before visiting Gary seems unlikely and makes it improbable that Gary would use the expression of 'a few days' after the prize-giving. Considering that there was no televised appearance of 'Maggie May' in July, then, in the absence of any better theory, 19 August 1971 must go down in history as the day the Bishop of Stepney magically appeared in Rotherfield Street with his cassette recorder.

APPENDIX 2

Rocking at the Roxy

TWO OF THE OWNERS of the Roxy in 1977 were a self-styled 'art designer', Jean Justice, who, in truth, designed very little art, and a barrister, Jeremy Dacre Fox: male lovers who had met at a gay club in Knightsbridge in 1955 while they were both in their late twenties. They were a particularly interesting couple who first made it into the public eye in 1960 following a three-week orgy of alcohol and sex with their friend and former car salesmen, dashing 43-year-old Jimmy Nugent, who preferred to be known as Baron Nugent of Clonlost. Although he was, for a while, labelled by some as 'The Phoney Baron' because his title was Austrian and thought to be dubious in origin, it was real enough; King Edward VII had granted a royal warrant in 1908 for it to be used in the United Kingdom.

The Baron had become a minor celebrity in 1956 when he was chosen to co-host an American television show to be called *The Lady and the Lord*, his celebrity arising not from the show itself, which was never made, but from the public way in which he defeated a number of other English peers to secure the job (in what might be considered an early non-singing newspaper version of *The X Factor*) and then became miserable and impoverished out in Los Angeles after the American production company, having doubts about whether he was a genuine peer of the realm after all, cancelled the show. The news of his return to London in 1957 made the front page of the *Daily Mirror* and he was on the front page again when he supposedly gave notice, at Caxton Hall Register Office, of his intention to marry his intended American TV co-host, beautiful 24-year-old Vicki Benet, even though he had not asked the lady first and she was quoted in the press as saying, 'A wedding indeed! It's absolute nonsense...I'm never going to marry Jimmy.'

Anyone who was suspicious about the Baron's need to make it so publicly known that he wanted to get married might have felt their suspicions confirmed when, in May of the following year, he did marry a rather plump and dowdy woman called Rosemary Edwards, who was about the same age as him but looked much older, to the extent that anyone who saw them together would surely have assumed that she was his mother. The attraction to the Baron might have been that Miss Edwards was named in the will of her recently deceased grandfather who had left an estate of half a million pounds. Within a month of the wedding, the suddenly enriched Baron Nugent bought himself a nightclub in Soho's Berwick Street called the Nineteenth Club, the name of which he quickly changed to the Huntsman. His best friend, and the best man at his wedding, Captain David Browne, already owned an illicit homosexual club in Gerrard Street called the Kandy Lounge and it seems that the Baron desired a similar club of his own just a short distance away.

He did not, however, desire the newly created Baroness Nugent, who was reported in August 1958 to have been abandoned by her husband and left in poverty. It seems that the half a million pounds from her grandfather's will was shared between Miss Edwards' relatives and what was left to her did not last long once her husband got his hands on it. The *Daily Mail* quoted her as saying: 'I'm broke. I must look for a job. I've never been in such a position before. I'm inundated with debts. I owe hundreds of pounds.' In fact, the marriage was never consummated – the Baron simply refused to have sex with his wife – and in May 1960 the poor lady was granted a *decree nisi* so that the marriage was annulled.

At some point, the Baron and his friend Captain Browne appear to have befriended Jean Justice and Jeremy Fox. The Baron was a member of the Naval and Military Club in Piccadilly which was virtually next door to Jean Justice's flat in Half Moon Street so that might have been how they met. Or it might have been in Captain Browne's Kandy Lounge. At any rate, Justice was soon allowing the Baron the free use of his flat and it was there that a twenty-year-old former personal attendant to Cliff Richard called Forbes Grant Walker, who the Baron dubiously claimed had been employed as his valet for one week, stole £14 and a watch worth £205 and was sentenced to four months imprisonment for this crime on 10 May 1960. Shortly after this, on 24 May, it was the Baron's turn to appear in the dock when he pleaded guilty at Bow Street Magistrates' Court to being drunk and disorderly after he was caught madly knocking over dustbins in Soho.

Rather more serious trouble was to follow in the summer of 1960 after Jean Justice picked up an eighteen-year-old male prostitute called David Dart in the street outside his flat in Piccadilly, a notoriously well-known area to find rent boys, and offered him £2 for sex back at the flat, an offer which was readily accepted. Justice rather liked the young man and introduced him to his friends: Jeremy Fox, Baron Nugent and Captain Browne. They all travelled together to Surrey for three weeks of serious drinking and sex sessions at Justice's bungalow in Newdigate, Surrey. However, it all went wrong when Dart started to feel aggrieved at being used as a sexual plaything and demanded large sums of money from Justice. He brought a rather rough friend of his to the bungalow to impress upon Justice and the others the seriousness of his request and, at one point, a knife was brandished to support the claim.

Justice paid up but decided to report the matter to the police. Dart and his associate were arrested and tried at the Old Bailey in September 1960 for demanding money with menaces and blackmail as well as theft of various items. However, with homosexuality illegal, Justice felt compelled to claim during the trial that the reason Dart had been at his bungalow in the first place was because he had employed him as his manservant. He gambled that Dart would go along with this, and would be as unwilling to reveal himself a male prostitute as Justice was to reveal himself a client of one, but the gamble failed miserably and Dart's barrister started asking the prosecution witnesses some very awkward questions, such as what Dart's duties as a manservant had been and why he was plied with drink every afternoon and taken out for dinner in the evenings. When Fox was asked in the witness box to confirm that he, Justice and Baron Nugent had all 'stripped absolutely naked' when they arrived at the bungalow, he replied, with quite unintentional hilarity, 'There were occasions when we did. It was very hot.' Baron Nugent, similarly, claimed that they only wanted to go sunbathing. In the end, following predictably sensational reporting of the trial in the tabloids, the two accused men were cleared by the jury.

The following year, Justice and Fox found themselves in the dock at Bow Street Magistrates' Court where they were convicted of unruly behaviour following a drunken jape which involved them holding open the doors, and pulling the communication cord, of a packed train at Clapham Common, thus delaying it for fifteen minutes, for which they were fined a total of £23. In 1962, Justice was bizarrely caught by police with a stolen parking meter under his bed and arrested for receiving stolen property – although he was given an absolute discharge after two of his friends helpfully admitted stealing it and putting it under his bed 'as a joke'.

By this time, Justice had started to play the more serious role of amateur detective, investigating the case of James Hanratty, who was hanged in 1962 after having been convicted of the so-called 'A6 murder' in which a scientist, Michael Gregston, was shot in the head while his companion, Valerie Storie, was raped and shot but survived. With the help of Jeremy Fox, Justice managed to get hold of the address of a man who had originally been suspected by police of committing the crime but who had been eliminated from their enquiries. His name was Peter Alphon. Justice believed

Hanratty was innocent and that Alphon was the real murderer. He befriended him and the two of them began a strange, probably sexual, relationship, with Alphon apparently falling in love with Justice who was playing a dangerous game, attempting to entrap Alphon into confessing his guilt or at least to drop his guard and incriminate himself. He had some partial success but Alphon physically attacked him in Green Park while he was meeting Hanratty's mother and Justice was forced to take out an unsuccessful private prosecution after the police refused to act. When he was threatened by Alphon while he was on holiday in Vienna, Justice panicked and attempted to purchase a revolver for protection. This led to the Austrian authorities becoming involved and they incarcerated him in a lunatic asylum for five days on the basis of his apparent paranoia. Undeterred, in 1964 he published a book on the case, accusing Alphon of being the true killer. A BBC *Panorama* documentary based on the allegations was broadcast in November 1966.

By now Justice had become obsessed with the case and, in 1969, was arrested outside the House of Commons while carrying out a demonstration against Hanratty's execution of seven years earlier. This brought him back to Bow Street Magistrates' Court where he was fined seven pounds and ten shillings. Fox supported his partner in the campaign and stood up in front of Lord Denning during a dinner at Lincoln's Inn to claim that Hanratty was the victim of an Establishment conspiracy. This was shortly after Denning had refused Hanratty's family leave to bring a private prosecution for negligence against the Home Secretary who had refused to commute Hanratty's death sentence. Justice also became chairman of the A6 murder appeal committee and fought an unsuccessful by-election campaign against a former Home Office Minister, Dick Taverne, in Lincoln in 1973, standing as the Independent Hanratty Enquiry Campaign candidate. When a report by Lewis Hawser Q.C. confirmed the correctness of Hanratty's conviction in 1975, Justice was quoted in the press as saying that his report was 'completely unsatisfactory'. Alphon did end up in court but only for making threats against Justice and others for which he was convicted and fined.

Meanwhile, Jeremy Fox, having lived at Justice's Piccadilly flat for some years, moved to a large house in Charlbury Grove, Ealing, where he held lavish parties attended, according to a police source, by 'all the yobs, queers and junkies in West London.' In 1970, he formed a property investment company called Charlbury Grove Investments Limited which, three years later, acquired the lease to the premises at 41-43 Neal Street where a gay club called Chaguaramas – homosexuality now being legal – was operating. Jean Justice became a director of the company along with an urbane, one-armed, Austrian businessman called René Albert and a few others. In 1974, Jean Justice bought out half of the company and Jeremy Fox, who became the liquor licensee of the club, retained the other fifty per cent. Chaguaramas was renamed the Roxy in 1976.

The manager of the Roxy when the Makers played there was a man calling himself Kevin St John, although the authorities believed his real name was Elliot Weston. The son of a British policeman, he had been born in Shanghai in 1938 and, like many European children trapped in China at that time, including the young J.G. Ballard who wrote a fictional account of his experiences in *Empire of the Sun,* spent a number of unpleasant years in a Japanese internment camp during the Second World War. Leaving in 1946 for Australia, where he was suspected by British police of having been involved in extensive criminal activity, and spending some time in New Zealand also committing crimes, he subsequently made his way to Canada before ending up in New York from where he was deported to the UK as an illegal immigrant in May 1964. Safely arrived in London, now calling himself Kevin Moffatt, he was initially the doorman, then the manager, of the Huntsman Club at 40 Berwick Street, the very same club Baron Nugent had acquired in 1958. However, the Baron had got himself into some financial difficulty, having failed to pay the bill of the club's wine supplier, and had been pursued for the debt to bankruptcy, forcing him to sell up. The club was taken over by the Bartell brothers from North London but, in 1963, the older of the two brothers was disqualified from running a club for five years after allowing unlicensed refreshments (Pepsi-Cola in fact! – the licensing laws were *really* strict in those days) and unlicensed public dancing on the premises, forcing both of the Bartells to move on. Thus, while Moffatt was managing the club in 1964, the owner, or perhaps front man on behalf of the Bartells, was a Turkish man called Ahmet Nadji Hassan.

Being the manager of a Soho club at this time was not a particularly safe occupation. There were protection gangs crawling all over the area, including one run by the Kray twins, and Moffatt evidently refused to pay over the required percentage of the club's profits to one of them because the Huntsman was petrol bombed in November 1964, the flames scorching Moffat's hair and eyebrows. The following month, only a few days before Christmas, in the early hours of the morning, Moffatt was attacked outside the club by four men, one of whom can be connected, via an associate, to the armed robbers John McVicar and Ronald Dark, the latter being an acquaintance of some of the Great Train Robbers. This incident might have been related to the disappearance of some fruit machines from the club; in those days fruit machines were usually owned and operated by criminal gangs. During the attack, Moffatt was stabbed and, once released from hospital, put under police protection for a short time. His attackers were arrested on a charge of grievous bodily harm later the same day but this was not the end of the matter. At a hearing at Marlborough Street Magistrates' Court on 14 January 1965, one of the men in the dock somehow managed to wriggle free from custody and assault Moffatt again inside the courtroom. Two days later, Moffatt was himself arrested when police found a firearm and seven cartridges hidden at the Huntsman. Undercover police officers had also been observing the club for a number of days, one describing it as a 'cesspit' and 'a haunt of homosexuals and lesbians'. The owner, Hassan, was prosecuted for disorderly conduct and licensing offences while Moffatt and the barman at the club, Fehmi Elmass, were also found guilty of aiding and abetting disorderly conduct and fined.

After the firearm was discovered at the Huntsman, Moffatt and Elmass departed from Berwick Street and, following a brief partnership with Harry Bidney, a rather unsavoury character who was later to be convicted of living off immoral earnings, took over another gay and lesbian basement club in nearby Gerrard Street called the Grotto Dance and Coffee Club, formerly known as the Kandy Lounge, the same club Baron Nugent's best man, Captain Browne, had owned before he sold up to acquire a hotel in Sussex. The police, as we have seen, were not particularly keen on gay clubs and sent in undercover officers to observe what was going on. Even they were surprised when they saw one man accidentally drop a matchbox he had taken out of his pocket from which about twenty drinamyl (amphetamine and barbiturate) pills, known as purple hearts or 'sweeties', spilled all over the floor right in front of them, before his friend picked them up and swallowed some. The police were also careful to record in their statements that Moffatt was observed to kiss a man on the lips and that couples of the same sex were dancing with each other in full view of Moffatt. According to the police at the time, this amounted to disorderly conduct which, they defined, ludicrously, but in all seriousness as: 'Male persons dancing together, kissing and cuddling and fondling each other in an offensive manner.'

In January 1966, Elmass was convicted at Inner London Quarterly Sessions of unlawful gaming (the club having installed fruit machines without a licence) while Moffatt was convicted of keeping a disorderly house and fined a rather hefty total of £600. Only a few months later, in March 1966, Moffatt, who had taken over another gay venue in D'Arblay Street, housing the Rector's Club and the Salt Beef Bar, was back in court for allowing public dancing without a licence after 'persons were seen dancing to music supplied by a juke box' and fined £15. The following month, and rather more seriously, he was fined £500 for a drugs offence, after being caught in possession of 616 amphetamine sulphate tablets.

Now owing over £1,000 in fines for his various criminal offences, Moffatt was also in debt to the younger Bartell brother to the sum of £500 and, to add to the pressure on his finances, had acquired the lease of a café in Bounces Road, Edmonton, which needed costly refurbishment. Although he claimed to be earning £300 a week from his ongoing interest in the Grotto (now renamed the Alphabet Club), the D'Arblay Street clubs and a couple of outer London clubs – the Fiesta in Notting Hill and the Pledge in Kensington – this wasn't enough to pay his debts and, no doubt, it was his pressing need for funds which rashly led him to attempt to steal a safe, believed to contain £400 in cash but in fact holding less than £40, from the manager's office of a Bournemouth hotel in May 1966. One of his two accomplices in the crime, Stanley Farrington, was an old Scouse lag with a criminal record for theft and burglary as long as his arm who, almost ten years earlier, had been described as a 'menace and a pest' by a judge at Liverpool Crown Court. It was the elderly Farrington who was caught by a porter surreptitiously transporting the safe in the hotel's lift as Moffatt fled into a waiting getaway car. The driver of that car was detained shortly afterwards by police while buying petrol at a nearby garage but Moffatt once again escaped the clutches of the law, fleeing through a school playground, only to be arrested in London a few days later after the getaway driver, in the vernacular, 'grassed him up'.

Following attempts to intimidate and threaten both of his co-defendants during the trial as well as another (female) witness and one of the Bartell brothers who gave evidence against him – all of which played very badly with the judge – Moffatt was sentenced to seven years in prison, the type of stretch usually reserved for armed robbers. The judge at his trial, who called him 'a dangerous and determined criminal', took the unusual step of writing to the Home Office to request his deportation after release (which was refused because his father had been a British citizen), describing him, somewhat melodramatically, as 'a man of great evil power from whom the public needs protection.'

Soon after being released from prison in 1971, having served less than five years of his seven-year sentence, and with a new business partner, a hard as nails Glaswegian called Kenny MacDonald (no relation to Jock) who had spent much of his youth in various borstals with a string of convictions for housebreaking and theft to his name, Moffatt, now calling himself Kevin St John and living in Ealing, could be found running a gay club in Shepherds Bush called Valentino's, not too far from where Jeremy Fox was now based in Charlbury Grove. St John must have felt a sense of déjà vu when, in October 1976, the club was petrol bombed during the early hours of the morning by two disgruntled customers who had been thrown out earlier in the evening. The damage was quickly repaired but, following a campaign by local residents who objected to noise and trouble being caused by youths leaving the club in the middle of the night and who complained of a 'complete lack of responsibility' by the club's management, the police became interested and Moffatt/St John was again convicted of licensing offences in March 1977, with the local authority making attempts to close the club for good. It was shortly after this that St John, along with his Glaswegian friend Kenny and his old associate from the Huntsman Club and the Grotto, Fehmi Elmass, took control of the recently opened Roxy in complicated circumstances.

According to St John, now apparently flush with cash from Valentino's and whatever other shady operations he was involved in, he paid René Albert £5,000 for 51 shares in a company called Chaguaramas Club Limited which sub-let 41-43 Neal Street from the leaseholder, Charlbury Grove Investments Limited, and therefore, in effect, owned the Roxy. As the issued share capital of the company comprised 100 shares, this should have given him overall control but he subsequently discovered that Albert had secretly and, in his view, fraudulently, expanded the share capital to a total of 300 shares just two days before the sale so that he (St John) was only a minority shareholder with 51 out of 300 shares. However with the help of a convicted thief and fraudster, Charles Firth, he managed to take physical possession of the Roxy in May 1977. Firth was a close associate of so-called 'Soho Vice Boss',

David Calderhead, a former doorman of the Huntsman Club and subsequent owner of both the Huntsman (renamed the Coffee Pot Café) and the Grotto/Alphabet Club, who was, at the time, awaiting trial on charges of living off immoral earnings, soliciting and attempting to procure a sixteen-year-old boy to commit an act of gross indecency with St John's former business partner, Harry Bidney (for which he was sent to prison for 18 months).

Having taken over the Roxy, St John had the benefit of the weekly takings, although he had to give up a 50% share of the jukebox income to Firth. Nevertheless, in early September, police were required to intervene when Albert, Justice and Fox arrived in Neal Street to try and close the club, claiming that they were owed money, presumably unpaid rent, by St John. This tactic was similar to one used by Albert in April to evict the Roxy's previous manager, Andy Czezowski, but St John was made of sterner stuff and had instructed his burly associates not to allow Albert into the club, leading to the arrival of the police to sort out the dispute. Taking advantage of the situation, St John reported Albert to the police for swindling him out of £5,000 in respect of the sale of shares in Chaguaramas Club Limited and insisted charges be brought against him.

Nevertheless, Albert and his associates continued in their attempt to regain control of the money-making club, partly out of desperation because Jeremy Fox was in dire financial straits, in the process of being made bankrupt: a first meeting of creditors having taken place at the Royal Courts of Justice on 11 May 1977 with an examination due on 11 October. Kevin St John was, in fact, forced out of the club in the last week of September, following the service of a writ to remove him, but was back within a fortnight after some sort of deal was cut. He dropped charges of fraudulent dilution of share capital against Albert who decided to return to Austria, having finally given St John control of the club, perhaps in return for some kind of additional payment of rent or a profit sharing arrangement.

The incident stirred up a hornets' nest, however, because the Greater London Council, which licensed music venues in London, had believed that the company which owned the Roxy was Charlbury Grove Investments Limited but, during their investigation into the dispute between St John and Albert, the police had discovered that, while this company owned the lease of 41-43 Neal Street, it had had nothing to do with the actual running of the club since 1974 despite the fact that the music and dancing licence, which had been renewed by the GLC in controversial circumstances as recently as June, was in the company's name. The authorities were not happy to discover that they had been misled and refused to transfer the licence from Charlbury Grove Investments Limited to Chaguaramas Club Limited, the company actually running the club, especially once police informed them of St John's criminal record. This was the least of the club's problems, though, because a public enquiry had already ruled that the Roxy should close following numerous complaints from local residents of drunken and violent punks causing extreme trouble and vandalism in and around Neal Street virtually every night of the week, often involving police intervention. Although the club had appealed, the Environment Department rejected the appeal in September 1977, a decision which was itself the subject of an (ultimately fruitless) appeal.

This was the context in which the Makers, now managed by Steve Dagger, played their first big gig at the Roxy.

APPENDIX 3

Spandau and the Music Press

A LONGSTANDING MYTH ABOUT Spandau Ballet, which lingers to this day, is that, at the start, they religiously avoided 'the black and white music press' (then *Melody Maker*, *New Musical Express*, *Sounds* and *Record Mirror*) who, in return, never gave the band 'a single line of support', as Gary Kemp claimed in a booklet accompanying the 2002 *Reformation* CD release. In fact, the notion of Spandau's disdain for the music papers has been so seductive that even a journalist writing for *Sounds*, which gave the band massive early publicity before it was signed, by way of Betty Page's article in September 1980, said in its issue of 28 March 1981 that, 'They did not rely on the pop papers for their initial exposure'. The hostility that this was supposed to have engendered amongst those pop papers was described by Steve Sutherland in *Melody Maker* of 10 January 1981, who referred to 'an angry rock press self-righteously miffed that Spandau's self-sufficient success has questioned and undermined their traditional role as principal arbiters of taste.' Although the myth usually states that the band targeted the national or local dailies instead of the music papers, some versions claim that the band kept away from the press entirely. According to *Smash Hits* of 30 October 1980, for example: 'Since their formation in November of last year, they have carefully avoided contact with the press and concentrated on cultivating an air of elegant mystique...'. For Mike Nicholls in *Record Mirror* of 11 April 1981, 'Spandau crossed from cultdom to the charts without relying on media patronage.'

While it is true that Spandau Ballet did not advertise their gigs in the music press, as was traditional, and this may have alienated some journalists, they nevertheless did have a reasonably close relationship with the music press as a whole in the early days. Steve Dagger sent Robert Elms into the offices of the *NME* with a review of the Scala gig in March 1980 and Dagger was happy for *Record Mirror* to carry a feature on the band in April. The *NME* ran a friendly piece in August 1980 about the band's time in St Tropez, a further positive article followed in November by Paul Rambali and the band had an ally inside the *NME* in the form of journalist Adrian Thrills who was responsible for some good reviews of the band's early singles and wrote the article for which Gary and Martin appeared on the cover in August 1981 under the banner 'Soul Boys of the Western World'. *NME* themselves referred to Thrills as 'NME's token Spandau camp follower'. Paul Morley in the *NME* also gave the band some good reviews during 1981, including one of the live performance at Sundown in March. Betty Page in *Sounds* likewise reviewed the early material favourably and Tony Hadley could be found on the front cover in February 1981, with a Betty Page centrespread on the band inside. *Melody Maker* put them on the front cover of its issue of 10 January 1981 with the comment 'Kilt heroes'. *Smash Hits* was always open minded and regularly carried features and colour photographs of the band.

Although their first single was not universally welcomed, it was really only with the release of *Journeys to Glory* and the Nazi controversy which accompanied it that their relations with the press actually broke down, especially with *Record Mirror*. However, those relations quickly improved and 'Instinction' was well reviewed by *Record Mirror*. From September 1982, a newly glossy *Record Mirror* redirected itself to the mass pop market and over the next twelve months, with Betty Page on board – not to mention Simon Tebbutt's 'Private Files' gossip page, which seemed to mention the band every week – became far more Spandau friendly.

A heated argument between *NME* journalist Paolo Hewitt and Robert Elms in Bournemouth in April 1983, followed by Gary refusing to speak to Hewitt for a planned interview (followed by Hewitt and Elms nearly coming to blows at the Camden Palace shortly afterwards, followed by libel proceedings instituted by Elms against the *NME*, culminating in a humiliating apology published by the *NME* for some insults they had rashly hurled at him), didn't help the band's relations with that publication but even then, in the same month, Penny Reel was declaring 'True' a hit in the *NME* (even though she didn't like the song herself) and the paper's reviewer of their Bournemouth gig admitted that he could not help but dance to their music.

Robert Elms and David Johnson were allies writing about the band not only in *The Face* and the *Evening Standard* respectively during 1980 but also in the short-lived *New Sounds, New Styles* in 1981 and 1982 while Paul Simper, having already positively reviewed both 'Instinction' and a live gig by Spandau in Glasgow for *Melody Maker*, became friends with the band after he wrote a *Melody Maker* cover page feature about the band's Bournemouth visit in April 1982, gave the *True* album a great review in *Melody Maker* in March 1983 and then, two months later, moved to the newly-established *No.1* magazine in which he wrote many favourable pieces.

There was some possibly fair criticism from the band that publications such as the *NME* and *Melody Maker* were happy to put their name or photograph on the cover to sell copies but then pan their records and write disparagingly about them. This could only be said to apply to the first few years of the band, mind you, as Spandau Ballet did not feature on many front pages of the 'serious' music press after 1984.

Between 1980 and 1983, however, when they did grace the covers, they did also receive the odd positive article and good notice. Take the reviews of 'Chant No. 1' from July 1981. In *Melody Maker*, Steve Sutherland said it was 'simply sensational', in the *NME*, Adrian Thrills described it as 'a dazzling dance floor stormer', in *Record Mirror*, Robin Smith called it 'a rare classic of its genre' and only *Sounds* of the black and white music press was ambivalent, with Robbi Millar, while not giving it a bad review, saying, 'You'd be better off purchasing a real Beggar & Co 45'. While the band seem to have been very lucky in having their single reviewed by sympathetic journalists on this occasion, it shows that praise from the serious rock press was by no means closed to them. Furthermore, from March 1982, when it introduced colour to its cover pages, *Melody Maker* made a conscious effort to change from a folk/rock-centred publication to one more interested in pop music and, for a while, bands like Spandau Ballet were welcome in its pages and on the cover. Indeed, in September 1983, *Melody Maker* published a Spandau Ballet special magazine, which was given away free with the main newspaper, and the band were happy to co-operate with them over such ventures. It wasn't only *Melody Maker* which was friendly at this time as *NME* in January 1984 ran an article by David Dorrell headlined 'The Godlike Genius of Gary Kemp', although that might not have been an entirely sincere reflection of the editorial view. In that article, which featured an interview with Gary Kemp, Dorrell asked Gary if he was doing the interview to regain some lost credibility (after the *True* album) to which Gary replied, 'Oh God no! No...I don't need the NME directly. Fuck, I don't need the NME, I just like to talk to people...Talking to the NME is just talking to another paper.' Clearly, relations between them weren't brilliant at this point but it was only with the *Parade* album that papers like the *NME*, *Melody Maker* and *Sounds* really turned against the band en masse in a musical sense.

Regarding the notion that the band targeted the Fleet Street dailies rather than the music press, it is true that Steve Dagger was keen to cultivate newspaper journalists in the early days but, in practice, this seems to have been limited to David Johnson at the *Evening Standard*. It was without Dagger's knowledge that Johnson invited a *Daily Star* journalist to the Scala gig which led to a Spandau Ballet interview being published in that most unlikely of newspapers. Even the big break of being featured in the LWT documentary seems to have come about by chance, without the band having done anything themselves to bring it about. The truth is that, in the days before being signed to Chrysalis, the band was happy for publicity wherever they could get it and they got quite a bit. Between late 1980 and early 1983 they certainly received their fair share of positive articles and reviews from the music press as a whole. After this it was only *Smash Hits, No.1* (later *Number One*) and *Record Mirror* who stayed loyal, or rather, in the case of *Record Mirror*, became loyal, providing plenty of articles through the Eighties, usually accompanied by colour photographs, but, even then, good reviews could not be guaranteed from any of these magazines and Spandau Ballet were often left fighting for themselves as best they could.

Overall, it appears to be the quality of the music which dictated the response of the music press to Spandau Ballet rather than any grudge about having been ignored or sidelined. The truth of the matter, therefore, is not quite as clear cut as the myth would have us believe.

APPENDIX 4

Spandau Ballet v.1 Images

Poster designed by Mick Robinson for planned gig at Ampthill Youth Club on 30 August 1978.

Mick Austin with Mark Robinson's huge Spandau Ballet banner, circa late summer 1978. (*Photograph by courtesy of Michael J. Austin*)

The original Spandau Ballet performing at the Hope & Anchor, 6 May 1979
(Mick Austin plays guitar marked 'SPANDAU BALLET'
and Gordon Bowman is on drums).
(Photograph by courtesy of Michael J. Austin)

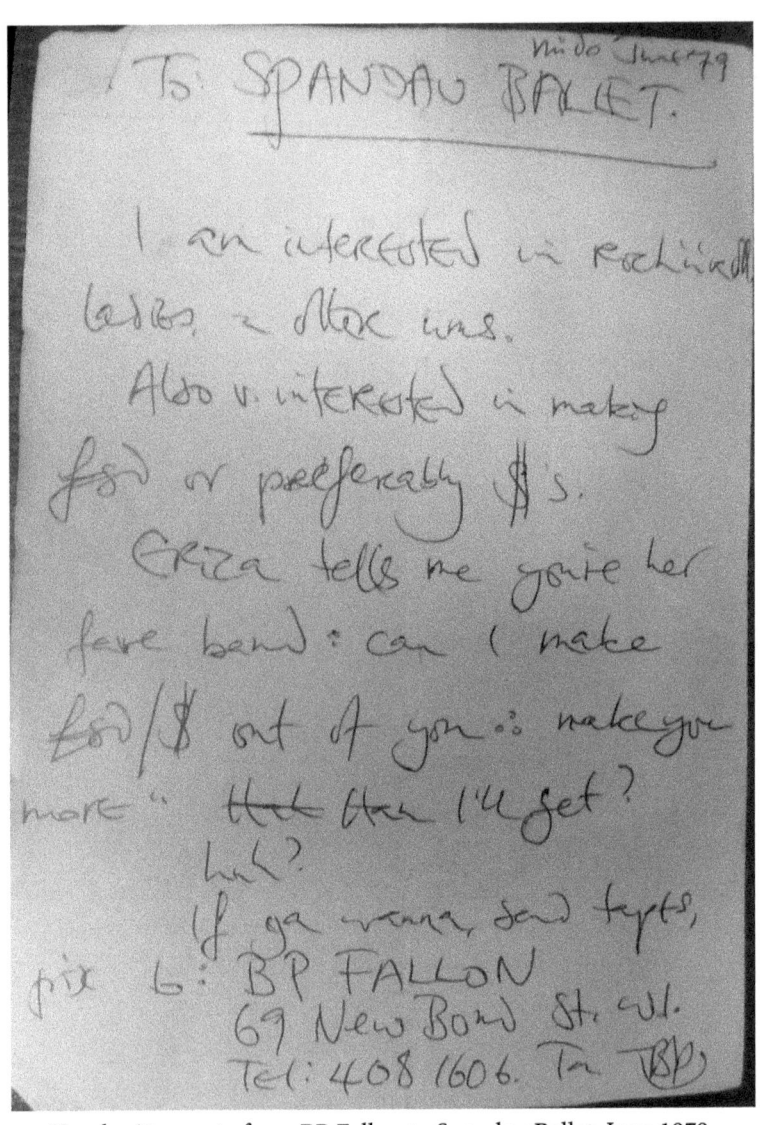

Handwritten note from BP Fallon to Spandau Ballet, June 1979. (*Courtesy of Michael J. Austin*)

> Sunday 29th 1979
>
> Dear Dave,
> Oh yes, I do remember you, the point is I hid your letter for safety and couldn't find it for a week, My hiding places in the house are even too good for me! I was looking forward to hearing from you so as to hear you rehearsing as I don ot hear live music very often. Thanks for writing. It seems a shame that even before starting Spandau Ballet it ceased, but as you said your looking for other musicians, to get something together I wish you luck. Hoping that you will let me know when your playing or rehearsing anywhere so that I could come hope to see you soon. Love Jean.

Letter written by 'Jean' to David Wardill on 29 July 1979 in which she refers to Spandau Ballet having ceased (the surviving envelope is postmarked 'CLAPHAM 10-AM 30 JULY 1979 S.W.A.' and addressed to 'Dave, 32, Sibley Grove, Manor Park, E.12.').
(*Courtesy of David Agar Wardill*)

Composite photograph of the original Spandau Ballet at the Hope & Anchor in May 1979 (from left to right: Mick Austin, Mark Robinson, Gordon Bowman and Dave Wardill).

APPENDIX 5

―◁○▷―

Spandau Ballet v.2 Images

Spandau prepare to invade St Tropez…this photoshoot was on 30 June 1980, shortly before the band left for St Tropez where they wore very similar outfits. (*Trinity Mirror/Mirrorpix/Alamy*)

One of the photographs from Virginia Turbett's photoshoot at the Ritz Hotel in August 1980; it was the images from this shoot which inspired Alan Lewis and Betty Page to refer to the band, for the very first time, as 'New Romantics' in a *Sounds* headline the following month.
(*Getty Images*)

Champagne Day in a golden year. (*Getty Images*)

Spandau at War: Hadley, Norman and Keeble arrive at the High Court near the Temple to crucify the Chosen One; they did not succeed. (*Rex Features*)

Band Reunited…but only for a while. (*Shutterstock*)

We will, presumably, never see the like of this again. (*Shutterstock*)

ACKNOWLEDGEMENTS

Many thanks to: Mike Ellison, Mick Austin, David Wardill, Mark Robinson, Michael Harvey, Victoria Allison (née Bird), Ray Foulk, Deanne Greenwood (née Pearson), Kim Bowen, Sonia Byrne, Vicky Hart (née Silvester), Liz Chalk (née Silvester), Alan Lewis, Sandie Maley, Bob Abrahams, Beverley Glick (Betty Page), Nick Logan, Virginia Turbett, Andy Hilton, Tim Shorten, Gill Newman (née Morris), Laura, David Johnson, Peter York and Marion Lowman. And last, but not least, to my proofreading team of Sidney, Jenita and Rachel Barrat although, of course, any errors which have slipped through the net are my responsibility.

BIBLIOGRAPHY

BOOKS

Alsen, Eberhard (ed), *The New Romanticism: A Collection of Critical Essays*, Garland, 2000

Ant, Adam, *Stand and Deliver*, Pan Books, 2007

Atkins, John, *The Who On Record; A Critical History 1963-98*, McFarland & Co, 2000

Bainton, Roy, *The Long Patrol: The British in Germany since 1945*, Mainstream, 2003

Birch, Ian (ed.), *The Book With No Name*, Omnibus Press, 1981

Blackford, Andy, *Disco Dancing Tonight*, Octopus Books, 1979

Blacknell, Steve, *The Story of Top of the Pops*, Patrick Stephens Ltd, 1985

Bromley, Tom, *Wired for Sound*, Simon & Schuster UK, 2012

Burgess, Richard James, *The Art of Music Production*, Omnibus, 2002

Cashmore, E. Ellis, *No Future: Youth and Society*, Heinemann, 1984

Complete NME Album Charts, Osborne Books, 1995

Denniston, Robin, *Trevor Huddleston: A Life*, Pan, 2000

Docherty, Geoff, *A Promoter's Tale: Rock at the Sharp End*, Omnibus Press, 2002

Evans, Richard, *Remember the 80s: Now That's What I Call Nostalgia!*, Portico Books, 2008

Ewbank, Tim & Hildred, Stafford, *Rod Stewart: A Biography*, Headline, 1991

Foot, Paul, *Who Killed Hanratty*, Penguin, 1988

Foster, Richard Jackson, *The New Romantics: A Reappraisal of the New Criticism*, Indiana University Press, 1962

George, Boy & Bright, Spencer, *Take It Like A Man*, Pan Books, 1995

Geldof, Bob, *Is That It?*, Sidgwick & Jackson, 1986

Gilmour, Sarah, *20th Century Fashion of the 70s: Punks, Glamour Rockers and New Romantics*, Gareth Stevens Publishing, 1999

Gittins, Ian, *Top of the Pops: Mishaps, Miming and Music, True Adventures of TV's no.1 Pop Show*, Random House, 2007

Goda, Norman, J.W., *Tales from Spandau: Nazi criminals and the cold war*, Cambridge University Press, 2008

Gray, Alvin, *Spandau Ballet: A Success Story*, Telstar, 1987

Haden-Guest, Anthony, *The Last Party: Studio 54, Disco and the Culture of the Night*, William Morrow, 1997

Hadley, Tony, *To Cut A Long Story Short*, Sidgwick & Jackson, 2004

Hardy, Phil & Laing, Dave, *The Faber Companion to 20th Century Popular Music*, Faber & Faber, 1990

Herman, Gary, *The Who*, Studio Vista Ltd, 1971

Holmes, Thomas B., *Electronic and Experimental Music*, Charles Scribner, 1985

Jackson, Laura, *The Art of Stone: The Unauthorised Life of Mick Jagger*, Smith Gryphon, 1997

James, Sally, *Almost Legendary Pop Interviews*, Eel Pie Publishing, 1981

Jones, Alan & Kantonen, Jussi, *Saturday Night Forever: The Story of Disco*, Mainstream, 1999

Jones, Dylan, *An Event That Rocked The World*, Preface, 2013.

Justice, Jean, *Murder Vs Murder: The British Legal System and the A6 Murder Case*, Olympia Press, 1964

Kemp, Gary, *I Know This Much: From Soho to Spandau*, Fourth Estate, 2009

Kemp, Martin, *True*, Orion, 2000

Le Tissier, Tony, *Farewell to Spandau*, Ashurst, Buchan & Enright, 1994

Larkin, Colin (ed), *Encyclopedia of Popular Music*, 4th edition, 2006

Marchbank, Pearce, *Spandau Ballet. In Their Own Words*, Omnibus Press, 1983

Marko, Paul, *The Roxy London WC2*, Punk 77 Books, 2007

McColvin, Kenneth Roy & Baumfield, Brian H., *The Literary Student's London*, Association of Assistant Librarians, 1961

McGrandle, Piers, *Trevor Huddleston: Turbulent Priest*, Continuum, 2004

Nicholson's London Guide, Nicholson, 1977
Nicholson's London Night Life, Nicholson, 1977
Nicholson's London Night Life, Nicholson, 1980
Numan, Gary, *Praying To the Aliens*, André Deutsch, 1998
O'Byrne, Robert, *Style City: How London Became A Fashion Capital*, Frances Lincoln, 2009
Palmer, Myles, *New Wave Explosion*, Proteus Books, 1981
Reynolds, Simon, *Rip It Up And Start Again: Postpunk 1978-1984*, Faber & Faber, 2005
Ridgers, Derek, *When We Were Young* (ed. Val Williams), Photoworks, 2004
Rimmer, Dave, *New Romantics The Look*, Omnibus Press, 2003
Seaton, Pete with Down, Richard, *The Kaleidoscope: British Television Music & TV Guide II – Top Pop: 1964-2006*, Kaleidoscope, 2007
Shapiro, Peter, *Turn the Beat Around: The Secret History of Disco*, Faber & Faber, 2005
Simmers, William, *Duran Duran*, Octopus, 1984
Simpson, Jeff, *Top of the Pops 1964-2002*, BBC, 2002
Smith, Graham & Sullivan, Chris, *We Can Be Heroes: Punks, Poseurs, Peacocks and People of a Particular Persuasion*, Unbound, 2012
Southall, Brian, *Pop Goes to Court*, Omnibus Press, 2009
Strange, Steve, *Blitzed*, Orion, 2002
Strong, Martin C., *The Great Rock Discography*, Mojo Books, 5th edition, 2000
Swenson, John, *The Who*, Star, 1979
Travis, John, *Spandau Ballet: The Authorised Story*, Sidgwick & Jackson, 1986
Ure, Midge, *If I Was...*, Virgin Books, 2004
Vickers, Graham, *Rock Music Landmarks of London*, Omnibus Press, 2001
Westwood, Vivienne and Kelly, Ian, *Vivienne Westwood*, Picador, 2014
Woffinden, Bob, *Hanratty: The Final Verdict*, Macmillan, 1997
Wright, Chris, *One Way Or Another: My Life in Music, Sport & Entertainment*, Omnibus Press, 2013
York, Peter, *Modern Times*, William Heinemann, 1984
York, Peter, *Style Wars*, Sidgwick & Jackson, 1980

ORIGINAL FILES

GLC licensing files for the Gargoyle Club, Gossips, the Roxy and The Huntsman held at the London Metropolitan Archives

Archbishop Trevor Huddleston's files held at the Bodleian Library, University of Oxford

File relating to the arrest and conviction of Kevin Moffatt held at the Dorset History Centre, Dorchester

MAGAZINES (selected)

Chartbeat, Issue No. 6

Gay News – 1975-1980

Mayfair News, 19 November 1976

Bailey & Litchfield's *Ritz* Newspaper, 1977 onwards [N.B. these are not dated by month and the monthly dates given in the text are a reconstruction based on internal evidence]

Superpop – 1979 issues

Tatler –1979-80 issues

The Bugle Call Rag – Spring & Summer 1990 issues

Time Out – 1975-1980

Viz – 1980

What's On In London – 1970-1980

ARTICLES

Adzgery, Sandy, 'Lush Life', *Only Music Magazine*, May 1987

Anon, 'Dandies for Dancing', *Evening Standard*, 8 May 1980

Anon, 'In London, An Escape Into Fantasy', *Time*, 8 September 1980

Anon, 'Spandau Ballet's Fashion Sense…', *Look-in*, 7 March 1981

Anon, 'Ballet On Their Toes!', *Look-in*, 6 June 1981

Anon, 'Spandau Ballet: From Early Days to Fame and Fortune', *Kim*, 1 May 1982

Anon, 'A Day in the Life of Tony Hadley', *Smash Hits Yearbook*, 1984

Anon, 'The Spandau Ballet Story', *Smash Hits*, 22 September 1986

Anon, 'Ye Olde Tale of Spandau Ballet', *Jackie*, 13 December 1986

Appleyard, Christena, 'Blitz Kids Let Their Hair Up', *Daily Mirror*, 3 March 1980

Appleyard, Christena, 'Coming Up Poses', *Daily Mirror*, 22 October 1980
Arar, Yardene, 'Duran Duran says it's not a New Romantic Band', *Free Lance-Star*, 24 October 1981
Archer, Keith, 'Number one soul boys', *Islington Gazette*, 8 May 1983
Associated Press, 'Blitz Kids latest London Fad', *Syracuse Herald-Journal*, 25 March 1980
Associated Press, 'London's Newest Cultists Call Themselves 'Blitz Kids'', *Indiana Evening Gazette*, 26 March 1980
Barker, Lynden, 'The Aryan freeze-out', *Melody Maker*, 28 February 1981
Birch, Ian, 'The Brothers', *Smash Hits*, 30 September 1982
Birch, Ian, 'New Romantics', *Smash Hits Yearbook*, 1984
Blau, Robert, 'Spandau Ballet's Moment of Truth', *RockBill*, June 1983
Bohn, Chris, 'Ultravox – 'rage 'n bull'', *New Musical Express*, 24 October 1981
Braitnauer, Jai, '23 Hours in the Life of Tony Hadley', *Sunday Express S Magazine*, 25 May 2003
Bradley, Lloyd, 'Manning The Barricades', *Rock Express*, February/March 1987
Brookes, Rosetta, 'Blitz Culture', *ZG*, No. 1
Burgess, Richard James 'Journeys To Glory Producers Notes', spandauballet.com, 11 March 2011
Burkham, Chris, 'Sun, Sea and Spands', *Sounds*, 1 May 1982
Cain, Barry, 'John – I'm Only Posing', *Record Mirror*, 12 April 1980
Cargill, Edward, 'The London Night Scene', *Pacific Islands Monthly*, May 1972
Calvert, Gemma, 'Spandau star dumps his wife for PR beauty', *News of the World*, 16 November 2003
Cameron, Samuel, 'Rock, Pop and Judicial Efficiency: Economic Considerations in the Spandau Ballet Decisions', *Journal of Interdisciplinary Economics*, 2006, Vol 17, pp.327-344
Catchpole, Charles and Phillips, Kathy, 'The Guy and the Girls', *Daily Mail*, 11 December 1978
Cavendish, Lucy, 'I had a jag and a big pink house. Then it all went wrong', *Evening Standard*, 4 August 2003

Clarke, Steve, 'Johnny Goes A-Courting', *New Musical Express*, 17 February 1979

Collingbourne, Huw, 'Strange Tales', *Kicks*, August 1982

Collingbourne, Huw, 'Journey To Glory: The Spandau Story', Flexipop Publication, 1983

Collingbourne, Huw, 'Spandau', Lionbond, 1984

Cooper, Mark, 'The Young Pretender', *Record Mirror*, 29 November 1980

Cooper, Mark & Sunie, 'The new New Romantics', *Record Mirror*, 7 August 1982

Cooper, Tim, 'Rock Around the Dock at the High Court', *Evening Standard*, 2 March 1999

Coulson, Andy, and Hoare, Sean, 'Pop stars all sue in Spandau bally-hoo – Court battle over cash', *Sun*, 25 May 1996

Coulthard, Alan, 'Copyright in Musical Arrangements: Spandau Ballet and beyond', *NIPC Newsletter*, Spring 2000

Court, Angela, 'Tony Hadley: Still living the dream', *Woman's Weekly*, 6 February 2007

Couzens, Cathy, 'Weirdies', *Daily Star*, 29 May 1980

Craven, John, BACK STAGE, *Radio Times*, 8 May 1982

Da Whallay, Chas, 'A Life In the Day of Gary Kemp', *Record Mirror*, 28 November 1981

Denselow, Robin, 'Spandau Ballet', *Guardian*, 31 December 1980

Denselow, Robin, 'Striking poses in the night', *Guardian*, 2 February 1981

Derringer, Liz, 'Mick Jagger: The man behind the mascara', *High Times*, June 1980

Dorrell, David, 'The Godlike Genius of Gary Kemp', *New Musical Express*, 7 January 1984

Duce, Richard, 'How Spandau Ballet lost their harmony', *Times*, 6 February 1999

Duce, Richard, 'Musical judge rejects £1m claim', *Times*, 1 May 1999

Ducie, Sonia, 'How success is turning Steve Strange Ordinary', *Daily Express*, 21 December 1981

Earls, John, 'Journeys To Glory', *Classic Pop*, October/November 2014

Egan, Rusty, 'Strange Events', *New Sounds, New Styles*, Spring 1981
Eliezer, Christie, 'Aussie's Dream', *Record Mirror*, 27 April 1985
Elms, Robert, 'The Spandau Ballet', *New Musical Express*, 29 March 1980
Elms, Robert, 'Spandau Ballet: An Immaculate Conception', *The Face*, No. 6, September 1980
Elms, Robert, 'The Cult With No Name, *The Face*, No. 7, November 1980
Elms, Robert, 'In Memoriam', *The Face*, No. 8, December 1980
Elms, Robert, 'In Short, The Inside Story of Spandau Ballet', *The Face*, No. 9, January 1981
Elms, Robert, 'Young Hearts Run Free', *Trax*, 18 February 1981
Elms, Robert, 'The Pulse Of The City, The Heart of the Dance', *Trax*, 4 March 1981
Elms, Robert, 'The Managers', *International Musician and Recording World*, February 1983
Elms, Robert, 'Spandau Ballet's super salesman', *You*, 1983 [issue unknown]
Elms, Robert, 'Journeys To Glory', Spandauballet.com, 8 March 2011
Feinstein, Sharon, 'The Ballet Boys Kick Back', *News of the World* magazine, 28 October 1984
Finke, Nikki, 'Post-Punk Cult Blitzes London', *Daily Herald*, 7 May 1980
Finke, Nikki, 'London's Blitz Look: Outlandish Is In', *Los Angeles Times*, 15 May 1980
Fox, Chloe, 'True Romantic', *Daily Mail Weekend*, 27 January 2007
Gelly, Dave, 'Enter the Electronic Futurists', *Observer*, 15 March 1981
Gentleman, Amelia, 'Real Lives', *Guardian*, 5 May 1999
Gill, John 'Numanoid', *Sounds*, 2 June 1979
Glick, Beverley, 'New Romantics – I Was There', *Record Collector*, June 2004
Govender, Robert, 'Vince Howard of Gilly's', *West Indian World*, 13 June 1975
Grabel, Richard, 'Spandaus Invade America', *New Musical Express*, 16 May 1981
Green, Benny, 'City Life', *Spectator*, 28 August 1971
Green, Jo-Anne, 'Mission Accomplished', *Goldmine*, 16 January 1998

Hadley, Tony, 'Celebrity View', *Daily Mirror's The Look*, 15 March 2003
Haines, Perry, 'Me, Sir', *New Sounds, New Styles*, Spring 1981
Hardy, Rebecca, 'I'm just an old romantic!', *Daily Mail*, 26 August 2011
Headley, Jane, 'Duran Duran', *New Sounds, New Styles*, Spring 1981
Harries, Rhiannon, 'How We Met: Gary Kemp & Robert Elms', *Independent on Sunday*, 27 September 2009
Heal, Sue, 'After Punk – the New Romantics?', *Woman's Own*, 9 May 1981
Heath, Chris, 'Would You Throw Your Underwear At These Men?', *Smash Hits*, 8 May 1985
Heath, Chris, 'Spandau Ballet in Holland', *Smash Hits*, 22 October 1986
Heath, Chris, 'Who The Hell Does Gary Kemp Think He Is', Q, February 1987
Hennessy, Val, 'The Disco Detector', *Evening News*, 6 August 1980
Heathcote, Charlotte, 'Tony Pledges To Be True', *Sunday Express*, 2 August 2009
Hewitt, Paolo, 'To Cut A Short Story Very Short', *New Musical Express*, 16 April 1983
Hughes, Chris, 'The Sue Romantics', *Daily Mirror*, 28 January 1999
Hughes, Chris, 'Spand-Ouch Ballet', *Daily Mirror*, 1 May 1999
Hunter, Mark, 'Their Aim Is True', *Record*, February 1984
Innes, John, 'Judge 'assimilates' Spandau Ballet and keeps the CD', *Scotsman*, 2 February 1999
Jaffe, Michel, 'I Dress, Therefore I Am, I Think', *Sunday Times*, 27 April 1980
Jelbert, Steve, 'To cut a long story short, he's back', *Independent*, 19 May 2000
Jenkins, Jo-An, '18th-century punk', *Los Angeles Times*, 12 December 1980
John, Andy, 'Just Dandy', *Daily Star*, 8 April 1980
John, Andy, 'Stranger Than Fiction', *Flexipop*, Issue No. 5
Johnson, David, 'Strange Days', *Evening Standard*, 24 January 1980
Johnson, David, 'How Now...', *Evening Standard*, 10 July 1980
Johnson, David, 'Striking a pose...', *Evening Standard*, 18 September 1980

Johnson, David, 'Private worlds of the New Young', *Evening Standard*, 16 October 1980

Johnson, David, 'Ballet On Broadway', *New Sounds, New Styles*, July 1981

Johnson, David, '69 Dean Street', *The Face*, No. 34, February 1983

Johnson, David, 'The Right Face At The Right Time', *Observer Music Monthly*, 4 October 2009

Jones, Dylan, 'First of the Old Romantics', *Mail on Sunday Live Magazine*, 13 March 2011

Jones, Paula, 'I've Buried The Ghost of Spandau Ballet', *Now*, 7 May 2003

Kinnersley, Simon & Phillips, Kathy, 'Dressing up – it's today's way of dropping out..!', *Daily Mail*, 13 February 1981

Kinnersley, Simon, 'The group with the gift of the garb', *Daily Mail*, 11 March 1981

Labadedi, Iman, 'Spandau Ballet Want You To Dance. That's All', *Creem*, August 1981

Lakemeier, Traute, 'Spandau Ballet's Stilted Dance', *International Music and Recording World*, April 1981

Lea, Andy, 'Spandau boys in comeback as rift healed', *Daily Star on Sunday*, 3 August 2008

Levy, Eleanor, 'I'm Martin, Fly Me', *Record Mirror*, 15 September 1984

Lott, Tim, 'Confessions of an honest poseur', *Record Mirror*, 9 June 1979

Luther, Marylou, 'Soft clothes for hard times', *Los Angeles Times*, 9 May 1980

Luther, Marylou, 'Punks and Posers Create Another London Blitz-Krieg', *Los Angeles Times*, 28 October 1980

Maillard, Chris, 'Kemp on Parade', *International Musician and Recording World*, December 1984

Maillard, Chris, 'Storm The Barricades', *International Musician and Recording World*, December 1986

Martin, Nancie S., 'Spandau Ballet Tell The Truth', *Tiger Beat Presents Rock!*, Vol 1 No. 6

Martin, Peter, 'A Ticket To The World', *Smash Hits*, 5 January 1984

Martin, Peter, 'Made in Hong Kong', *Smash Hits*, 1 October 1984

Massey, Fraser, 'Is Tony Hadley Going Through A Midlife Crisis?', *Now*, 14 January 2004

Meyer, Marianne, 'There's More To Us Than Music', *New Sounds*, March 1984

Mohan, Dominic, 'Gary may be back in Ballet', *Sun*, 1 May 1999

Morgan, Sally, 'Me and My Girl', *The Look*, 7 September 2002

Mott, Joe, 'Tony's Old Gold', *Star Mag*, 11 May 2002

Nicholls, Mike, 'Posing Dahn the Palace', *Record Mirror*, 21 February 1981

Nicholls, Mike, 'Prancing The Night Away', *Record Mirror*, 11 April 1981

Nicholls, Mike, 'Pas De Deux', *Soundmaker*, 29 January 1983

Nicholls, Mick, 'A New Romance', *Sunday Times*, 4 May 2003 (and correction on 15 June 2003)

Norman, Steve, 'If My Memory Serves Me Well', 18 March 2011, Spandauballet.com

Odell, Michael, 'They called us Thatcher's spawn. I honestly didn't care', *Times*, 10 May 2014

Oddy, Jane, 'I Was Stupid And Selfish', *Closer*, 3 January 2004

O'Hanlon, Brian, 'Blitz – It Gets My Five-Star Symbol', *Where To Go*, 10 February 1977

O'Hanlon, Brian, 'Blitz – It Reminds Me of My Youth', *Where To Go*, 6 October 1977

O'Hanlon, Brian and Slinn, Tony, 'Vince You Haven't Changed At All!', *Where To Go*, 14 April 1977

Ottewill, Jim, '21st Century Soul Boy', *M*, April 2014

Owens, Peter, 'The Dancing Years', *Hot Press*, 24 June 1983

Page, Betty, 'The New Romantics', *Sounds*, 13 September 1980

Page, Betty, 'Stranger In Town', *Sounds*, 6 December 1980

Page, Betty, 'Muscle Band', *Sounds*, 7 February 1981

Page, Betty, 'Futurist flashback', *Sounds*, 28 February 1981

Page, Betty, 'Resurrecting America', *Sounds*, 30 May 1981

Page, Betty, 'Let's Spand The Night Together', *Record Mirror*, 12 February 1983

Page, Betty, 'Eight Years In The Raw', *Record Mirror*, 3 September 1988

Panos, Andrew, 'The Dance Goes On', *No.1*, 8 November 1986

Patterson, Sylvia, 'A Round With Spandau Ballet', *Q*, September 2009

Pead, Debbie, 'Spandau Ballet', *Record Collector*, May 1983

Polhemus, Ted, 'What Makes Steve Strange', *Tatler*, November 1979
Polhemus, Ted, 'The 80's Set of '79', *Tatler*, February 1980
Polhemus, Ted, 'Saturday Night Creatures', *Tatler*, March 1980
Polhemus, Ted, 'The Other Society', *Tatler*, May 1980
Polhemus, Ted, 'The denizens of Hell', *Tatler*, July 1980
Powell, Lucy, 'Going from Ballet to theatre in True style', *Times The Knowledge Supplement*, 5 November 2005
Price, Simon, 'A Wild Nobility', thequietus.com, 27 April 2010
Rainbird, Ashleigh, 'Tony Hadley quit Spandau Ballet..', *Daily Mirror*, 3 July 2017
Rambali, Paul, 'Talking Threads', *New Musical Express*, 29 November 1980
Rambali, Paul & Callard, Sarah, 'The British Supermarket of Style', *Independent on Sunday Fashion Magazine*, 25 September 1994
Rapport, Steve, 'Dynasty (the three minute version)', *No.1*, 8 September 1984
Reid, Jim, 'Spandau Ballet', *Record Mirror*, 13 August 1983
Reid, Jim, 'Stockholm is where the heart is', *Record Mirror*, 12 November 1983
Reid, Jim, 'Spandau Works Report', *Record Mirror*, 21 April 1984
Reid, Jim, 'To Cut A Long Story Short', *Record Mirror*, 20 October 1984
Reid, Jim, 'Spandau Ballet: A Contract of Art', *Record Mirror*, 2 August 1986
Rhodes, Nick, 'How we opened the door to the 1980s', *Daily Telegraph Arts & Books supplement*, 22 April 2006
Ridley, Jane, 'I am in love with Alison but still friends with my wife…it's all a balancing act', *Daily Mirror*, 7 May 2004
Rimmer, Dave, 'Five Go Mad In Musikland', *Smash Hits*, 7 June 1984
Rimmer, Dave, 'The hair, synths and secret cool of the New Romantics', *ShortList*, 21 May 2009
Roberts, Yvonne, 'The Electronic Eighties', *New Society*, 7 February 1980
Rose, Cynthia, 'At Home They're Purists: Street Fashion Mag Takes Brave New Twirl', *New Musical Express*, 16 August 1980
Ross, Ron, 'The Best Part of Making Up', *NY Rocker*, May 1981
Salewicz, Chris, 'Café Society and the Social Disease', *The Face*, No. 8, December 1980

Salewicz, Chris, 'Just Fine and Dandy', *New Musical Express*, 31 January 1981
Salewicz, Chris, 'A Revolt Into Style', *The Face*, No. 16, August 1981
Sandall, Robert, 'The Return of Spandau Ballet', *Sunday Times Magazine*, 27 September 2009
Senior, Jaynie, 'Eeek! They're Back', *Number One*, 17 September 1988
Sexton, Paul, 'The Thoughts of Tony Hadley', *Record Mirror*, 11 August 1984
Shah, Deepah, 'I've Put Fame Before My Family', *Closer*, 15 March 2003
Sherwin, Adam, 'Liberty is death for old pop group', *The Times*, 23 January 2002
Shirley, Ian, 'Spandau Ballet', *Record Buyer*, October 2000
Silverton, Pet, 'Passion without sex', *Sounds*, 31 May 1980
Simper, Paul, 'Sand, Sea and Spandau', *Melody Maker*, 17 April 1982
Simper, Paul, 'A Girl's Best Friend', *New Sounds, New Styles*, May 1982
Simper, Paul, 'The Journey To Glory of Spandau Ballet', *No.1*, 28 May 1983
Simper, Paul, 'The Spandau Ballet Interviews', *No.1*, 11 June-9 July 1983
Simper, Paul, 'Spandau Over Europe', *No.1*, 12 November 1983
Simper, Paul, 'Our Triumphant Year', *No.1*, 31 December 1983
Simper, Paul, 'Spandau Ballet', *No.1*, 21 January 1984
Simper, Paul, 'The Spandau Ballet Guide To Holidays In The Sun', *No.1*, 17 March 1984
Simper, Paul, 'Spandau Ballet On Parade', *No.1*, 2 June 1984
Simper, Paul, 'Parade To Portugal', *No.1*, 25 August 1984
Simper, Paul, 'The Price of Fame', *No.1*, 13 October 1984
Simper, Paul, 'In the Searchlight', *No.1*, 22 December 1984
Simper, Paul, 'Round & Round the Globe with Martin Kemp', *No.1*, 16 February 1985
Simper, Paul, 'The Trip of A Lifetime', *No. 1*, 27 April 1985
Simper, Paul, 'I'm A Born Again Spandau', *No. 1*, 12 July 1986
Simper, Paul, 'Glow for Gold', *No.1*, 20 December 1986
Simper, Paul, 'Star Parts: Singing by Tony Hadley', *The No.1 Book 1987*, 1987
Simper, Paul, 'The Hazy Krazy Days of Spandau', *Number One*, 14 February 1990
Slinn, Tony, 'Gems and Junk, Letters and Leftovers', *Where To Go*, 21 February 1976

Sloan, Ben, '60 Second Interview: Tony Hadley', *Metro*, 7 March 2003
Sloan, Billy, 'Around the World in Disco Daze', *Record Mirror*, 1 August 1981
Sloan, Billy, 'Only Loch And Loll', *Record Mirror*, 17 April 1982
Smart, Norman, 'On their way go Jet Sell girls!', *Daily Express*, 25 March 1969
Smith, Christine, 'I haven't said a word to the Kemp boys since that court case and I won't ever again', *Daily Mirror*, 22 September 2001
Smith, Liz, 'The trad bunch', *Evening Standard*, 3 December 1979
Smith, Liz, 'Dandies in hand-me-downs', *Evening Standard*, 17 March 1980
Soave, Daniela, 'Brave New Face – Spandau Ballet', *Record Mirror*, 29 November 1980
Soave, Daniela, 'Mind of a boy', *Record Mirror*, 18 April 1981
Soave, Daniela, 'Nancy Boys Not Us Say Duran Duran', *Record Mirror*, 15 August 1981
Soave, Daniela, 'A Life In The Day of David Band', *Record Mirror*, 4 June 1983
Spencer, Kathryn, Carpenter, Julie and Bohdanowicz, Kate, 'Tony goes into battle again over Spandau', *Daily Express*, 29 January 2003
Stand, Mike, '....art Nouveaux...', *Smash Hits*, 2 April 1981
Stand, Mike, 'Spandau Ballet', *Smash Hits*, 20 August 1981
Steels, Mark, 'Strange Tales', *Trax*, 11 March 1981
Street-Porter, Janet, 'Me, Spandau Ballet and an outbreak of flowing scarves', *Independent*, 25 March 2009
Stephenson, David, 'Band of Gold', *Sunday Express S:2*, 25 August 2002
Strike, Andy, 'Socks 'n' Surrealism', *Record Mirror*, 2 June 1984
Sullivan, Caroline, 'Once more with girdles', *Guardian*, 2 October 2009
Sunie, 'Ruff Treatment', *Record Mirror*, 25 September 1982
Sutherland, Steve, 'Stranger Than Fiction', *Melody Maker*, 27 December 1980
Sutherland, Steve, 'Kustom Kilt Kommandos', *Melody Maker*, 10 January 1981
Sutherland, Steve, 'Shaking the west awake', *Melody Maker*, 31 January 1981
Sutherland, Steve, 'Spandau Ballet', *New Sounds, New Styles*, Spring 1981
Sutherland, Steve, 'Stepping out in the futurist disco', *Melody Maker*, 4 April 1981
Swift, Greg, 'To cut a long story short, I'm pleased I lost Spandau battle', *Daily Express*, 22 January 2001

Sykes, John and Spence, Dinah, 'Spandau Ballet Case; Group Members' Contributions Ruled Not Significant Enough', *Music & Copyright*, 2 June 1999

Sykes, Homer, 'Fantasy At The Disco', *Sunday People*, 15 June 1980

Tatty, Jack, 'No Tat In these Lad's Lives', *New Musical Express*, 2 August 1980

Taylor, Steve, 'Blitz: we love the nightlife (disko round)', *Melody Maker*, 8 December 1979

Taylor, Steve, 'Spandau Ballet', *Smash Hits*, 11 December 1980

Taylor, Steve, 'People are Strange', *The Face*, No. 9, January 1981

Taylor, Steve, 'The Mutant Disco', *The Face*, No. 11, March 1981

Taylor, Steve, 'Moog Music', *Observer* (Magazine), 15 March 1981

Tennant, Neil, 'Shout to the Top', *Smash Hits*, 31 January 1985

Thomas, David, 'The Lost Weekend', *The Face*, No. 37, May 1983

Thomas, Pat, 'Spandau Ballet: We're Back But We Haven't Been Away', Number One, 30 August 1989

Thrills, Adrian, 'Always Passion in the Same Car', *New Musical Express*, 1 December 1979

Thrills, Adrian, 'Spandau Ballet a solar eclipse on the social calendar' (a.k.a 'The Rise and Rise of Spandau Ballet'), *New Musical Express*, 1 August 1981

Thrills, Adrian, 'Behind Blue Eyes', *Uncut*, October 2002

Tickell, Paul, 'Top of the Fops', *New Musical Express*, 13 December 1980

Timmins, Rene, 'Journeys To Glory', *The History of Rock*, Volume 10, Issue 118, 1984

Tong, Pete, 'A change has gotta come...', *Blues & Soul*, 11 August 1981

Ungar, Stanford J., 'Sniffles, Not Snuggles', *The Billings Gazette*, 12 May 1968

Vague, Tom, 'Classix Nouveaux', *Zigzag*, May 1981

Vaziarni, Shoba, 'We're a big extended family', *New!*, 5 May 2003

Vincent, Alice, 'Spandau Ballet: inside the messiest pop break-up in pop history', *Daily Telegraph*, 4 July 2017

Vincent, David, 'Diamond Geezer: An interview with Martin Kemp', Amazon.co.uk, 2000

Wade, Judy, 'Putting on the Blitz!', *Sun*, 10 February 1981

Walden, Celia, 'Boys Will Be Boys', *Mail On Sunday – Night & Day*, 8 September 2002

Waller, Johnny, 'Kemp Comments', *Blitz*, September 1984

Watson-Smyth, Kate, 'Spandau face ruin after lost court case', *Independent*, 1 May 1999

Watts, Michael, 'A New Dress Code On The British Scene', *Los Angeles Times*, 5 April 1981

Wells, Matt, 'Songwriter accused in royalties row', *Scotsman*, 28 January 1999

Westcott, Sarah, 'True! Spandau Ballet are big hit with judge', *Independent*, 2 February 1999

Westcott, Sarah, 'Singer's money troubles', *Independent*, 4 February 1999

Westcott, Sarah, 'Spandau Ballet songs 'all mine' says Kemp', *Independent*, 6 February 1999

White, William, 'Almost Too Good To Be True', *Melody Maker*, 4 June 1983

Williams, Richard, 'Spandau Ballet', *The Times*, 31 December 1980

Winship, Joanne, 'Full fashions show element of self-style', *Daily Herald*, 13 May 1980

Woods, Catherine, 'This Much Is True', *Hot Stars*, 11 May 2002

Wootton, Dan (Bizarre column), 'Spandau Battle', *Sun*, 3 July 2017

Wright, Elisa, 'Gary Kemp Converses', *Debut*, Issue 4

INTERNET

Goldmine interview – www.lizardkingduran.com/gold

www.youtube.com

www.shapersofthe80s.com